The Impact Entrepreneur Breakthrough

The Impact Entrepreneur Breakthrough

A Field Manual for the Regenerative Economy

Laurie Lane-Zucker

Berrett-Koehler
PUBLISHERS

Berrett-Koehler Publishers, Inc.
1333 Broadway, Suite P100
Oakland, CA 94612-1921
(510) 817-2277
bkconnection.com

Ordering Information
Quantity sales. Special discounts are available on quantity purchases by corporations, associations, individuals, and others. For details, please go to bkconnection.com to see our bulk discounts or contact bookorders@bkpub.com for more information.
Textbook exam/desk copies. Please consult the General FAQ at bkconnection.com.
Bookstore orders for trade or textbook use. For print books, please contact Penguin Random House Publisher Services at customerservice@penguinrandomhouse.com. For ebooks, contact your favorite distributor.

Distributed to the US trade and internationally by Penguin Random House Publisher Services.

The authorized representative in the EU for product safety and compliance is
EU Compliance Partner, Pärnu mnt. 139b-14, 11317 Tallinn, Estonia,
www.eucompliancepartner.com, +372 5368 65 02.

All illustrations were created by the author using the following AI-assisted design tools: Nano Banana AI, Pixelmator Pro, Canva, and Adobe Illustrator.

Printed in the United States of America

Berrett-Koehler books are printed on long-lasting acid-free paper. When it is available, we choose paper that has been manufactured by environmentally responsible processes. These may include using trees grown in sustainable forests, incorporating recycled paper, minimizing chlorine in bleaching, or recycling the energy produced at the paper mill.

Library of Congress Cataloging-in-Publication Data
Names: Lane-Zucker, Laurie author
Title: The impact entrepreneur breakthrough : a field manual for the regenerative economy / Laurie Lane-Zucker.
Description: First edition. | Oakland, CA : Berrett-Koehler Publishers, Inc, [2026] | Includes bibliographical references and index.
Identifiers: LCCN 2026008143 (print) | LCCN 2026008144 (ebook) | ISBN 9798890572318 paperback | ISBN 9798890572325 pdf | ISBN 9798890572332 epub
Subjects: LCSH: Entrepreneurship | Investments
Classification: LCC HB615 .L269 2026 (print) | LCC HB615 (ebook)
LC record available at https://lccn.loc.gov/2026008143
LC ebook record available at https://lccn.loc.gov/2026008144

First Edition
35 34 33 32 31 30 29 28 27 26 10 9 8 7 6 5 4 3 2 1

Book production: Happenstance Type-O-Rama
Cover design: Ashley Ingram
Author photos: Christina Rahr Lane

For Anna, Liam, and Silas,
and the seven generations to come

Contents

Why Impact Entrepreneurs? ix
How to Use This Book xvii

Part I: Foundations—From Crisis to Coherence

1 The Impact Entrepreneur: Who We Are and Why We Matter . . 9

2 From Single-Bottom-Line to Systemic Intelligence 21

Part II: Possibility—What We Could Build

3 Enterprises That Heal: Design for Regeneration 43

4 Ownership as Justice 63

5 Capital as Custodian. 79

6 Markets That Reflect What Matters 93

Part III: Protection—The Five Pillars of Real Security

7 The Misallocation of Defense. 119

8 Who Really Keeps Us Safe 139

9 From Militarization to Mutualism: The Strategic Case for Cooperation 149

10 Defense as a Service: The Operating Model 165

Part IV: Integration—The Architecture of a Regenerative Economy

11 The Culture We Keep Alive 191

12 The Stories That Shape the Possible 207

13 The Attention Commons: Defending Cognitive Infrastructure 217

14 Identities That Remember the Whole. 227

Part V: Reclamation—A Civilization Worth the Name

15 Reclaiming the Commons: From Ownership to Belonging . . 261

16 The Work of Reclamation: A Field Manual for Civilizational Renewal 275

Breakthrough 289

Acknowledgments 297
Glossary 305
Notes 313
Index 335
About the Author 349
About Impact Entrepreneur 353
About the Art 355

Why Impact Entrepreneurs?

In 2011, I gave a name to something I was seeing emerge across sectors and geographies: the *impact entrepreneur*.

Not a social entrepreneur adding a charitable component to business. Not a sustainability consultant helping corporations greenwash. Not a philanthropist writing checks from wealth extracted elsewhere.

Something different. Someone building enterprises where financial return and systemic regeneration are inseparable—where success *requires* healing rather than merely tolerating harm.

I founded Impact Entrepreneur, PBC—a media platform and network—to support these pioneers, and to argue that they represented not a niche but a necessary evolution in how we organize economic life.

Fifteen years later, that argument has only become more urgent. What felt like emergence in 2011 now feels like *breakthrough*—a critical mass of practitioners, tools, and proof points that can no longer be dismissed as marginal or utopian.

The Crisis Is Here

We are living through converging breakdowns (see figure 1). Climate systems are breaching tipping points—melting ice sheets, intensifying storms, expanding droughts—and the window to prevent catastrophic warming is closing.[1] Ecosystems are collapsing at rates unseen since mass extinctions, with biodiversity loss, soil depletion, and ocean acidification threatening the foundations of food security and planetary stability.[2] Social fabric is fraying as inequality reaches historic extremes, trust in institutions falls to historic lows, and democratic governance comes under assault from authoritarianism and concentrated wealth.[3] Democratic institutions are eroding as authoritarian movements gain ground, disinformation corrodes civic trust, and concentrated wealth captures governance—making collective action nearly impossible precisely when it's most needed.[4]

Economic systems optimized for short-term extraction are accelerating all of this—unable to price ecological destruction, unwilling to address structural inequity, incapable of coordinating collective action at the scale and speed required.

These are not separate crises. They are symptoms of a single system failure: an economy designed for extraction rather than regeneration. And the conventional responses—environmental, social, and governance (ESG) screening; corporate social responsibility; impact investing as currently practiced—are insufficient. They operate at the margins, trying to make extraction slightly less harmful rather than transforming the logic itself.

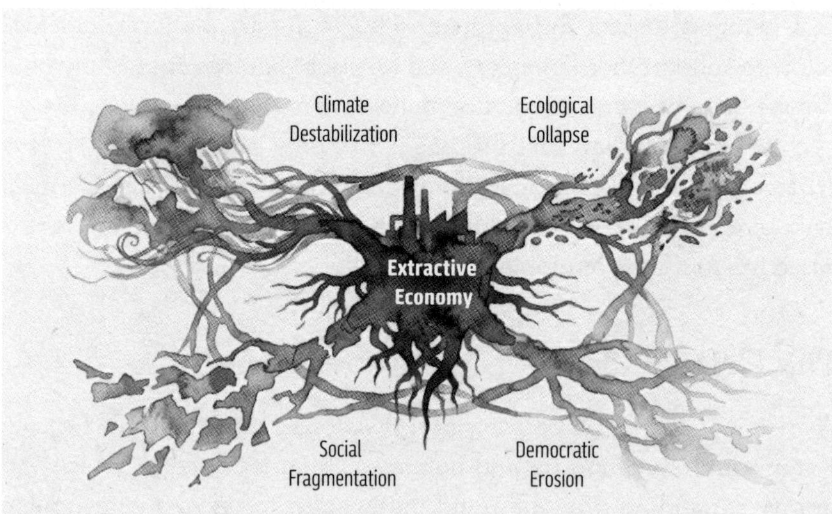

Figure 1. The Polycrisis—Converging Symptoms of Extinction

Why This Book, Why Now

When I coined the term "impact entrepreneur" in 2011, I was naming something I saw emerging. This book documents the breakthrough that emergence has become. It provides the *intellectual architecture*, showing how enterprises, ownership, capital, markets, security, culture, and identity all need to transform together. It offers *practical tools*—not just theory but tool kits, case studies, and pathways for implementation. And it issues an *invitation* to join a breakthrough that is already building the alternative to extraction, one enterprise and investment and community at a time.

The book is both field manual and manifesto. It is designed to be *used*, by entrepreneurs building regenerative businesses, investors deploying aligned capital, policymakers creating enabling frameworks, educators shaping consciousness, and community leaders building power from the ground up.

Introducing the Impact Entrepreneur

An impact entrepreneur is someone who rejects incremental tinkering—the add-on fixes, the attempts to make extraction slightly less harmful. Someone who makes regeneration, equity, and ecological restoration central to how value gets created—not as an afterthought, but as the foundational logic. This is not about sacrifice or charity. It is about *structural redesign*—building enterprises that cannot succeed unless the systems they're embedded in become healthier, more just, and more resilient.

The economy they are building—what this book calls the *Impact Economy*—is fundamentally a regenerative economy: one that heals rather than extracts, restores rather than depletes, distributes rather than concentrates. Chapter 1 explores what distinguishes impact entrepreneurs from adjacent approaches and maps the architecture of the Impact Economy in detail. Here, it is enough to say: This is not individual heroism. It is movement building. The Impact Economy will not be constructed by lone visionaries but by networks of practitioners who see themselves as part of a larger civilizational project, achieving this breakthrough together.

Impact Entrepreneurs as Systems Architects

Impact entrepreneurs are systems architects. They work at the intersection of four transformative domains. *Enterprise design* means building businesses that heal rather than extract—where the business model itself generates positive outcomes for people, planet, and community, not as a side effect but as the core logic of value creation. *Capital innovation* means structuring financing that rewards regeneration, not just return—patient capital that measures success in systemic health, aligned incentives that make long-term thinking economically rational, and investment structures that share risk and reward with all stakeholders. *Ownership justice* means distributing power through cooperatives, trusts, and stakeholder governance—ensuring that those who create value share in its benefits and that concentrated wealth cannot capture the enterprises meant to serve communities. *Market transformation* means changing what gets valued and how—building measurement systems that account for true costs and benefits, pricing mechanisms that internalize externalities, and market structures that reward regeneration over extraction.

Who This Book Serves

This book serves movement builders across multiple domains.

Enterprise builders creating regenerative businesses who seek comprehensive frameworks for impact integrity. Investors deploying aligned capital who need due diligence tools and strategic vision. Coaches, consultants, and advisors guiding organizations toward systemic solutions who need frameworks that integrate technical, cultural, and structural dimensions. Policymakers creating enabling frameworks for stakeholder capitalism and community wealth-building. Educators shaping tomorrow's consciousness through impact curricula. Community leaders organizing collective power through cooperatives and democratic economic development. Nonprofit and foundation leaders catalyzing systems-level change. Cultural workers—artists, storytellers, media makers—shaping narratives that make regeneration compelling. And anyone recognizing that extraction is terminal and wanting to help build what comes next.

Standing on Shoulders

The Impact Economy did not emerge from nothing. It stands on the shoulders of pioneers who proved, decades before the frameworks existed, that business could be both profitable and principled—that goodness and performance could work hand in hand.

In the second half of the 20th century, entrepreneurs like Tom and Kate Chappell at Tom's of Maine, Anita Roddick at The Body Shop, Ben Cohen and Jerry Greenfield at Ben & Jerry's, and Jeffrey Hollender at Seventh Generation stepped out to make business a moral as well as a financial enterprise—often at considerable risk, with modest capital, against prevailing wisdom that said values were a distraction from shareholder returns. They built companies that donated profits, empowered employees, sourced responsibly, and proved that markets would reward integrity.[5]

These pioneers demonstrated the market viability of values-driven enterprise before "impact" had a name. Their proof of concept made everything that followed possible: B Corporations, benefit corporation legislation, impact investing, the entire ecosystem this book describes. We are their inheritors.

Yet the pioneers also revealed the limits of values alone. When Unilever made an offer for Ben & Jerry's in 2000, the founders resisted. There were legal defenses to a forced sale, but the practical pressures proved overwhelming: Shareholder expectations, board dynamics, and the relentless logic of maximizing financial returns created what felt like an impossible situation. Ben Cohen, reflecting on that period, noted that he required emergency bypass surgery shortly after the sale closed, adding: "One could say that losing Ben & Jerry's literally broke my heart."[6] When Anita Roddick sold The Body Shop to L'Oréal in 2006, she called it a "Trojan horse" strategy—but relying on infiltration rather than structure is precarious.[7] These stories are not failures of the founders' vision; they are lessons in why mission needs to be encoded into structure itself.

This is precisely why the structural innovations explored in these pages—benefit corporation status, steward ownership, golden shares, purpose trusts—matter so urgently. They are attempts to encode the pioneers' values so deeply into enterprise design that the mission becomes difficult to abandon even when the founders are gone—or when they're overruled.

This is not a critique of what came before. It is gratitude, and continuation. The Impact Economy is what happens when the pioneers' moral imagination meets structural innovation at scale.

My Journey to This Work

Before founding Impact Entrepreneur, I spent decades in the intersecting worlds of ecology, systems theory, and place-based education—fields that taught me how to think relationally, how to listen to land and community, and how to understand resilience not as robustness but as right relationship. I created one of the earliest founding B Corps (Hotfrog), closed the first private equity investment on an impact investing exchange, and worked deeply within the nascent movements of impact investing and benefit corporations.

I believed—and still believe—that a new kind of economy could emerge, one grounded in custodianship rather than extraction, in coherence rather than opportunism. But I was also wary. Even as the language of "impact" spread, I saw the looming risk of co-optation. The legacy business paradigm, with its machinery of short-term incentives, opaque governance, and monocultural thinking, had a habit of neutralizing insurgent ideas.

Impact Entrepreneur was born from this tension: a refusal to accept marginality, and a commitment to building an intellectual, cultural, and professional platform that could both protect and advance the deeper vision. Today, that platform includes *Impact Entrepreneur Magazine* with correspondents worldwide, educational webinars with impact luminaries, field-building summits, and deep dives into regenerative finance, just transition, and democratic renewal.

Through this work, I've learned that transformation requires more than good intentions. It requires structures that embed values, cultures that sustain commitment, and movements that build collective power. This book distills that learning.

What You'll Find Here

The book is organized into five parts. Part I establishes what the Impact Economy is and why systemic intelligence matters. Part II explores the technical architecture—enterprises that heal, ownership as justice, capital as custodian, markets that reflect what matters. Part III introduces the Five Pillars of Real Security, the Prevention Dividend, and Defense as a Service, reimagining security from militarization to mutualism. Part IV examines the cultural infrastructure of story, attention, and identity that determines whether technical solutions endure. Part V addresses the commons as foundation and the work of civilizational renewal.

Each part builds on the previous one, moving from diagnosis to design to implementation. Each chapter includes a tool kit—practical exercises and frameworks you can apply immediately. Throughout, you'll meet impact entrepreneurs and aligned investors, policymakers and organizers, scholars and practitioners who are already building what comes next.

An Invitation

If you're reading this, you likely already sense that the extractive economy is unsustainable—ecologically, socially, morally. You may be building alternatives, funding them, teaching about them, or organizing movements around them. This book is for you. It will give you language to name what you're doing, frameworks to strengthen it, and connection to a global movement of people doing the same work in different contexts.

The Impact Economy is not a distant possibility. The breakthrough is happening now—in ten thousand places simultaneously, by people who refuse to accept that extraction is inevitable. The question is not whether it's possible. The question is whether you will participate.

Welcome to the breakthrough.

—Laurie Lane-Zucker
Sheffield, Massachusetts

How to Use This Book

This book is designed to be read sequentially, each part building on what came before. But your preferred entry point and area of focus may differ depending on your role and your journey:

IF YOU'RE AN ENTERPRISE BUILDER—A FOUNDER, BUSINESS LEADER, OR ORGANIZATIONAL ARCHITECT CREATING REGENERATIVE ENTERPRISES:

Parts I and II are your foundation. Chapter 1 establishes what distinguishes impact entrepreneurship from adjacent movements, while Chapter 2 introduces systemic intelligence as the essential capacity. In Part II, pay particular attention to Chapter 3 (how business models can reward healing, not just minimize harm), Chapter 4 (ownership structures that align governance with mission), and Chapter 5 (capital that serves rather than extracts).

Don't skip Part IV. The cultural and identity dimensions covered there—especially Chapter 11 on organizational culture and Chapter 14 on the interior work of leadership—determine whether your structural innovations will hold under pressure.

IF YOU'RE AN INVESTOR OR CAPITAL ALLOCATOR, DEPLOYING ALIGNED CAPITAL THROUGH IMPACT INVESTING, PHILANTHROPY, OR FOUNDATION STRATEGY:

Chapters 5 and 6 speak most directly to your role and will give you frameworks for due diligence, capital structure, and market shaping.

But the argument of this book is that capital follows culture, so Part IV's treatment of narrative infrastructure and cultural foundations isn't optional context; it's essential for understanding why aligned capital so often gets captured by extractive logic.

Part III's reframing of security and prevention (particularly Chapter 10 on Defense as a Service) opens significant opportunities for preventive investment that traditional risk frameworks miss entirely.

IF YOU'RE A COACH, CONSULTANT, OR ADVISOR, GUIDING ORGANIZATIONS TOWARD SYSTEMIC SOLUTIONS AND HELPING LEADERS TRANSLATE VALUES INTO OPERATIONAL REALITY:

Your role is to multiply impact by enabling others to build well. You need frameworks that integrate technical, cultural, and structural dimensions, because your clients will face challenges across all three. Part II (Chapters 3–6) introduces the enterprise architecture you'll help clients implement. Part IV (Chapters 11–14) presents the cultural and identity frameworks that determine whether structural changes hold. Chapter 10's Defense as a Service model offers a powerful frame for helping organizations think about prevention and resilience.

Pay special attention to the tool kits at each chapter's end—these can be adapted for client engagements. The three-layer framework (cultural foundation + economic architecture + systemic infrastructure) provides a diagnostic model for assessing where clients need the most support.

IF YOU'RE A POLICY OR SYSTEMS-CHANGE PROFESSIONAL, WORKING ON REGULATORY FRAMEWORKS, INSTITUTIONAL REFORM, OR SYSTEMS-LEVEL STRATEGY:

Part III (Chapters 7–10) engages most directly with your domain, reframing security, prevention, and public investment. Chapter 10's Defense as a Service operating model offers a concrete framework for policy innovation. Chapter 6 addresses the institutional and regulatory levers that shape capital flows.

But policy change that lacks cultural foundation tends to be either captured or reversed. Part IV's treatment of narrative warfare, attention commons, and cultural infrastructure explains why technically sound policies often fail—and what conditions enable them to succeed.

IF YOU'RE AN EDUCATOR, DESIGNING CURRICULA, LEADING PROGRAMS, OR SHAPING HOW THE NEXT GENERATION UNDERSTANDS ECONOMY AND ENTERPRISE:

The book's sequential structure maps naturally to a course arc, moving from foundational concepts through economic architecture to systemic infrastructure and cultural integration. The tool kits at each chapter's end can serve as discussion prompts, reflection exercises, or assignments.

Also consider organizing around the three-layer framework that structures the book: cultural foundation (Part IV) → economic architecture (Part II) → systemic infrastructure (Part III). Students might read the book sequentially the first time, then return through this developmental lens.

The part-opening narratives model a pedagogy of place and story that you may want to foreground in your teaching.

IF YOU'RE A CULTURAL WORKER—AN ARTIST, STORYTELLER, JOURNALIST, OR MEDIA MAKER SHAPING THE NARRATIVES THAT MAKE REGENERATION IMAGINABLE:

Part IV is your home territory. Chapter 12 (on the stories that shape what becomes possible) and Chapter 13 (on the attention commons and the struggle against manufactured distraction) address your work directly. Chapter 11's treatment of culture as infrastructure, not decoration, reframes the strategic importance of cultural work.

But cultural workers operating without economic and systemic literacy often find their work absorbed and neutralized. Parts II and III provide the structural understanding that gives narrative work traction.

FOR COMMUNITY LEADERS, NONPROFIT EXECUTIVES, AND ANYONE ELSE BEGINNING THIS JOURNEY:

If you're a community leader working in cooperative development, democratic economic organizing, or place-based change, you'll find yourself across multiple pathways. Your organizational work draws from enterprise builders; your systems advocacy from policy professionals; your public narrative work from cultural workers. Let your current focus guide your entry point, and return to other parts as your work evolves.

If you lead a nonprofit or foundation, your pathway depends on whether you're primarily deploying capital (see investors and capital allocators), building organizational capacity (see enterprise builders), or shaping policy and narrative (see policy professionals and cultural workers).

And if you're simply someone who recognizes that extraction is terminal and wants to help build what comes next—welcome. Begin with Part I, which establishes the foundations. Follow your curiosity from there. The book will meet you where you are.

FOR EVERYONE:

The part-opening narratives are not optional preambles. They carry the book's animating vision—and they model the kind of place-based, embodied knowing that the Impact Economy requires. Don't skip them.

The "Breakthrough" section at the end offers a reflective close that many readers find essential. It's where the book's argument becomes personal.

Table 1 provides a summary that readers can use as a quick reference.

Table 1. Reading Pathways

READER TYPE	CORE CHAPTERS	ALSO ESSENTIAL	KEY INSIGHT
Enterprise builders *Founders, business leaders, org architects*	Part I (Chs. 1–2) Part II (Chs. 3–5)	Ch. 11 Ch. 14	Structural innovations only hold under pressure when supported by cultural and identity work.
Investors and capital allocators *Impact investors, philanthropists, foundations*	Ch. 5 Ch. 6	Part IV (Chs. 11–14) Ch. 10	Capital follows culture. Aligned capital gets captured by extractive logic without cultural foundations.
Coaches, consultants, and advisors *Guides translating values into operations*	Part II (Chs. 3–6) Part IV (Chs. 11–14)	Ch. 10 All chapter tool kits	The three-layer framework (cultural + economic + systemic) provides a diagnostic model for client engagements.
Policy and systems-change professionals *Regulatory, institutional reform, strategists*	Part III (Chs. 7–10) Ch. 6	Part IV (Chs. 11–14)	Technically sound policies often fail without cultural foundation. Part IV explains why—and what enables success.
Educators *Curriculum designers, program leaders, faculty*	Sequential (all parts) All chapter tool kits	Part-opening narratives Three-layer framework	Sequential first read maps to course arc; second pass reorganizes as cultural foundation (IV) → economic architecture (II) → systemic infrastructure (III).
Cultural workers *Artists, storytellers, journalists, media makers*	Part IV (Chs. 11–14)	Parts II & III	Cultural work without economic and systemic literacy gets absorbed and neutralized. Structure gives narrative traction.

(CONTINUED)

Table 1. Reading Pathways (*continued*)

READER TYPE	CORE CHAPTERS	ALSO ESSENTIAL	KEY INSIGHT
Community and nonprofit leaders *Cooperative developers, organizers, foundations*	Multiple pathways apply—enter by focus (enterprise builders, policy professionals, cultural workers, investors)		Your work spans domains. Let your current focus guide your entry; return to other parts as your work evolves.
For everyone: Begin with Part I, which establishes the foundations all pathways build from. The part-opening narratives are not optional preambles—they carry the book's animating vision. "Breakthrough" offers a reflective close where the argument becomes personal.			

Part I

Foundations

From Crisis to Coherence

The seagulls were fighting to stay aloft (figure 2). Late autumn on Cape Cod, 1991—the kind of gray November day when the wind comes hard off the Atlantic, slicing through every seam and gap, rattling windows in their frames. Those that could rode the gale, wings locked, bodies rigid against the buffeting. Others had surrendered, huddled alone on the beach, backs to the weather, waiting.

Figure 2. Cape Cod, November 1991

Inside the old Coast Guard lighthouse and retreat center, we had gathered around tables scarred by decades of use, the wind working through cracks in the walls with the persistence of water finding fissures in stone. I was twenty-six, newly arrived as a work-study intern at *Orion* magazine, tasked with helping organize this first convening of environmental writers and naturalists—people whose names I had encountered reverently in college seminars, whose books had taught me that language could be an act of witness.

Orion had spent nearly a decade cultivating deep relationships with many of the leading practitioners of the long and esteemed tradition of nature writing—pioneering thinkers like Wendell Berry, Barry Lopez, Peter Matthiessen, Jane Goodall, Wes Jackson, E.O. Wilson, Homero Aridjis. Their work shaped the magazine's vision, their voices resonating through every issue.

That November weekend brought together Terry Tempest Williams, Gary Paul Nabhan, Ann Zwinger, Robert Michael Pyle, Richard Nelson, Scott Russell Sanders, John Elder, Jan DeBlieu, David Abram, Robert Finch, and John Hay, grandson of Abraham Lincoln's personal secretary, whose own seven-decade writing career we had come to celebrate with the establishment of a lifetime achievement award.

Lighthouses are threshold architecture, built at the edge between land and sea, safety and danger, the human world and the wild. They exist to mark boundaries, to warn of where solid ground ends and chaos begins. But they also exist precisely *at* that boundary, inhabiting the liminal zone, neither fully of land nor of sea—a threshold space where the old dissolves and something new becomes possible. And they exist to enable passage—to guide vessels through dangerous waters, to make breakthrough possible where otherwise there would only be wreckage.

That weekend on Cape Cod, we inhabited that between-space. The writers gathered at the retreat had spent their careers at the boundary between human and more-than-human, between the articulate and the ineffable, between what could be named and what could only be witnessed. They were lighthouse keepers of a different kind, marking the edges of what language could reach, warning of where human understanding dissolved into mystery, standing vigil at the threshold between the known world and the wild one.

For three days, we inhabited that wind-battered building and talked: about craft and calling, about the particular demands of bearing witness to the more-than-human world, about the writer's obligation when ecosystems unravel and species vanish. The conversations moved like the weather, circling, intensifying, breaking briefly into lightness before the weight returned.

The absent voices were present too, carried in through quoted passages, through the ideas that had shaped everyone in that room.

"There are no unsacred places," Wendell Berry had written. "There are only sacred places and desecrated places."

The retreat's participants understood desecration intimately—the strip-mined mountains, the clear-cut forests, the poisoned rivers, the silenced marshes. But they also knew the sacred with a precision that came from years of patient attention.

Terry Tempest Williams—whose book *Refuge* had just been published that year—spoke of the birds she watched at Great Salt Lake, how the rising waters were drowning the marshes, how bearing witness to loss was itself an act of love. "I pray to the birds," she said, "because they remind me of what I love rather than what I fear. And at the end of my prayers, they teach me how to listen."[1]

David Abram had published his first essay in *Orion* that summer—"The Ecology of Magic," drawn from his years apprenticing with Indigenous shamans.[2] At one point, he stood and performed sleight-of-hand tricks while describing how shamans use illusion not to deceive but to shift perception, to break the habitual ways of seeing that keep people trapped in suffering. "The magician's art," he explained, making a stone disappear and reappear, "is to show that what we think is solid and fixed is actually fluid, participatory, alive with possibility." The healing wasn't in the trick; it was in the perceptual shift the trick enabled. Many of us sat transfixed, understanding that what he described wasn't primitive superstition but sophisticated epistemology: Transformation requires changing not just external structures but the consciousness that creates and maintains them. Five years later, that essay would become the foundation for his book *The Spell of the Sensuous*, but we witnessed its core insight that November afternoon—that perception itself is participatory, that how we attend to the world shapes what the world becomes.

Another in the room quoted Barry Lopez on wolves: "The wolf exerts a powerful influence on the human imagination. It takes your stare and turns it back on you." What we project onto the wild, Lopez suggested, reveals what we cannot yet see in ourselves.[3]

These were not romantic pastoralists mourning a lost Eden. They were rigorous observers bearing witness to catastrophe in real time—the accelerating extinctions, the collapsing fisheries, the warming that would soon make "climate change" the defining crisis of the century. Robert Michael Pyle, the world-renowned lepidopterist, spoke of pollinators in crisis, not as charming subjects for nature essays but as keystone species whose collapse would cascade through entire ecosystems. Someone read aloud from Wes Jackson's work on topsoil loss, his documentation of how industrial agriculture's extractive logic was treating living soil as dead substrate, mining fertility that had taken millennia to build. E.O. Wilson's urgent accounting of biodiversity loss—his catalog of what we stood to lose if we continued on our current trajectory—threaded through conversation after conversation, a drumbeat of warning we could no longer ignore.

But what stayed with me, what worked its way into my understanding the way that November wind worked through the walls, was how they *thought*. Not in isolated problems but in systems. Not in single causes but in cascading effects. They saw what Aldo Leopold had seen a half-century before: "A thing is right when it tends to preserve the integrity, stability, and beauty of the biotic community. It is wrong when it tends otherwise."[4]

They understood: Not individual species but communities. Not isolated acts but integrity. Not static preservation but dynamic stability.

Orion itself—the magazine I had joined just a few months before—was practicing this "systems intelligence" through its editorial vision. While mainstream environmentalism still largely focused on conservation and pollution control, and social justice movements fought economic inequality and civil rights, *Orion* insisted these were not parallel struggles but interwoven ones. An economy that extracted from nature and from people operated by a single logic. A culture that could not see the sacred in rivers would not see it in workers. The poisoning of land and the poisoning of communities flowed from the same source: a worldview that saw both as resources to be exploited until exhausted.

This was not yet the common language. In 1991, "environmental justice" was just beginning to coalesce as a named framework. The Principles of Environmental Justice had been drafted and adopted at the First National People of Color Environmental Leadership Summit held that October in Washington, DC.[5] The connections were being drawn, the intersections named, but the full architecture of systems thinking—the feedback loops, the leverage points, the emergent properties that Donella Meadows would later crystallize in *Thinking in Systems*—was still largely the province of ecologists and Indigenous knowledge holders, not yet translated into economic and organizational design.[6]

"We can't solve problems by using the same kind of thinking we used when we created them," Einstein had said.[7] The writers in that lighthouse keeper's building understood this instinctively. The way forward could not be through incremental improvement of extractive systems. It required different premises, different questions, different measures of what mattered.

During a break between sessions, I walked the beach. The wind had not relented. I found a gull alone on the sand, one wing dragging, clearly broken. It tried to lift when I approached, but managed only an awkward hop before settling again, exhausted. The tides would take it by evening, or the cold, or something with sharper teeth. It was not equipped for the storm it found itself in.

I thought of that gull often in the years that followed—as founding director of The Orion Society, which grew out of that coastal convening, and especially through the 2000s as I moved into what was then called "social entrepreneurship." The field was animated by genuine commitment, by people who wanted business to serve more than shareholder return. We spoke about "doing well by doing good," about "double bottom lines" and "blended value." We celebrated enterprises that hired from marginalized communities, that used sustainable materials, that donated portions of profits to worthy causes.

But something was missing. Something fundamental. The enterprises we celebrated were more humane versions of extractive models—gentler, more thoughtful, more generous, but still operating within the same systemic logic. They treated symptoms, not causes. They asked, "How can we do less harm?" rather than, "How do we participate in healing?" They optimized for efficiency within the existing paradigm rather than questioning the paradigm itself.

By 2009, as impact investing began to crystallize as a distinct field, I watched capital flow toward enterprises that could deliver financial returns with some measurable social or environmental benefit—often genuine benefit, meaningfully improving lives or reducing harm. But the fundamental extractive architecture remained intact. We were not redesigning systems. We were adding social programs to business as usual and calling it transformation.

The broken wing became my metaphor. Without systems intelligence—without the capacity to see how economies participate in ecologies, how ownership structures shape power, how capital either concentrates or distributes, how markets reflect or distort what matters—all our good intentions would leave us hobbled, unable to navigate the intensifying storms.

In 2011, I founded Impact Entrepreneur with a different premise: that transformation requires redesigning economic systems from their foundations, not incrementally improving extractive ones. That true "impact" is not what we add to business but what we *build into* its structure—its ownership, its governance, its capital, its measures of success, its relationship to community and ecosystem and future generations.

The writers whose work shaped that Cape Cod gathering in 1991 had taught me to think in systems, to see integrity as indivisible, to understand that the health of human communities and the health of living communities are not separate concerns but expressions of the same underlying relationships. They understood that you cannot heal what you do not see as whole.

What the Impact Economy Is and Why Systemic Intelligence Matters

This part of the book begins where that understanding begins: with the foundational recognition that the Impact Economy is not a sector or a strategy but a *civilizational redesign*. It requires us to understand what systems *are*, how they function, where they resist change, and where leverage lies. It requires us to see economy not as separate from ecology but as nested within it—a subsystem that either supports or undermines the larger living systems it depends upon.

As you read, you're already part of this transformation. Every design choice—product, deal terms, metrics, story—either rehearses the extractive past or prototypes a regenerative future. The seagulls that survived that November storm were the ones whose wings were intact, whose instincts and structures allowed them to navigate turbulence. The same is true for the enterprises, investments, policies, and communities that will navigate what comes next.

This is about building those wings. Not stronger versions of broken structures, but fundamentally different designs—capable of flight, capable of elegance, capable of meeting the wind on its own terms. Capable of breakthrough.

•

Every transformation worth making begins with a reckoning. Before we can build the architecture of a regenerative economy, we must first examine the foundations upon which the current system rests—and ask whether they can bear the weight of a more just and life-giving future. These opening chapters uncover the moral fractures and structural habits embedded in our economic life, revealing not only why they fail us but how they might be reimagined. Here, we meet the impact entrepreneur not as a lone innovator but as a moral architect, shaping ownership, capital, governance, and markets to serve a larger whole.

You cannot build on unstable ground. Before exploring what regenerative enterprises look like or how to finance them, we need shared understanding. What is the Impact Economy? Who are impact entrepreneurs, and how do they differ from adjacent approaches? Why does conventional thinking—even well-intentioned—fail to address systemic crises? And what cognitive capacity does transformation actually require?

The two chapters ahead answer these questions in sequence. The first names who we are and what we're building—the identity of the impact entrepreneur and the architecture of the Impact Economy. The second cultivates how we think—the systemic intelligence required to design solutions that work with complexity rather than against it. You cannot practice impact entrepreneurship without systemic intelligence; you'll produce unintended consequences or get co-opted back into extraction. And you cannot apply systemic intelligence without the structural innovations of impact entrepreneurship; understanding complexity without power to act accomplishes nothing.

Together, these chapters establish the foundation for everything that follows. Without this groundwork, the architectures of Part II, the security reimagining of Part III, the cultural integration of Part IV, and the commons reclamation of Part V risk becoming disconnected tools rather than integrated transformation.

This is where we begin. Everything else builds from here.

1

The Impact Entrepreneur

Who We Are and Why We Matter

In 2006, Muhammad Yunus won the Nobel Peace Prize for pioneering microfinance through Grameen Bank. The Nobel Committee praised him for proving that markets could serve the poor—that financial innovation could be a tool for social change. But here's what they didn't say: Yunus didn't just create a better banking product. He redesigned the entire architecture: ownership (borrower-owned institution), capital structure (patient, relationship-based), governance (women-led community groups), and success metrics (social outcomes alongside financial sustainability). He wasn't optimizing within the existing system. He was building a different one.[1]

This is what distinguishes an *impact entrepreneur* from every other kind of changemaker (see figure 3). Not the intention to do good—that's necessary but insufficient. Not the willingness to measure social outcomes—that's become table stakes. Not even the commitment to sustainability—that's increasingly expected. What defines the impact entrepreneur is *structural innovation in service of systemic transformation.*

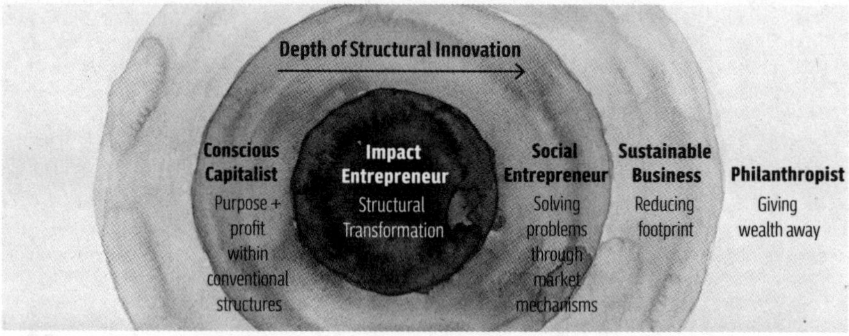

Figure 3. The Impact Entrepreneur—A Distinct Identity

It's the recognition that you cannot solve systemic problems with conventional tools, and the courage to redesign those tools at their foundation.

What Is an Impact Entrepreneur?

An impact entrepreneur is someone who builds enterprises where regeneration is not an add-on to the business model—it *is* the business model.

They understand that enterprise design shapes outcomes. You cannot extract your way to regeneration, and the structures you choose (legal, governance, ownership, capital) determine whether your enterprise can heal or only minimize harm. They recognize that impact requires integration. Social, environmental, and economic outcomes are not separate objectives to be "balanced" but interdependent dimensions of a living system, and true impact means strengthening all three simultaneously. They know that transformation is the goal. Impact entrepreneurs are not trying to succeed within the extractive economy but to build the regenerative economy that replaces it, one enterprise, one investment, one community at a time. And they embrace movement building—no single enterprise transforms systems, so impact entrepreneurs see themselves as part of a larger movement, learning from and strengthening one another.

A note on terminology: When this book uses "extractive," it refers to a systemic logic—one deeply entangled with capitalism as currently practiced, but not reducible to profit seeking itself. Extractive logic externalizes costs onto communities and ecosystems, concentrates wealth rather than distributing it, depletes commons rather than regenerating them, and optimizes for short-term gain at the expense of long-term flourishing. Many profitable enterprises reject this logic entirely. They internalize costs, distribute wealth, strengthen communities, and build for generations. These are not extractive—they are prototypes of the regenerative economy, often built by pioneers who took enormous risks to prove that values and viability could coexist.

The critique in these pages is directed at extractive logic as a system default—not at entrepreneurship, not at wealth creation, not at the pioneers who showed us another way was possible. Indeed, the Impact Economy depends on entrepreneurs creating wealth. The question is whether that wealth creation heals or harms the systems it touches.

How Impact Entrepreneurs Differ

To clarify what impact entrepreneurship is, it helps to distinguish it from related but different approaches.

Social entrepreneurs solve social problems through market mechanisms. They build sustainable revenue models for social missions—schools, healthcare, clean water. They're driven by mission but often accept conventional ownership and capital structures. Impact entrepreneurs share the mission focus but go further: They redesign the structures themselves, asking not simply "How do we fund this mission?" but "How do we build enterprises where mission cannot be compromised?"

Conscious capitalists believe business should serve all stakeholders, not just shareholders. They advocate for purpose-driven leadership and stakeholder-oriented management. But they often work within conventional corporate structures, relying on enlightened leaders to maintain stakeholder focus. Impact entrepreneurs ask what happens when the enlightened leader leaves, and they build structures that survive leadership transitions.

Sustainable business leaders minimize environmental harm through operational improvements: reducing emissions, eliminating waste, sourcing responsibly. These practices matter enormously, but they can exist within fundamentally extractive business models. Impact entrepreneurs ask whether the business model itself should be redesigned so that success requires ecological health rather than merely tolerating reduced harm.

ESG practitioners integrate ESG factors into investment analysis and corporate reporting. This surfaces important information but often treats environmental, social, and governance concerns as risks factors to manage rather than transformation goals to achieve. Impact entrepreneurs regard these dimensions as interconnected design principles, not compliance checkboxes.

The Core Characteristics

Across sectors and geographies, impact entrepreneurs share distinctive practices.

Systems-level thinking means they see enterprises as participants in larger ecosystems—ecological, social, economic—and design accordingly. Every decision considers ripple effects, feedback loops, and long-term consequences.

Structural innovation drives them to experiment with ownership models (cooperatives, trusts, distributed), governance (multistakeholder, consent-based), and capital structures (patient, blended, community-sourced) that embed mission into the DNA of the enterprise.

Stakeholder integration goes beyond consultation—impact entrepreneurs give stakeholders governance voice. Workers, communities, ecosystems, and future generations are represented in decision making, not just considered.

Transparency and accountability mean they measure and share both successes and failures, open-source learnings, and acknowledge complexity rather than oversimplifying for marketing.

Movement consciousness shapes how they see their work—as a contribution to a larger transformation. They mentor others, share resources, build coalitions, and recognize that collective success matters more than individual "unicorn" status.

Cultural intentionality leads them to cultivate organizational cultures aligned with regenerative values, rejecting burnout, extractive productivity, and domination in favor of care, sustainability, and mutualism.

Impact Entrepreneurship as Journey

Impact entrepreneurship is rarely a singular founding moment—it's an iterative process of progressively embedding mission into structure. Each decision that moves from discretionary gesture to structural commitment deepens alignment and makes regenerative purpose harder to compromise. This evolution often follows a recognizable pattern: from values-driven culture to operational integration, from voluntary practices to legal accountability, and ultimately to ownership structures that protect mission in perpetuity.

Patagonia's journey exemplifies this evolution: from its 1973 founding with strong environmental values but conventional structure, through decades of progressive decisions (1% for the Planet, organic cotton, B Corp certification, the Worn Wear program), culminating in 2022's transfer to a purpose trust ensuring profits fund environmental work in perpetuity. Far from a single founding moment, that's fifty years of structural deepening. The journey is as instructive as the destination, demonstrating that impact entrepreneurship is not a binary state but a practice of continuous structural evolution.

Why Impact Entrepreneurs Matter Now

We are living in a moment of civilizational decision. The extractive economy is producing cascading breakdowns—climate destabilization, ecological collapse, democratic erosion, social fragmentation—faster than incremental reforms can address.

Impact entrepreneurs matter because they are building the alternative at scale. They are demonstrating that regenerative models are economically viable, creating employment and livelihoods aligned with planetary health, innovating governance and ownership structures that distribute power, shifting cultural narratives about what business is for, and building movement infrastructure for systemic transformation.

They are not waiting for permission from governments, corporations, or markets. They are creating a new economic reality, one enterprise at a time, networked into a movement.

The Impact Economy: The Larger System

Individual enterprises are essential but insufficient on their own. What we need—what is emerging—is the *Impact Economy*: an integrated system where regenerative enterprises are the norm, not the exception (see figure 4).

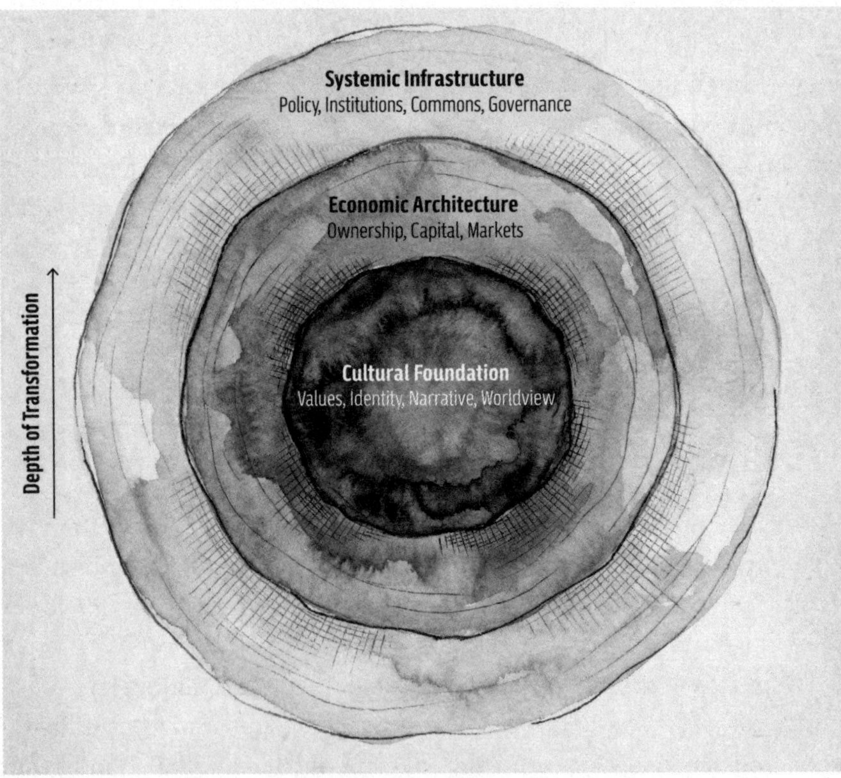

Figure 4. The Impact Economy—Three Nested Layers

The Impact Economy operates through eight interconnected dimensions, each reinforcing the others, organized across three layers:

- **Economic architecture:** Consists of *regenerative enterprises* (businesses designed to heal communities and ecosystems as they create financial value), *justice-oriented ownership* (cooperatives, trusts, and distributed models that prevent wealth concentration), and *custodial capital* (patient, aligned financing that rewards long-term regeneration).
- **Systemic infrastructure:** Includes *impact integrity* (mission embedded in legal structure, governance, and culture—not just stated in marketing), *transformed markets* (exchanges and valuation systems that price in externalities and reward stewardship), and *mutualistic security* (defense reimagined as prevention infrastructure—public health, ecological restoration, community resilience—rather than militarization).
- **Cultural foundation:** Comprises *cultural coherence* (stories, attention systems, and identities aligned with interdependence rather than extraction) and *protected commons* (land, water, knowledge, and democratic institutions reclaimed from enclosure and managed collectively).

This book maps the entire system, showing how each piece connects and how you can participate in building it.

The Essential Pairing

Naming who we are is only half the foundation. The other half is how we think. That's the subject of Chapter 2.

Impact entrepreneurs operate in complex systems where linear thinking fails, where well-intentioned interventions produce unintended consequences, where the very language we inherit shapes what we can see. The extractive economy persists not only because of misaligned structures but because of compartmentalized cognition—the habit of treating interconnected systems as separate problems with separate solutions.

Systemic intelligence—the capacity to perceive wholes, trace feedback loops, and identify leverage points—is not an optional upgrade to impact entrepreneurship. It is the prerequisite. Without it, even the most mission-driven enterprise will produce externalities it cannot see, get captured by dynamics it doesn't understand, or burn out fighting symptoms rather than causes.

Together, these two chapters form the foundation of everything that follows: who we are and how we must think to do this work effectively. Everything that follows—the enterprise architectures of Part II, the security reimagining of Part III, the cultural integration of Part IV, the commons reclamation of Part V—depends on both. Identity without intelligence produces earnest failure. Intelligence without identity produces clever co-optation.

You need both. Let's build the second.

Conclusion: The Work Begins with You

The Impact Economy will not be built by governments or corporations deciding from the top down to change course. It will be built by millions of people—entrepreneurs and aligned investors, policymakers and educators, community leaders and cultural workers—choosing to design enterprises, deploy capital, craft policy, tell stories, and organize movements differently.

You are already part of this. Even reading this book is an act of participation, equipping yourself to do the work more effectively. The question is not whether transformation is necessary. The question is how you will contribute to it.

Welcome to the movement. Let's begin.

TOOL KIT: THE IMPACT ENTREPRENEUR

Purpose: To help you assess whether you're operating as an impact entrepreneur, and to identify structural innovations that can deepen your impact.

1. Self-Assessment: Are You an Impact Entrepreneur?

   Honestly answer the following questions, organized across three dimensions:

   Enterprise design: Is regeneration core to your business model, or an add-on? Does your success require the systems you're embedded in to become healthier? If you scaled by a factor of one hundred, would the world be better or just have more of the same?

   Structural innovation: Have you redesigned ownership, governance, or capital structure to embed your mission? Are your stakeholders represented in decision making? Is your mission legally protected from future compromise?

   Movement consciousness: Do you see yourself as part of a larger transformation? Do you openly share learnings and resources? Do you actively support others doing similar work?

   If you answered "not yet" to most of those questions, that's okay—this book will show you how to move toward impact entrepreneurship step by step.

2. Identify Your Structural Innovations

   What aspects of your enterprise have you redesigned for impact? Consider your ownership model (cooperative, trust, distributed), governance (stakeholder voice, consent-based), capital structure (patient, blended, community-sourced), revenue model (circular, service-based, regenerative), supply chain

(CONTINUED)

(transparent, reciprocal, local), and culture (care-based, sustainable, mutualistic). Which areas need deeper innovation?

3. Map Your Ecosystem Position

   Where does your enterprise sit within larger systems? What ecological systems do you depend on? What communities are affected by your operations? What economic flows do you participate in? What cultural narratives do you reinforce or challenge? How could you strengthen those systems, not just extract from them?

4. Define Your Contribution to the Movement

   How does your work advance the Impact Economy beyond your enterprise? Do you mentor other entrepreneurs? Share intellectual property openly? Participate in coalitions and networks? Advocate for enabling policy? Fund or support movement infrastructure?

5. Assess Mission Permanence

   How protected is your mission from future compromise? Consider your legal structure (benefit corporation, cooperative, trust), governance (stakeholder voice, mission-lock provisions), capital (patient, aligned investors with limited exit rights), culture (strong enough to resist drift), and succession (plan for leadership transition). Where are the vulnerabilities? What would happen if you were acquired by a conventional corporation?

6. Commit to Next-Level Innovation

   Choose one structural innovation to implement in the next twelve months: convert to benefit corporation or cooperative, add stakeholder representation to governance, restructure capital with mission-aligned terms, implement transparent impact reporting, or join or form a coalition with aligned enterprises.

(CONTINUED)

Reflection Prompt

If your enterprise disappeared tomorrow, what would be lost that cannot be replicated by conventional businesses? If the answer is "not much," what structural innovation would make your impact irreplaceable?

Connects To

This foundational tool kit establishes the identity and structural innovations that all subsequent tool kits build upon. For building the cognitive capacity to implement these innovations, see Chapter 2. For specific structural design, see Chapters 3–5.

2

From Single-Bottom-Line to Systemic Intelligence

In the 1990s, many major clothing brands pledged to eliminate child labor from their supply chains. They audited factories, terminated noncompliant suppliers, and published sustainability reports celebrating progress. Twenty years later, child labor persists—sometimes

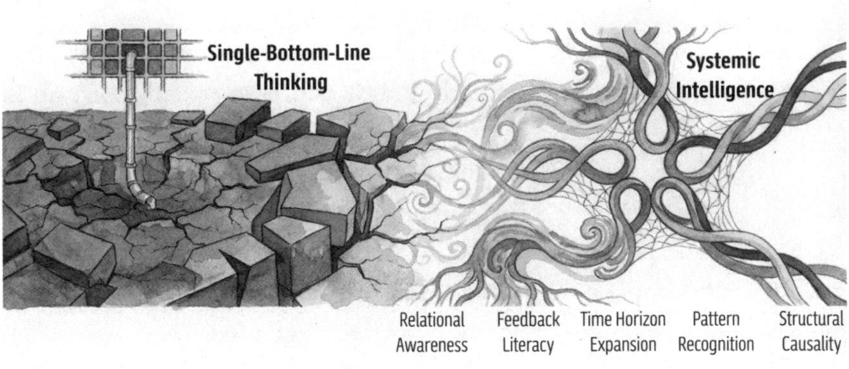

Figure 5. From Single-Bottom-Line to Systemic Intelligence

in the same regions, just pushed into smaller, less visible operations. Brands achieved compliance on paper while the underlying conditions that led to child labor (poverty, lack of education access, weak governance) remained unchanged or worsened.[1]

This is what happens when you try to solve systemic problems without systemic intelligence. You measure what's easy to measure. You address symptoms, not causes. You declare victory while root dynamics continue generating the harms you claim to combat.

Chapter 1 defined the impact entrepreneur as someone who designs enterprises where regeneration is core to the business model. But that design work requires a specific capability: *the ability to see, understand, and act within complex systems*. This is systemic intelligence (see figure 5). And without it, even the most well-intentioned structural innovations will produce unintended consequences, fail to scale, or be co-opted back into extraction.

The Failure of Single-Bottom-Line Thinking

For most of the modern era, business success has been defined by a single metric: profit. This reductionism seemed to work—at least for those measuring it. GDP grew. Markets expanded. Innovations proliferated. But the costs were systematically externalized: ecological degradation, social fragmentation, democratic erosion. These weren't counted because they weren't on the balance sheet.

The logic was elegant in its simplicity and devastating in its consequences: If it increases profit, do it. If it decreases profit, don't do it. Everything else is irrelevant or someone else's problem.

This approach seems sustainable as long as you can extract resources without pricing depletion, externalize pollution without liability, pay workers less than living costs (subsidized by families, communities, governments), concentrate wealth without social instability, and ignore long-term consequences beyond investment horizons.

But those conditions are collapsing. We've hit planetary boundaries. Social contracts are fracturing. Trust in institutions is eroding. The externalities are coming home. Single-bottom-line thinking didn't just fail morally; it failed strategically. It optimized for efficiency in ways that created fragility. It pursued growth that undermined its own foundations.

Why ESG and Impact Measurement Aren't Enough

The response from conventional business has been to add metrics: ESG scores, impact assessments, triple-bottom-line accounting. This is progress—but insufficient.

The problem is that you cannot solve for systemic health by adding variables to an extractive equation.

ESG typically measures environmental factors (carbon emissions, water use, waste), social factors (diversity stats, labor practices, community investment), and governance factors (board composition, ethics policies, transparency). These matter. But they're often *backward-looking* (reporting what happened rather than preventing what's coming), *siloed* (treating E, S, and G concerns as separate rather than interdependent), *compliance-oriented* (checking boxes rather than transforming structures), and *gameable* (optimizing for scores while maintaining an extractive core).

A company can score high on ESG while still extracting resources unsustainably, exploiting supply chain labor, structuring operations around extraction, and lobbying against climate policy. The metrics capture fragments while the system continues its destructive momentum.

What Systemic Intelligence Actually Is

Systemic intelligence is not a methodology or framework. It's a cultivated capacity—a way of seeing and acting within complexity that becomes increasingly intuitive with practice. It has five core dimensions (see figure 6):

- *Relational awareness* is the recognition that nothing exists in isolation. Every enterprise is nested within ecosystems (ecological,

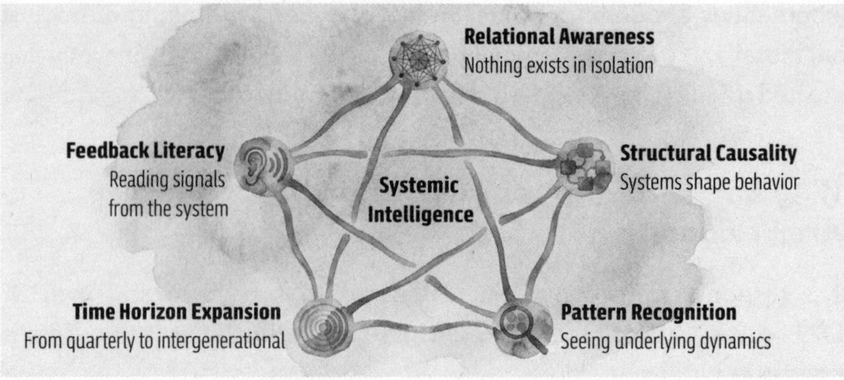

Figure 6. The Five Dimensions of Systemic Intelligence—Cultivating the Capacity to See and Act Within Complexity

social, economic, cultural), and every decision ripples through those systems. In practice, before launching a product, an impact entrepreneur asks not just "Will this sell?" but "What relationships does this strengthen or weaken? What feedback loops does it create? Who benefits and who bears costs—including nonhuman stakeholders and future generations?"

- *Feedback literacy* is the ability to read signals from the system—shifts in employee morale, customer sentiment, ecosystem health, regulatory climate—as information about alignment or drift. In practice, when turnover spikes, systemic intelligence asks "What is the system telling us?" rather than "How do we retain people more cheaply?" The answer might reveal misalignment between stated values and actual culture, or between compensation structure and cost of living.
- *Time horizon expansion* means moving from quarterly logic to intergenerational stewardship, recognizing that the longest time horizons often reveal the most important dynamics. In practice, a regenerative agriculture enterprise designs crop rotations on seven-year cycles (building soil health) rather than annual monocultures (depleting it), even though this requires patient capital and delayed returns.

- *Pattern recognition* is seeing the same underlying dynamics across different contexts—recognizing that extractive logic in labor markets, carbon cycles, and attention economies all stem from treating living systems as resources to be mined. In practice, an impact entrepreneur who sees how attention platforms commodify cognitive capacity can recognize the same pattern in gig economy worker exploitation, and design alternatives that resist both.
- *Structural causality* is understanding that individual behaviors are shaped by systems, not just by individual choices. Blaming people for systemic outcomes obscures root causes and prevents effective intervention. In practice, instead of blaming consumers for buying fast fashion, systemic intelligence examines why wages are too low for consumers to afford durable goods, why marketing manipulates insecurity, and how to restructure incentives throughout the system.

Case Study: Interface Carpets and Mission Zero

Ray Anderson, founder of commercial carpet manufacturer Interface, had a conversion moment in 1994 when challenged to articulate the company's environmental vision. He realized Interface was "plundering the earth" and committed to reaching *Mission Zero*—eliminating negative environmental impact by 2020.[2]

But this wasn't just about reducing emissions.

Anderson and his team applied systemic intelligence across all five dimensions (see figure 7). *Relational awareness* led them to recognize carpets as part of building ecosystems affecting air quality, waste streams, and occupant health. *Feedback literacy* meant listening to customers wanting sustainable options and employees wanting meaningful work. *Time horizon expansion* drove them to set a twenty-six-year goal (not two-year) and track progress in multiple dimensions. *Pattern recognition* revealed the extractive pattern across material sourcing, manufacturing, installation, and disposal, enabling redesign of the entire lifecycle. *Structural causality*

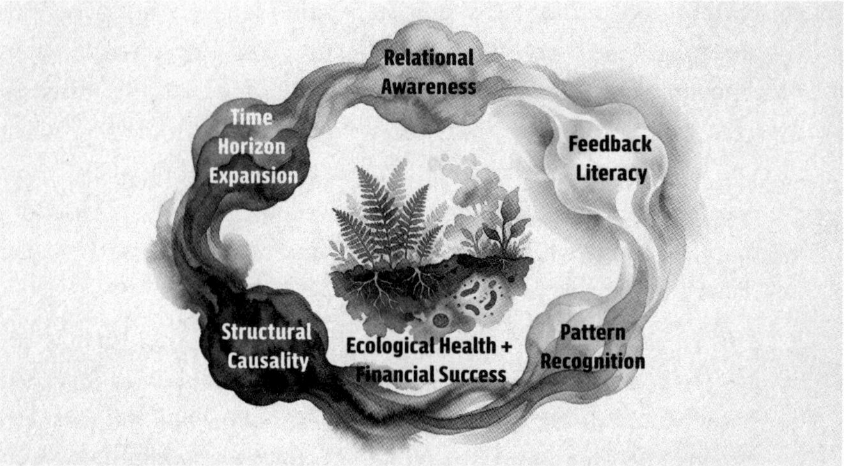

Figure 7. Interface Carpets—Systemic Intelligence in Action

led to attempts at fundamental shifts, such as experimenting with leasing rather than selling carpets (incentivizing durability over volume), even when these innovations faced market resistance.

By 2013, nearly half of the raw materials the company was using (approximately 49 percent) were from recycled or bio-based sources, resulting in estimated savings from avoided waste costs of $450 million. By 2019, a year ahead of schedule, Interface had achieved its Mission Zero goal of carbon neutrality, including a 96 percent reduction in greenhouse gas emissions and an 89 percent reduction in water use.[3]

This is systemic intelligence operationalized: Not just measuring harm reduction, but redesigning the enterprise so ecological health and financial success reinforce each other.

Cultivating Systemic Intelligence

Systemic intelligence can be learned. It requires both conceptual frameworks and embodied practice. The development happens across three complementary domains: the intellectual tools that help us map and analyze complexity, the personal practices that build our capacity to hold that complexity without reductive simplification, and the organizational structures that embed systems thinking into collective decision making.

Conceptual tools provide the analytical frameworks for understanding how systems operate. These aren't just abstract theories but practical instruments for seeing patterns, relationships, and leverage points that remain invisible to linear thinking. They include systems mapping (visualizing causal loops, stock-and-flow dynamics, feedback mechanisms), stakeholder analysis (identifying who is affected, including nonhuman and future stakeholders), scenario planning (exploring multiple futures to test assumptions and identify leverage points), and backcasting (working backward from the desired future to identify present actions).

Embodied practices cultivate the cognitive and emotional capacity to work with complexity. Systemic intelligence isn't just intellectual; it requires developing comfort with ambiguity, patience with emergence, and the ability to hold multiple perspectives simultaneously. This is done through contemplative practice (meditation, journaling, time in nature), long walks and slow thinking (creating space for nonlinear, integrative insight), dialogue across difference (regular engagement with stakeholders who see the system differently), and pattern journaling (noting recurring dynamics across contexts to train pattern recognition).

Organizational practices translate individual systemic intelligence into collective capability. Even the most systemically intelligent individuals will struggle within organizations designed for linear thinking. These practices create structures that surface blind spots, integrate diverse perspectives, and learn from complexity. They include premortems (before major decisions, imagining failure and working backward to identify risks), red teaming (designating someone to argue against proposals, revealing assumptions), learning reviews (regular reflection on what's working, what's not, and why), and cross-functional collaboration (breaking down silos so diverse perspectives inform decisions).

The Limits of Systemic Intelligence

Systemic intelligence is essential, but not sufficient. Three important caveats:

- *Complexity cannot be fully controlled.* No matter how sophisticated your systems thinking, surprises will emerge. The goal is not control but adaptability—building enterprises that can sense shifts and respond gracefully.
- *Analysis can become paralysis.* Systemic thinking can reveal so much complexity that action feels impossible. At some point, you must act with incomplete information, learn from results, and iterate.
- *Intelligence without power is ineffective—this is why structure matters.* This is perhaps the most crucial limitation. You can map every feedback loop, identify every leverage point, understand perfectly how systems perpetuate harm—but without the power to act on that understanding, nothing changes. A factory worker may see exactly how production systems destroy both human dignity and ecological health. A loan officer may understand precisely how financial structures trap communities in poverty. A teacher may recognize how educational systems reproduce inequality. But individual understanding without structural power results in nothing except frustration.

This is why impact entrepreneurs don't stop at systemic intelligence—they use it to inform structural innovation. They redesign ownership so workers have decision-making power. They restructure capital so patience is rewarded over extraction. They rebuild markets so regeneration becomes profitable. Intelligence guides the design, but it's the structures themselves—legal, financial, organizational—that create the power to transform systems.

Without structural innovation, systemic intelligence becomes merely sophisticated observation of problems you cannot solve. With it, intelligence becomes the blueprint for building alternatives that make extraction obsolete. This is why Part II focuses on the concrete structures—enterprises, ownership, capital, markets—that translate understanding into transformation.

From Intelligence to Action

Understanding systems is not the goal—transforming them is.

Systemic intelligence serves impact entrepreneurs by informing design choices (structuring enterprises to work with system dynamics, not against them), preventing unintended consequences (surfacing risks before they cascade), identifying leverage points (finding where small interventions create large shifts), building resilience (designing for adaptation rather than brittle optimization), and enabling collaboration (building the shared systems understanding that allows diverse actors to coordinate effectively).

The chapters ahead show how to apply systemic intelligence across every dimension of the Impact Economy: enterprise design, ownership structures, capital flows, impact integrity, market architecture, security infrastructure, cultural transformation, and commons stewardship. Each domain requires both the frameworks (what to build) and the intelligence (how to navigate complexity while building it).

Conclusion: The Difference It Makes

Two entrepreneurs see the same problem: food insecurity in their community.

Without systemic intelligence, one entrepreneur opens a food bank (addresses the symptom), depends on donations (fragile, unpredictable), distributes whatever food is available (often processed, low-nutrition), and succeeds by serving more people—but underlying causes persist.

With systemic intelligence, the other entrepreneur maps root causes (low wages, food deserts, industrial agriculture), designs a worker-owned grocery cooperative in the underserved area, sources from local regenerative farms (supporting ecosystem health), pays living wages (addressing the income dimension), structures ownership so the community controls food access permanently, and succeeds when the community becomes more food sovereign— with the underlying causes removed.

Both entrepreneurs have good intentions. Both work hard. But one addresses symptoms while the other transforms structures.

That's the difference systemic intelligence makes.

And it's the difference between impact entrepreneurship as noble effort and impact entrepreneurship as civilizational transformation.

The rest of this book builds on this foundation, showing you how to design, finance, protect, integrate, and scale enterprises that heal rather than extract. But all of it depends on the capacity cultivated here: the ability to see whole systems and act within them with wisdom.

TOOL KIT: FROM SINGLE-BOTTOM-LINE TO SYSTEMIC INTELLIGENCE

Purpose: To develop your capacity for systemic thinking and apply it to your enterprise or investment decisions.

1. Map Your System

   Choose one challenge you're facing and map it systemically. What are the visible symptoms? What underlying dynamics generate those symptoms? What feedback loops reinforce or balance those dynamics? Who are all the stakeholders (including nonhuman and future)? What would happen if you intervened only at the symptom level? Where are potential leverage points for deeper change? Create a simple causal loop diagram showing relationships between elements.

(CONTINUED)

2. Expand Your Time Horizons

   For your next major decision, ask: What does success look like in six months? Three years? Ten years? Fifty years? What dynamics only become visible at longer time scales? How would seven-generation thinking change this decision?

3. Identify Feedback Loops

   For your enterprise or investment, identify one reinforcing loop (where success builds on success) and one balancing loop (where growth triggers limiting forces). How can you strengthen positive loops and anticipate balancing ones?

4. Read System Signals

   List signals from your system: What are employees indicating about culture? What are customers indicating about value? What are ecosystems indicating about resource use? What are partners and suppliers indicating about relationship health? For each signal, ask: What is the system telling us? What would we do if we listened?

5. Seek Diverse Perspectives

   Identify three people who see your work differently: someone from a different sector, someone from an affected community, and someone from a different generation. Schedule conversations asking: What am I not seeing? What patterns do you notice? What concerns do I need to hear?

6. Run a Premortem

   Before your next major initiative, imagine it has failed spectacularly. Work backward: What went wrong? What systems dynamics did we miss? What feedback did we ignore? What structural flaws existed from the start? Use insights to redesign before launch.

(CONTINUED)

7. Build Systemic Intelligence Practices

   Commit to one practice for ninety days: weekly systems journaling (pattern recognition), monthly stakeholder dialogue (diverse perspectives), quarterly learning review (reflection and adaptation), or annual scenario planning (long-term thinking).

Reflection Prompt

Think of a decision you made recently that had unintended negative consequences. What systems dynamics did you miss? What would you do differently with stronger systemic intelligence?

Connects To

This tool kit builds on the identity established in Chapter 1 and provides the cognitive foundation for all the structural work that follows. Apply these systems-thinking practices when using the design tool kits in Part II (Chapters 3–6).

Part II

Possibility

What We Could Build

Race Brook Lodge, Berkshires, Massachusetts, July 2018. This is a landscape of deep memory, where the earth itself seems to speak in whispers. The area cradling the lodge is not just a place but a convergence, a hollow where geological time and human history press against each other, shadowed by the silent, watching presence of the mountains (figure 8).

The story begins with water. Race Brook, the lodge's namesake, is the valley's pulse, a cold, clear artery fed by the high-elevation springs

Figure 8. Race Brook Lodge

of the Taconic Range. It is a voice before it is a sight, tumbling over moss-slicked stones and slabs of ancient gneiss, carving the dark, hemlock-shaded ravine that gives the lodge its sanctuary. This brook is a worker, tirelessly sculpting the land, and its cascading falls are a sudden, thrilling revelation—a staircase of white water climbing toward the sky.

Above it all looms the great "Dome of the Taconics," Mount Everett. This is not the jagged, arrogant peak of a young range; this is old earth with a resilient, quiet intelligence—worn, weathered, and wise. Its slopes are dressed in a deep, steady forest of northern hardwoods, but its true magic lies at the summit. To climb it is to enter an entirely different realm, a "sky island" of ecological wonder.

Here, a rare and fragile forest of dwarf pitch pine and gnarled scrub oak clings to a shallow, rocky life. It is a tough, ancient community, sculpted by wind and ice, where the ground is a carpet of blueberry, huckleberry, and lichen. From this windswept summit, the world falls away into a 360-degree panorama, a sea of green ridges folding into the blue haze of the Hudson Valley to the west and the rolling Berkshire hills to the east.

This is the ancestral land of the Mahican people, "the people of the waters that are never still." They knew the murmur of these hemlocks and the thunder of the falls not as "wilderness," but as home—an indivisible weave of land and life, of sustenance and spirit. They moved through these mountains for centuries, their paths following the same logical contours of the land that hikers follow today. The Housatonic River, a silver ribbon in the valley below, was their lifeblood, and their consciousness is embedded in the very names of the region: Housatunnock, "beyond the mountain place"; Mahaiwe, "the place downstream"; Taconic, "steep ascent" or "place of trees."[1]

Then came the ring of the axe and the creak of the wagon wheel. The "Undermountain Road," now the scenic Route 41, became a vital artery of commerce and news, a muddy, rugged path for stagecoaches rattling between Hartford and Albany. The Stagecoach Tavern, the historic heart of Race Brook Lodge, was a haven for those weary travelers—a pinprick of firelight, rum, and news in the vast, shadowed forest. You can still feel that history in the hand-hewn beams and the low ceilings, a sense of shelter against the profound darkness of the mountain.

Each epoch left its own pattern of interdependence—natural, social, economic. It was into that palimpsest that we arrived in 2018, asking whether a new economy could root itself here with the same humility and reciprocity.

It is a landscape that molds its people, a place that demands introspection. This is what some have called the "ground of consciousness"—where standing between the wild, ancient mountain and the cultivated valley below reveals something fundamental about integration, about the relationship between place and how we see.

Today, to walk the trails from Race Brook Lodge is to walk through all these layers at once. You are following the path of the stagecoach, the footsteps of the Mahican, and the geological fault line of an ancient range, all while listening to the same timeless rush of water that has defined this hollow for millennia. Everything interpenetrates—ecology, economy, culture, consciousness. The pattern is the same.

One study, years ago, identified the Berkshires as possessing ideal proportions: ancient hills, meandering rivers, reclaimed northern forests, small working farms, well-constructed villages with engaged citizenry. Not wilderness, not suburb, not city—something in between. A landscape shaped by humans but not dominated by them. Reciprocal. Regenerative before we had language for it.

Twenty-seven years after that November gathering at Cape Cod described in Part I, I found myself here, convening forty systems change leaders from three continents around tables in Race Brook's great room. The questions had shifted. We were no longer asking *what's wrong with the system*—we knew what was wrong. Now we were asking: *What does it look like to build something else? Is it actually possible? And if so, how do we scale what's working?*

•

The first evening, before the work began, I invited Randy Weinstein, director of the W. E. B. Du Bois Center in Great Barrington, to welcome us. Great Barrington sits just a few miles up the road—where William

Edward Burghardt Du Bois was born in 1868, attended local schools, learned to see the world (figure 9).[2]

"Du Bois always said the Berkshires formed him," Randy told the room. "Not just the people—though they were crucial—but the landscape itself. He wrote about these hills, these rivers. About how being embedded in this place taught him that everything connects—that you can't separate social justice from economic justice from relationship with the natural world. He saw systems before we had frameworks for systems thinking."

Du Bois left the Berkshires but never stopped claiming them as the ground of his consciousness, the place that taught him what integration actually meant—not just racial integration, though that was central to his life's work, but the integration of all dimensions of human thriving with ecological health. You can't uplift people while destroying the land they depend on. You can't build a just economy while treating nature as commodity. Everything interpenetrates.

I understood. I've lived in these hills for thirty years, just a mile up the road from where we sat. This landscape has taught me too—the same lessons Du Bois learned a century before. That everything connects. That you can't separate economic justice from ecological health. That place forms consciousness in ways we don't fully understand but can't

Figure 9. W. E. B. Du Bois in the Berkshire Hills

ignore. When I chose Race Brook for this gathering, I wasn't just picking a convenient venue. I was bringing people to my home ground, to the watershed that shaped how I see, asking: *Can you see what this place teaches?*

"Du Bois was," Randy said, "what you might now call an impact entrepreneur. Someone who understood that transformation requires seeing the whole, changing structures, building alternatives that address root causes."

The room went quiet. We were gathering to map the Impact Economy, and here was its prototype—born up the road 150 years ago, formed by this place, showing us it had always been possible to see differently.

•

After Randy spoke, Susan Witt stood. Susan runs the Schumacher Center for a New Economics, also just miles from where we sat.[3] She'd brought samples of something most of the group had heard about but never held: BerkShares, the local currency that's been circulating in these hills since 2006.[4]

She passed them around the tables. They looked like dollars—same size, similar design—but instead of presidents, they featured local heroes. And they were printed by Crane & Co., the same Berkshire company that prints US currency, on the same cotton-fiber paper. Not play money—real currency with the same material integrity as what the Federal Reserve issues, but serving different values. Herman Melville on the $20, who wrote *Moby-Dick* at his Pittsfield home. Norman Rockwell on the $50, who spent his last decades painting American life from his Stockbridge studio. Robyn Van En on the $10, who founded the Community Supported Agriculture (CSA) movement at Indian Line Farm in South Egremont.

And W. E. B. Du Bois on the $5.

I held that bill, looking at Du Bois's face. Not Washington. Not Lincoln. Not Hamilton arguing for centralized banking. Du Bois—the integrative thinker, the one who saw that liberation required economic transformation, that economic transformation required ecological wisdom, that none of it could be separated.

"This is real currency," Susan said. "Accepted at three hundred businesses across the county. Not a protest. Not a symbol. An operating alternative to extractive finance, grounded in place, building local resilience."

The Impact Economy isn't theory, I thought. *It's already here in embryo. We're not inventing it—we're recognizing it, naming it, scaling what already works.*

•

Over three days, we mapped.

Heather Grady from Rockefeller Philanthropy Advisors and I had spent months designing this convening. We'd reached out to leaders working at the intersection of philanthropy, impact investing, systems change, and new economy design. Foundation executives who'd moved billions toward justice. Impact entrepreneurs who'd built enterprises nobody thought viable. Regenerative capital practitioners who'd structured deals finance professors said couldn't work. Community organizers who'd reclaimed land. Blockchain designers who saw distributed ledgers as tools for distributed power.

The invitation had been simple but ambitious: *Come help us map the path to an economy that serves all life, not just shareholders.*

What we hadn't articulated but what became clear within hours was that many already were building it. Not theorizing. *Building.* The question wasn't whether the Impact Economy was possible—it was how to make visible what was emerging, how to connect the nodes, how to move from scattered experiments to coherent alternative.

John Fullerton from the Capital Institute stood at a whiteboard, windows open to birdsong and the sound of the brook below. Ceiling fans rotated slowly overhead in the barn's high space as he sketched circles within circles—the regenerative systems thinking he'd developed over years of working in finance and then leaving it for something truer.[5]

"We're nowhere near smart enough to know how to shift our economic system to where it needs to be," he said. "But we can study systems that have sustained themselves for long periods of time—ecosystems, Indigenous societies. We can learn principles and then apply those principles to finance, to enterprise, to markets."

He wasn't talking about sustainability anymore. Sustainability meant "do less harm"; maintain current degradation without making it worse. He was talking about regeneration—the difference between "do less harm" and "actively heal." The pattern that shows up everywhere from cells to forests to healthy economies: Symbiotic. Mutual. Win-win at every scale.

Someone asked what this meant practically. Regenerative agriculture was proving you could build topsoil while growing food, sequester carbon while feeding communities, make profit while healing land. Could we do that with capital? With ownership structures? With markets?

"We have to," John said. "Because extraction is ending whether we choose it or not. The question is whether we build alternatives before collapse or after."

•

We worked in small groups, then reconvened. Identifying what was already operational. Naming gaps. Finding patterns.

By the final morning, something had shifted in the room. Not optimism exactly—everyone present was too aware of the scale of crisis for naive optimism. But something else: recognition. The recognition that comes just before breakthrough—when scattered efforts suddenly see themselves as a coherent whole. We weren't alone. The work we'd each been doing in isolation was part of a larger pattern trying to emerge. The Impact Economy wasn't utopian fantasy—it was already being born in ten thousand places simultaneously, by people who might not even know each other's names but were following the same deep coding toward something more alive.

•

On my last morning at Race Brook, I walked down to the brook before breakfast. Clear water moving over stone, ferns thick on both banks, light filtering green through leaves. The sound of it—constant, ancient, utterly present.

I thought about Du Bois, born a few miles from here, formed by a landscape that taught integration before he had language for it. About BerkShares with his face on them, circulating as proof that alternatives aren't theoretical. About John Fullerton's circles within circles, Susan Witt's local economics, Heather Grady's commitment to shifting how foundations deploy capital. About forty people in a room deciding to make visible what's trying to be born.

The Impact Economy was already here—in this watershed, these hills, this community that had been practicing regenerative relationship for longer than any of us had been alive. Our work wasn't to invent it. Our work was to recognize it, to name it, to build the scaffolding that would let it scale from embryo to ecosystem.

The brook kept moving, as it had for millennia, finding its way around obstacles, carving channels, feeding the valley, demonstrating what regeneration looks like when you pay attention.

We just had to follow the pattern.

The pattern that brook revealed—and that our gathering confirmed—was this: Regeneration isn't built through master plans imposed from above, but through aligned innovations at every level of economic life. The forty leaders at Race Brook had shown us the proof points. Enterprises already demonstrating that healing could be profitable. Ownership structures already distributing power rather than concentrating it. Capital already flowing patiently toward long-term regeneration. Markets already beginning to price what actually matters. Each innovation reinforced the others, creating the nucleus of an entirely different economy.

What we needed now was to make these patterns visible, replicable, scalable. To show not just that alternatives to extraction exist, but exactly how they work—the precise structures, frameworks, and design principles that make regeneration economically viable. The next four chapters map those structures, moving from the enterprise itself outward through the concentric circles of ownership, capital, and market architecture that either enable transformation or prevent it.

From Diagnosis to Design

In Part I, we established what the Impact Economy is and who is building it. We named the crisis of single-bottom-line thinking and introduced the systemic intelligence required to navigate complexity. Now we shift from diagnosis to design—from *what's wrong* to *what works*.

Possibility without foundations is fantasy—ideas unmoored from the systems they claim to transform. But foundations without possibility is paralysis—endless analysis that never translates into action. Part I gave us the intellectual architecture. Part II translates that understanding into structures.

The four chapters ahead address interconnected dimensions of regenerative design. Change one and leave the others extractive, and the system will revert. Change all four in alignment, and regeneration becomes self-reinforcing: An enterprise designed for healing cannot sustain itself if ownership concentrates power in extractive hands. Distributed ownership cannot function without patient capital that doesn't demand premature exits. Custodial capital cannot scale if markets reward extraction over regeneration. And markets that reflect what matters cannot exist without enterprises demonstrating that regenerative models work.

Each dimension reinforces the others. Together, they create a coherent system—which is why the Impact Economy is not a sector but a paradigm, requiring simultaneous innovation across operations, ownership, finance, and exchange.

This is where we move from understanding to building.

3

Enterprises That Heal

Design for Regeneration

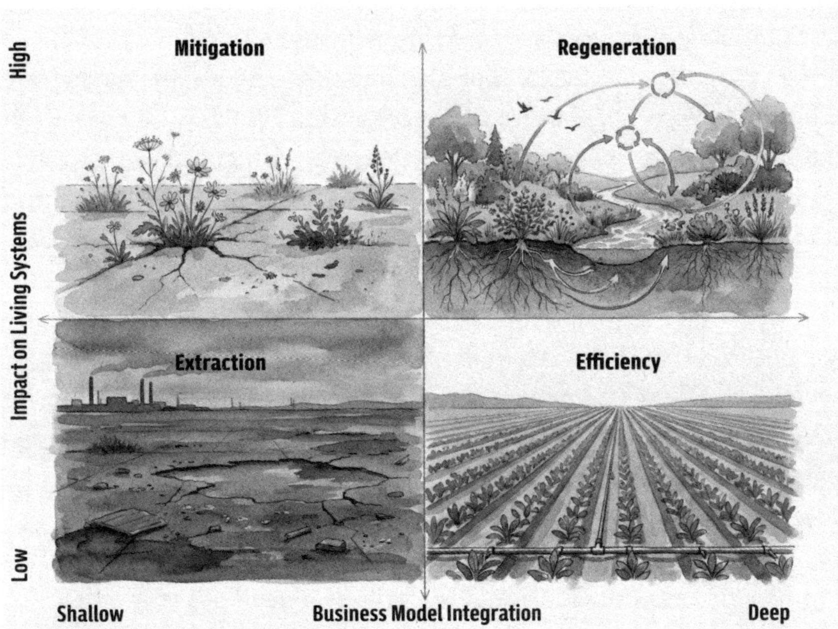

Figure 10. Enterprises That Heal

Beyond "Do Less Harm"

For most of the modern industrial era, business has measured its success in the language of extraction. Labor, resources, attention, time—all pulled from somewhere else, transformed, and sold for more than they cost to acquire. The surplus went to the enterprise. The losses—degraded ecosystems, frayed communities, eroded trust—were left for someone else to bear.

This model did not pretend to heal. At best, it aspired to "do less harm," usually as a late-stage add-on: a carbon offset here, a philanthropic donation there, a glossy sustainability report that framed damage mitigation as progress.

The Impact Economy asks a more radical question: *What if enterprises could heal what the old economy harmed?*

Not as metaphor. Not as corporate charity. But as the central operating logic, embedded in the design of products, services, supply chains, ownership structures, and governance systems.

Enterprises that heal reject the zero-sum assumption that profit must come at someone's or something's expense (see figure 10). They create value in place, with health, trust, and ecological vitality as outcomes, not externalities. They measure their worth in the resilience they cultivate.

This is not wishful thinking. It is already happening—in soil and schools, in rivers and governance charters, in ways ancient and new. But scaling this vision requires a shift away from sustainability as maintenance toward regeneration as strategy—repair, reciprocity, and relational restoration as the standard of excellence.

And it requires something more: *impact integrity*. The alignment between what an enterprise claims and what it actually does, between stated values and operational reality, between marketing narrative and governance structure.

This chapter explores both what regenerative enterprises look like and how to design them so that integrity is embedded in their DNA—making mission drift difficult and healing inevitable.

Ancient Roots of Regeneration

The regenerative vision is not an invention of 21st-century entrepreneurs. It is a rediscovery of knowledge that has been present for millennia in Indigenous, Eastern, and African traditions—wisdom systems that see life as interdependent, responsibility as reciprocal, and economic activity as inseparable from ecological stewardship.

Consider the Haudenosaunee Confederacy, whose Great Law of Peace insists that decisions be made with the well-being of seven generations ahead in mind—a principle that treats short-term gain at long-term expense as a form of theft from those not yet born.[1] Or the Māori practice of *rāhui*: temporary restrictions placed on harvesting to allow ecosystems to regenerate, a model of governance rooted in ecological cycles rather than quarterly returns.[2] The African ethic of *Ubuntu*—"I am because we are"—recognizes that economic vitality depends on collective well-being, countering the hyperindividualism of modern capitalism.[3] And the Taoist principle of *wu wei* teaches action in harmony with the natural order, favoring flow over force, alignment over domination.[4]

These principles remind us that regeneration is not a contemporary innovation. It is an ancient norm—one we have strayed from and must learn to embody again.

From Sustainability to Regeneration

Sustainability, as a concept, was a step forward. It shifted business discourse toward efficiency, footprint reduction, and harm minimization. But sustaining a broken status quo is not enough in a world already overshooting planetary boundaries.

Regeneration is a higher bar.

It means restoring degraded soils and waterways, not merely slowing their decline. It means repairing the social fabric fractured by inequity and disinvestment, not just documenting the tear. It means designing ownership structures that distribute power rather than consolidate it, embedding circularity from product inception rather than as an afterthought, and treating customers as collaborators in value creation rather than consumers to be captured.

Regeneration is about returning more than you take—in resources, in trust, in cultural vitality. It makes "How does this make the world more alive?" the most important design question.

Let me be clear: Regenerative enterprise is not a vow of poverty. The impact entrepreneur who starts with $5,000 and builds a company worth $130 million—while distributing profits to employees, donating to community, and strengthening rather than depleting the systems they touch—is not a contradiction. They are the proof of concept. Wealth creation is not antithetical to regeneration; it is fuel for it. The question is never *whether* to create wealth but *how*: whether the journey concentrates or distributes, extracts or regenerates, depletes or renews.

The practitioner's burden is real: the steep climb, the risk, the years of uncertainty. This book does not minimize that burden. It offers structural tools to ensure that when success comes, it compounds healing rather than harm—and that the wealth created expands alongside trust, not at its expense.

The Architecture of Regenerative Enterprise

What makes an enterprise capable of healing rather than merely minimizing harm? The answer lies not in intentions but in architecture—structural choices that make regeneration inseparable from success.

It begins with the business model itself. The conventional model profits from throughput: The faster resources flow from extraction to disposal, the greater the return. Regenerative models invert this logic. Interface doesn't sell carpet tiles; it leases them, maintaining ownership so that durability and recyclability become profit centers rather than threats to revenue.[5] MUD Jeans leases denim, recovering materials at end of use.[6] In these service-based models, the enterprise succeeds only when products last longer, not when they fail faster.

Circular models take this further, designing for endless material recovery where what one process discards becomes what another requires. Restorative models go further still, tying revenue directly to ecosystem regeneration—regenerative farms earning carbon credits while rebuilding soil, watershed restoration funded by downstream water users who benefit from the healing. And community wealth models make local economic development the business itself, as community development financial institutions and cooperative networks demonstrate daily.

But business model alone isn't enough. What you make matters as much as how you make money from it. Products designed for healing are durable and repairable, built for longevity, not planned obsolescence. They use materials that enrich rather than degrade: compostable textiles, bio-based compounds that sequester carbon, inputs that can return to soil or industry without toxicity. They're designed for local conditions rather than one-size-fits-all extraction, adapted to place rather than imposed upon it.

The supply chain extends this logic into every relationship. Transparency and traceability become nonnegotiable—not as compliance exercises but as the foundation for reciprocal partnerships built on mutual benefit. Local sourcing keeps wealth circulating within communities. Fair conditions and living wages throughout the chain recognize that extraction from workers is no different than extraction from ecosystems: Both deplete what the enterprise depends upon.

Stakeholder integration gives voice to all who are affected. Workers gain ownership stakes, profit sharing, and governance representation. Communities move from consultation to codesign and shared decision making. Some enterprises have created formal mechanisms for nonhuman stakeholders—board seats representing "future generations" or "watershed health"—recognizing that ecological systems have interests even if they lack voices. Customers become collaborators in value creation rather than targets for extraction.

And beneath all of this lies culture: the internal environment that either reinforces or undermines every structural choice. Enterprises that heal reject burnout culture, building rest and renewal into operations. They create psychological safety, so people can bring wholeness, speak truth, and take risks. They treat failures as learning opportunities, encouraging experimentation. They celebrate interdependence, recognizing success as collective rather than individual heroism.

These elements—business model, product design, supply chain, stakeholder voice, and culture—are not separate initiatives to be pursued in sequence. They are the integrated architecture of regeneration. Each reinforces the others; weakness in any one creates vulnerability in all.

Impact Integrity: The Soul of the Enterprise

All of this design work fails if there's a gap between what an enterprise says and what it does. Impact integrity is the discipline of closing that gap until there is none.

Every enterprise has a public story—mission statement, values, origin myth polished for the "About Us" page. But beneath that story lies another one, harder to tell and harder to hide: the lived reality of how it operates.

In the Impact Economy, the distance between these two stories is the measure of integrity.

Integrity is not perfection. In a world of complexity, compromise is inevitable. But coherence is possible. And coherence is what gives enterprises moral gravity—the ability to hold their course when pressures mount; when shortcuts beckon; when capital, customers, or crises demand speed over substance.

Integrity as Design, Not Aspiration

We tend to think of integrity as a personal virtue—something that depends on the character of founders, the vigilance of leaders, the culture of a particular team. But people leave. Cultures drift. Markets pressure. What begins as fierce commitment erodes under the relentless friction of operations.

This is why regenerative enterprises design integrity into structure rather than relying on intention alone. When values are encoded in architecture, they outlast individuals and resist the erosion that time and pressure inevitably bring.

Every structural element becomes a vessel for values. Ownership structure determines who holds power and whose interests ultimately govern—cooperatives, trusts, and distributed models concentrate decision making in those most affected by outcomes, making extraction mechanically difficult. Governance models either share power and make accountability visible or concentrate authority and obscure responsibility. Revenue mechanics either allow mission to guide growth or force mission drift to meet targets that patient capital would never impose. Hiring and compensation practices either uphold economic dignity or undermine the very values the enterprise claims. Supply chains either embody transparency and reciprocity or hide exploitation behind contractual distance. Community relationships either invite shared stewardship or perform consultation while retaining all real power.

When these elements align, they reinforce one another, creating architecture that can withstand both external shocks and internal temptations. When they're misaligned, cracks are inevitable—and through those cracks, impact-washing seeps in.

Case Study: Patagonia—Integrity Through Iterative Design

Patagonia exemplifies the journey from values to structure—not as a single transformative decision, but as decades of layered choices, each making backsliding harder than the one before (see figure 11):

1973: Founded with environmental ethos but conventional corporate structure—Patagonia could have remained a company that cared about the outdoors while operating like any other apparel business. Instead, it began encoding its values into its architecture.

1985: 1% for the Planet commitment—structural, not discretionary giving that could be cut when margins tightened. The commitment was locked into the company's operating DNA.

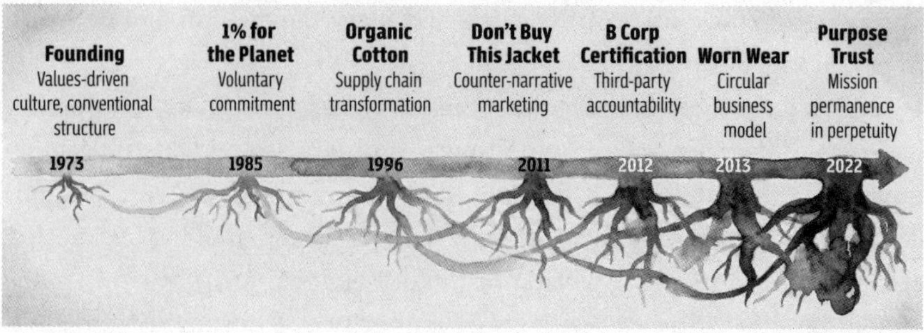

Figure 11. Patagonia's Journey: From Values-Driven Culture to Mission Permanence

1996: Switch to 100 percent organic cotton despite significant cost increases—operational alignment with values even when the market didn't reward it. This was integrity as sacrifice, proving the commitment was real.

2011: "Don't Buy This Jacket" Black Friday ad—not marketing cleverness but countercultural positioning that attracted customers who shared the company's values and repelled those who didn't. The brand became a filter.

2012: B Corp certification and benefit corporation status—third-party validation paired with legal restructuring for stakeholder accountability. Values now had governance teeth.

2013: Worn Wear program—a business model that rewards durability over volume, making the company's financial success dependent on products lasting longer.

2018: Mission-locked $1 million annually to grassroots environmental groups—activism made structural rather than dependent on leadership preference.

2022: Ownership transferred to purpose trust and nonprofit. Yvon Chouinard didn't just donate his company to environmental causes—he engineered an ownership structure that makes it mechanically impossible for future leaders to prioritize profit extraction over planetary healing.[7]

Each layer makes backsliding harder and integrity more structural.

The result: a company whose operational DNA makes it difficult to compromise mission. Revenue flows fund environmental work. Governance protects values. Culture reinforces stewardship. Supply chain transparency exposes contradictions early.

This is integrity by design.

Case Study: Fairphone—Integrity in the Supply Chain

Fairphone, founded in Amsterdam in 2013, set out to create a smartphone designed for longevity, repairability, and ethical sourcing, in an industry notorious for the opposite. The challenge was immense: Smartphones sit at the nexus of some of the world's most complex and often exploitative supply chains, from conflict minerals in the Democratic Republic of Congo to labor conditions in Chinese assembly plants.

Rather than claiming purity it couldn't deliver, Fairphone designed for integrity through radical transparency and structural alignment. Modular components make repair easy, reducing e-waste and extending product life—design choices that encode values into the physical object itself. Published supplier lists (rare in electronics), partnerships with conflict-free mines, and worker representation in manufacturing decisions extend that integrity through the supply chain. The revenue model aligns with the mission: Fairphone sells repair parts directly and offers repair guides, profiting from durability rather than replacement. B Corp structure ensures mission permanence beyond current leadership.[8]

Perhaps most importantly, Fairphone publicly acknowledges its limitations. No complex hardware company can fully escape existing systems, but the operational DNA makes backsliding difficult and transparency unavoidable. When contradictions emerge—and in global supply chains, they inevitably do—the structure forces acknowledgment rather than concealment.

The lesson: Integrity is not a veneer. It's a structure.

Designing for Integrity: A Living Practice

Integrity is not static. Markets shift, cultures evolve, stakeholder needs change. An enterprise with true impact integrity treats alignment as an ongoing design process, not a one-time certification.

This requires assessment and transparency: mapping mission against operations at least annually, with independent verification where possible. The questions are simple but demanding: Are our stated values reflected in actual decisions? Where are the gaps between what we say and what we do? What structural changes would close those gaps? Publishing decisions, metrics, and trade-offs—not just successes but challenges and failures—makes integrity accountable to those watching.

It requires governance and structure that bring affected stakeholders into decision making: workers represented in major decisions, community members on advisory boards, formal mechanisms for ecosystem and future generation consideration. And it requires adaptive structures: governance and contracts built with flexibility to respond to new knowledge, while protecting the core mission from erosion.

Perhaps most importantly, it requires cultural reinforcement: training, storytelling, and rituals that keep values alive in daily operations. Onboarding that transmits culture, not just tasks. Regular storytelling about mission alignment. Celebration of decisions that chose integrity over expediency. Without this cultural layer, even the most carefully designed structures eventually hollow out.

The Moral Economy of Design

All this structural work—the auditing, the stakeholder inclusion, the transparency—reveals a deeper layer of questions that regenerative enterprises must confront. Every design decision carries moral weight, encoding values into operations whether we acknowledge them or not. The structures we build don't just organize work; they distribute power, allocate risk, and determine who thrives and who merely survives.

This is why we must move beyond asking whether our designs function to interrogating what values they embody and whose interests they serve.

Asking "Does it work?" is not enough. We must also ask: What does it work *for*? *Whom* does it serve? What does it cost, and *who bears* that cost?

These questions force us to confront the moral economy embedded in every design decision. A company may claim to prioritize living wages, yet outsource production to regions with no labor protections—the structure contradicts the claim. A platform may commit to diversity, yet structure equity distribution so that only founders and early investors accumulate meaningful wealth—the ownership undermines the values. A nonprofit may champion environmental restoration, yet rely on grant funding from extractive industries that undermine the very ecosystems it aims to heal—the capital structure corrupts the mission.

Designing for impact integrity means pulling these contradictions into the open and redesigning the enterprise so that stated commitments are not only operationally feasible but structurally inevitable.

Why Integrity Is a Resilience Strategy

Some leaders still see integrity as a moral luxury—something to be pursued only when there's enough surplus time or capital. But the Impact Economy reframes it as a core resilience strategy.

Enterprises with integrity build trust capital that outlasts market swings and reputational crises. They attract mission-aligned talent motivated by more than compensation, increasing retention and reducing recruitment costs. They create transparent systems that identify mission drift early, before it becomes crisis. They navigate disruption without losing stakeholder confidence. They generate loyal customers who become advocates and partners rather than transactions to be optimized.

The paradox is that designing for integrity often slows growth in the short term but accelerates durability in the long term. It's the difference between sprinting and endurance running: Only one can take you the full distance.

Enterprises as Ecosystem Participants

The industrial economy imagined businesses as machines—self-contained, predictable, interchangeable. In reality, every enterprise is an organism nested within larger systems: ecological, social, cultural, psychological. Enterprises that heal act as ecosystem participants, attuned to place, responsive to feedback, and committed to reciprocal exchange.

This means rooting operations in local capacities and needs rather than extracting resources and exporting them elsewhere. It means building trust-based relationships with suppliers, workers, and communities—valuing long-term partnerships over transactional efficiency. It means designing for durability over dominance, building resilience into the system rather than just the enterprise. And it means recognizing that resilience comes from right relationship: You cannot insulate yourself from systems you depend on; you can only strengthen them.

An enterprise that behaves as an ecosystem participant doesn't just survive shocks—it helps buffer the system from collapse. It becomes part of the immune system of the world.

Case Study: Everlane—When Transparency Claims Meet Reality

Everlane built its brand on a single word: transparency. "Radical Transparency," they called it—publishing factory locations, breaking down costs, promising customers could see exactly where their clothes came from and who made them. The market responded. Everlane grew from a small San Francisco startup to a company valued at over $250 million.

Then the cracks appeared—not in their supply chain, but in their own house. In late 2019, Everlane's customer experience team announced plans to unionize, citing pay below living wage, unpredictable schedules, and benefits withheld by capping hours just below full-time thresholds. The company's response revealed a gap between its public values and internal practices: Management sent emails discouraging unionization, warning that collective bargaining would "reduce transparency."

In March 2020, as the pandemic struck, Everlane laid off the majority of that same customer service team—precisely the workers who had been organizing. Critics, including Senator Bernie Sanders, called it union busting. Months later, former employees published accounts of a workplace culture at odds with the brand's progressive image. The company that had trademarked "Radical Transparency" found itself accused of the opposite.[9]

What makes Everlane's story instructive isn't the failure itself—every enterprise faces contradictions. It's what the failure reveals: *Transparency as marketing is not the same as transparency as structure.*

Everlane had built elaborate systems to show customers where products came from. But it had not built governance structures that gave workers voice, ownership mechanisms that aligned internal practices with external claims, or accountability systems that would surface contradictions before they became crises. The transparency was outward-facing—a brand promise, not an operational reality.

The lesson is sobering. Integrity built on narrative rather than architecture is fragile. When pressure came—economic crisis, labor organizing, public scrutiny—the gap between story and structure was exposed. And once exposed, that gap is extraordinarily difficult to close. Everlane has made incremental improvements since 2020, but years later, the company still lacks comprehensive third-party certifications, still faces skepticism about the depth of its commitments, and still carries the reputational weight of promises broken.

This is the cautionary tale every impact entrepreneur must internalize: *You cannot market your way to integrity.* The enterprises that heal are not those with the best transparency campaigns but those that embed accountability into ownership, governance, and operations from the beginning—making the story and the structure indistinguishable.

Healing in Practice: Three Enterprises, Three Continents

Theory matters, but proof matters more. The following enterprises demonstrate that regenerative design isn't aspirational—it's operational, across radically different sectors, scales, and geographies. Each has embedded healing into its core architecture in ways that make extraction structurally difficult:

- **Tanka Bar (USA)** is a Native American-owned food company reviving the buffalo economy of the Lakota people. Tanka Bar has built a regenerative supply chain that restores prairie ecosystems, supports cultural sovereignty, and creates jobs on reservations historically defined by economic deprivation.[10] Ecological restoration and economic dignity are treated as inseparable goals. What makes this enterprise significant isn't just what it produces—it's that the business model itself cannot succeed without healing land, culture, and community simultaneously.
- **Riversimple (UK)** is a hydrogen fuel cell car company structured as a multistakeholder trust. Riversimple doesn't sell cars; it provides mobility as a service, aligning incentives with long-term ecological health and user satisfaction.[11] Governance ensures that environmental, customer, and community interests are represented equally alongside financial ones. The structure makes it impossible for any single stakeholder group to capture the enterprise for extractive purposes.
- **Grameen Shakti (Bangladesh)** is a solar energy enterprise that, by bringing affordable solar energy to millions of rural households, reduces energy scarcity, lowers resource competition, and boosts local economic resilience—a triple layer of stability that is security work as much as development work.[12] The enterprise demonstrates that regeneration scales: what began as a pilot now has installed over 1.8 million solar home systems, benefiting more than 12 million people, proving that healing design is not limited to boutique operations.

These are not exceptions. They are templates—proof points that others can study, adapt, and replicate.

Healing as Strategy

Healing is often dismissed as "soft"—the language of nonprofits or therapists, not boardrooms. This is a costly misunderstanding.

Watch what happens in enterprises designed for healing from inception. Patagonia doesn't make outdoor gear and then donate to environmental causes—the gear itself is designed to reduce harm and restore ecosystems. Fairphone doesn't make smartphones and then offset the damage—the phone itself challenges extractive supply chains. Grameen Shakti doesn't provide solar panels and then talk about empowerment—the business model itself distributes ownership and builds local capacity.

The healing isn't what they do with their profits. The healing is the business.

As David Abram demonstrated at that Cape Cod gathering described in Part I, where he described watching Indigenous shamans, healing isn't treating symptoms—it's shifting the entire system so that health becomes natural rather than requiring constant intervention. You don't heal a person by giving them medicine while they continue drinking poison. You heal them by transforming the conditions that created illness in the first place.

Enterprises that heal transform conditions. They don't extract from ecosystems—they participate in regeneration. They don't extract from communities—they build capacity. They don't extract from future generations—they enhance inheritance. The business model itself creates the conditions for health.

And here's what these enterprises demonstrate: Healing is more viable than extraction. Not morally superior—though it is. Not feel-good—though it does. *More viable*. More resilient. More likely to survive over decades. More capable of attracting talent, building loyalty, weathering crisis, adapting to change.

Because enterprises designed for healing are designed for life. And life—unlike extraction—is a pattern that sustains itself, that creates additional life, that builds rather than depletes, that becomes more rather than less over time.

The choice isn't between profit and impact. It's between enterprises designed for death—taking until nothing remains—and enterprises designed for life—creating conditions for ongoing flourishing.

Everything that follows—the tool kit, the implementation guides, the measurement frameworks—exists to help you build for life.

Not because it's virtuous. Because it works.

Conclusion: Design for What You Want to See Multiply

Every enterprise is a template. When it succeeds, others will replicate its patterns—for better or worse.

Extractive enterprises that succeed teach the market that extraction works. Regenerative enterprises that succeed teach the market that healing works.

This is why design matters so profoundly. You're not just building a business. You're creating a pattern that others will copy, adapt, and spread.

The question is: What pattern do you want to see multiply?

If you design for integrity from inception—embedding values in ownership, governance, capital, operations, and culture—you create an enterprise that cannot succeed unless the world becomes healthier.

And when that enterprise thrives, it becomes proof that regeneration is not idealism—it's strategy.

That proof is what the Impact Economy needs most. Not more arguments, but more examples. Not more theory, but more templates.

Your Next Forty-Eight Hours

If this chapter has moved you from contemplation to commitment, here's your immediate action: Within the next forty-eight hours, conduct a single-point integrity audit. Choose one core value your enterprise claims—just one. Map it against three concrete decisions you made this week. Ask: Did those decisions strengthen or compromise this value? What structural change would make future decisions automatically align with this value? Who wasn't in the room who should have been?

This isn't a comprehensive assessment—that comes later. This is a practice run, a way to train your perception to see gaps between stated values and operational reality. Do it with curiosity, not judgment. The goal isn't perfection; it's honest recognition of where you are versus where you claim to be.

Then take one action—however small—to close that gap. Change one supplier contract term. Add one stakeholder to a decision process. Shift one metric from extraction to regeneration. Make one structural choice that makes integrity easier tomorrow than it is today.

Start there. Start now. Not because you have to, but because once you see the gap, you can't unsee it. And once you begin closing it, you've already joined the ranks of enterprises that heal.

The rest is replication.

TOOL KIT: ENTERPRISES THAT HEAL

Purpose: To embed regeneration and integrity into the core design of your enterprise, moving from "less harm" to active healing.

1. Assess Your Business Model

   Begin with an honest examination of how your enterprise creates value. Does your revenue depend on throughput and disposal, or on durability and regeneration? Ask where the money actually comes from: Are you paid more when customers need to replace what you sell, or when what you provide lasts and deepens? Map the flow of materials through your enterprise—where do they come from, where do they go, and what happens to them afterward? Consider what "success" means for your business model at scale: If you grew a hundred-fold, would ecosystems and communities be healthier or just more depleted?

2. Redesign Products and Services

   Examine what you actually deliver. Are your offerings designed for durability, repairability, and positive impact, or for obsolescence? Choose one product or service and trace its full lifecycle: extraction, production, use, and end of life. Identify one concrete change that would extend its useful life, enable repair, or ensure the use of regenerative materials. Consider how you might shift from selling products to providing services—leasing, sharing, or stewardship models that align your incentives with longevity rather than replacement.

3. Transform Supply Chain Relationships

   Map your supply chain with honesty about what you know and what remains opaque. Is it transparent, reciprocal, and fair, or invisible and transactional? Identify one relationship to shift from arm's-length purchasing to genuine partnership. Ask what your

(CONTINUED)

suppliers need to thrive, not just to deliver. Consider whether those who extract raw materials or provide essential labor share in the value your enterprise creates. Design one structural mechanism—profit sharing, long-term contracts, capacity building—that would make your supply chain more reciprocal.

4. Expand Stakeholder Voice

   Audit who has meaningful input into decisions and who doesn't. Do those affected by your choices—workers, communities, ecosystems, future generations—have a voice in making them? Start with one decision-making process and ask: Who bears the consequences but lacks a seat at the table? Design one mechanism to include a missing perspective: worker representation on key committees, community advisory boards, or formal processes to consider ecological and intergenerational impacts. Remember that voice without power is theater. What structural changes would make stakeholder input actually binding?

5. Close the Integrity Gap

   Every enterprise has a gap between stated values and operational reality. Acknowledge yours. What do you claim publicly? What decisions actually get made, and why? Where are the structural failures that allow drift between aspiration and action? Institute a regular integrity review, a quarterly mapping of stated values against actual decisions. For each gap identified, ask whether the solution is behavioral (change what people do) or architectural (change what the structure incentivizes). Prioritize structural changes; behavior follows incentives.

6. Take First Steps

   Complete the forty-eight-hour integrity audit described in "Your Next Forty-Eight Hours." Once you've identified one gap between stated values and operational reality—and taken

(CONTINUED)

one action to close it—choose your next step: a full integrity audit with independent verification, exploration of ownership transition (cooperative conversion, purpose trust, multistakeholder model), or redesigning capital structure for patient, mission-aligned investment.

7. Triage: If Your Organization Is in Integrity Crisis

   When the gap between stated values and operational reality has become public—or is about to—defensiveness accelerates credibility collapse. Instead: Pause before defending. Map the full gap by documenting what you claim versus what is actually true and identifying where structural failures allowed this. Communicate transparently by acknowledging the gap before others expose it further. Commit to structural change, not just behavioral adjustment; ask what architecture allowed this gap to grow. Invite accountability by bringing affected stakeholders into the redesign process.

Reflection Prompt

If your enterprise multiplied a hundred-fold, would the world be healthier or just have more of the same problems? What one structural change would ensure multiplication creates healing?

Connects To

This tool kit applies the systemic intelligence developed in Chapter 2 to enterprise design. For protecting your regenerative design through ownership structure, see Chapter 4. For financing it with aligned capital, see Chapter 5. For the market context it operates within, see Chapter 6.

4

Ownership as Justice

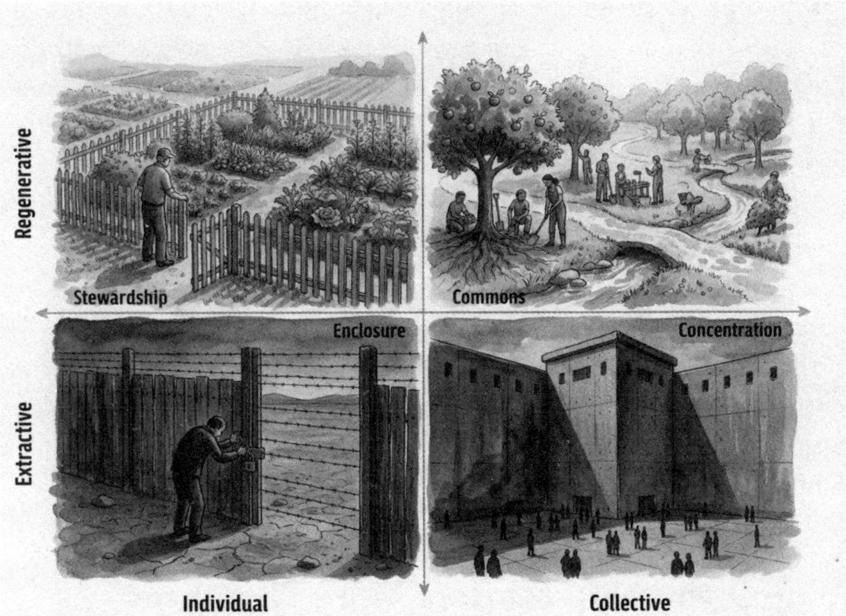

Figure 12. Ownership as Justice

The Architecture of Belonging

Ownership is not merely a legal arrangement. It is the architecture of belonging—a set of invisible lines that define who counts, who decides, and whose future is secured.

Every society encodes its moral order into ownership. In feudal Europe, land ownership drew the map of obligation and privilege. In the age of colonial expansion, ownership became a weapon, redefining territory, labor, and even identity itself in service to empire. Modern capitalism has abstracted ownership further, turning it into paper claims on assets and algorithms, severed from place and the people whose lives are shaped by those claims.

Across these epochs, the pattern is familiar: Ownership determines power, and power shapes possibility. When ownership is concentrated, the benefits of civilization—wealth, security, and influence—flow narrowly, while the risks and harms disperse broadly.

Today, we face another hinge in history. The concentration of ownership—of land, housing, data, intellectual property, infrastructure—has reached levels unseen since the Gilded Age. This is not only a moral crisis but a functional one: Societies fracture when too much is held by too few. Ecological collapse accelerates when land and resources are managed as disposable. Innovation stagnates when its fruits are enclosed.

And yet, ownership remains an unfinished story. It is not fixed; it is rewritten in every era, often in moments of rupture. We are in such a moment now—one that demands a reimagining of ownership not as dominance, but as stewardship; not as exclusion, but as a structure of shared belonging.

To speak of ownership as justice is to recognize that the way we design ownership systems will either perpetuate the deep inequities of history or become the foundation for a more equitable and regenerative future (see figure 12).

Why Ownership Matters More Than Ever

Ownership determines where value begins, where it flows, and where it rests. It shapes whether the wealth generated by climate adaptation,

AI deployment, regenerative agriculture, and infrastructure renewal will reinforce the old order or nourish a new one.

When we treat ownership as an afterthought, we replicate harm. We may "innovate" new industries only to watch their profits accrue to the same concentrated interests that have long dictated the terms of life and labor.

But when we place ownership at the center of design, the possibilities shift. Workers can accumulate wealth alongside the enterprises they sustain. Communities can retain sovereignty over land, housing, and the digital commons. Indigenous governance systems can be restored to guide collective stewardship. Wealth can circulate locally instead of leaking upward and outward.

This is not speculation. From community-owned renewable energy cooperatives in Germany to Black-led credit unions in the American South, from land-back agreements in Canada to steward-owned companies in Denmark, viable ownership alternatives are already functioning at scale.

The question is not whether they can work. It is whether we have the courage to make them the norm.

The models presented here represent proven patterns that have demonstrated viability at scale across different contexts and cultures. While not exhaustive, each offers a different answer to the fundamental questions of who decides, who benefits, and who belongs. Together, they form a tool kit for those ready to move from ownership as domination to ownership as relationship.

From Extractive Control to Shared Stewardship

Extractive ownership seeks control without relationship. It divorces rights from responsibilities. It rewards distance—the further the owner is from the place, people, and consequences of their decisions, the greater the profit.

The alternative is *shared stewardship*—a structural acknowledgment that value creation is inherently collective and that governance should reflect that interdependence. This means ownership models where decision making is distributed among those who create value and are affected by outcomes, where benefits flow to stakeholders rather than just shareholders, where mission is protected from acquisition or shareholder pressure, and where long-term stewardship is incentivized over short-term extraction.

Models of Shared Ownership

The landscape of shared ownership includes several proven models, each addressing different contexts and needs.

Worker cooperatives are enterprises owned and democratically controlled by workers, operating on the principle of one worker, one vote, with profits distributed based on contribution. Governance ensures those who create value share in decision making and wealth. Mondragon in Spain, with more than eighty thousand worker-owners, demonstrates this model at massive scale, while Cooperative Home Care Associates (CHCA) in the Bronx, with over two thousand worker-owners, stands as the largest worker co-op in the United States.[1]

Consumer cooperatives are owned by those who use the service, with democratic governance ensuring the enterprise serves member needs rather than investor profits. REI in outdoor gear,[2] credit unions globally, and rural electric cooperatives across America exemplify this model's reach and resilience.

Multistakeholder cooperatives include workers, consumers, producers, and community representatives in governance, recognizing that multiple groups have legitimate stakes in outcomes. Quebec's cooperative childcare networks and Italy's multistakeholder food co-ops show how this complexity can be managed for collective benefit.

Community land trusts (CLTs) hold land in perpetual trust for community benefit. Housing, agriculture, or cultural use remains affordable because land is removed from speculative markets. The community governs use, while individuals may own buildings. The Dudley Street Neighborhood Initiative in Boston, Massachusetts,[3] and the Champlain

Housing Trust in Vermont[4] have protected communities from displacement for decades.

Steward ownership is a legal structure where voting shares are held in trust, preventing sale or acquisition. Economic shares can be traded, but control remains with mission-aligned stewards. Patagonia's purpose trust structure, the search engine Ecosia,[5] and many European Mittelstand companies operate this way, demonstrating that mission protection and financial viability reinforce each other.

Purpose trusts transfer enterprise ownership to a trust that exists solely to advance mission. Profits fund the purpose, governance protects values, and no individual or investor can sell or redirect the enterprise. Bosch in German engineering, Zeiss in optics, and the Novo Nordisk Foundation in pharmaceuticals have operated this way for generations, proving that purpose trusts create durability conventional ownership cannot match.[6]

Indigenous ownership and governance manages land and resources according to traditional governance structures and seven-generation thinking. Sovereignty is exercised through tribal corporations, land trusts, or comanagement agreements. Tribal enterprises on sovereign lands and comanagement of national parks with Indigenous nations demonstrate how traditional ecological knowledge and modern legal structures can work together.

Ownership and the Repair of History

No conversation about ownership is complete without reckoning with history. Much of today's concentrated wealth rests on dispossession—stolen Indigenous lands, centuries of forced and unpaid labor, exclusionary policies that denied communities of color access to property, credit, and markets. Without confronting these legacies, ownership reform risks becoming cosmetic—a change in form without a change in justice.

Repair is possible when ownership is designed to address historical harm directly.

Land-back movements are returning territory to Indigenous nations—not as symbolic gesture but as restoration of sovereignty and self-determination. The return of comanagement at Bears Ears National Monument to tribal nations[7] and the Wiyot Tribe's restoration of Tuluwat Island in California[8] show what's possible when colonial assumptions about ownership are challenged.

Restorative finance directs capital into Black- and Brown-owned enterprises, cooperative development in historically disinvested communities, and reparations trust funds. RUNWAY Roots supporting Black entrepreneurs, Shared Capital Cooperative's BIPOC co-op lending, and the Northeast Farmers of Color Land Trust returning farmland to Black and Indigenous farmers in Vermont and New York demonstrate how capital can flow toward repair.[9]

Cooperative equity programs grant shares to descendants of exploited workers and build community ownership in neighborhoods subject to extraction or displacement. Worker ownership transitions in historically Black neighborhoods and cooperative development in formerly redlined areas show how ownership structure itself can become a mechanism of redress.

This is not charity. It is *structural accountability*—embedding redress into the DNA of enterprise and recognizing that justice delayed is not only justice denied but wealth compounded through theft.

Case Study: Mondragon Cooperative Corporation

Mondragon, a federation of worker cooperatives in Spain's Basque region, demonstrates how ownership structure shapes outcomes across decades.[10]

Founded in 1956 by priest José María Arizmendiarrieta and local workers, Mondragon established a model of democratic governance where every worker has one vote, regardless of position. Pay ratios are democratically capped, typically between 3:1 and 6:1, though some larger cooperatives have expanded to 9:1—compare this to the 300:1+ ratios common in conventional corporations. Profits are distributed according to a formula that allocates approximately 10 percent to community benefit, with the remainder split between reinvestment in the enterprise and distribution to workers (the specific ratios vary among cooperatives and have evolved over time). An internal solidarity fund supports struggling cooperatives, ensuring that no member enterprise faces crisis alone.

Today, Mondragon comprises over eighty cooperatives with over eighty thousand worker-owners generating approximately €11–14 billion in annual revenue across sectors from manufacturing to finance to education (figures vary by reporting methodology). The outcomes speak for themselves: Workers accumulate wealth through ownership stakes rather than depending solely on wages. The federation has proven more resilient through economic crises because cooperative mutual support prevents the failures that cascade through conventional corporate structures. Income inequality within the federation remains far lower than in conventional firms. Worker satisfaction and retention exceed industry norms. And community investment strengthens the regional economy rather than extracting from it.

The key insight is structural: Ownership creates different incentives. Worker-owners think long term because they can't extract and exit. Democratic governance prevents concentration. Solidarity mechanisms distribute risk. This is ownership as justice operationalized at scale.

Case Study: Community Land Trusts

The Dudley Street Neighborhood Initiative in Boston shows how CLTs prevent displacement and build community wealth.

Roxbury and North Dorchester were historically Black and Latino neighborhoods marked by high disinvestment and abandonment. In 1988, residents organized and achieved something unprecedented: They became the first community organization in the United States to gain eminent domain power. They used it to create a community land trust.

The structure is elegantly simple: The land trust owns land in perpetuity. Residents own buildings but lease the land affordably. A community board governs land use. Restrictions prevent speculation and ensure permanent affordability.

The outcomes have been transformative: over 225 affordable homes built, commercial space for local businesses, community gardens, parks, and cultural spaces. Most significantly, the neighborhood has experienced no displacement through gentrification, while surrounding areas have seen massive displacement. Wealth stays in the community across generations.

The key insight is that removing land from speculative markets protects communities. Democratic governance ensures decisions serve residents. Permanent affordability breaks cycles of displacement.

Resilience Insight: Nova Vida Cooperative

However, distributed ownership is not automatic or easy. It requires careful attention to governance and trust building.

In southern Brazil, a group of small farmers formed Nova Vida, pooling land and resources into a cooperative. Within three years, disputes over profit sharing and governance fractured trust. Key members left, threatening the cooperative with collapse.

But instead of dissolving the organization, the remaining members paused operations, brought in facilitators, and rewrote bylaws to prioritize transparency, accountability, and conflict resolution. Nova Vida recovered—leaner, but stronger—and became a regional model for cooperative governance.

The lesson: Ownership models that distribute power must also distribute the skills and structures to sustain trust. Without them, even the most promising shared stewardship efforts can fail.

Distributed ownership requires clear governance processes, conflict resolution mechanisms, transparency and accountability, cultural practices that reinforce cooperation, and training in democratic participation. Organizations like the Democracy at Work Institute, the Sustainable Economies Law Center, and regional cooperative development centers provide training, templates, and technical assistance for building these governance capacities. The up-front investment in developing these skills is typically paid back within two years through reduced conflict, faster decision making, and stronger stakeholder commitment.

When these are present, distributed ownership outperforms extraction. When they're absent, it struggles.

The Economics of Distributed Ownership

Critics claim concentrated ownership is more efficient.

Evidence suggests otherwise.

Studies across sectors show that worker cooperatives achieve higher productivity per worker, prove more resilient through economic downturns with lower closure rates, demonstrate better worker retention and satisfaction, and are more likely to invest in worker training and community benefit.

Community ownership keeps wealth circulating locally through multiplier effects, creates enterprises more responsive to local needs, builds social capital and trust, and establishes accountability structures that extractive ownership lacks.

Steward ownership enables long-term thinking free from quarterly pressure, protects mission from acquisition, attracts mission-aligned talent and customers, and often proves more profitable over the long term despite slower initial growth.

The efficiency argument for concentrated ownership only works when you externalize costs. When you account for social fragmentation, ecological degradation, and democratic erosion, distributed ownership is far more efficient at creating durable prosperity.

Ownership and Power: The Core Question

At its heart, ownership is about power: who gets to decide how resources are used, who benefits from their use, and who bears the costs.

Concentrated ownership concentrates power. A small group decides; benefits flow narrowly; costs are externalized to those with no voice.

Distributed ownership distributes power. Those affected participate in decisions; benefits circulate; costs are internalized and addressed collectively.

The question every impact entrepreneur must answer is: *Are we designing ownership to concentrate power (even if benevolently) or to distribute it?*

Because in the long run, concentrated power—no matter how well intentioned—tends toward extraction. And distributed power—when well structured—tends toward stewardship.

Ownership Models and Enterprise Types

Different ownership structures fit different contexts. Worker cooperatives work best for labor-intensive services, manufacturing, and professional services where worker knowledge is core value. Consumer cooperatives fit essential services—housing, food, credit, utilities—where user needs should drive decisions. Multistakeholder models suit enterprises where multiple groups have legitimate stakes, such as healthcare involving patients, workers, and community.

Community land trusts are ideal for land-based assets needing permanent affordability. Purpose trusts work for large enterprises where founders want mission permanence beyond their lifetime. Steward ownership serves mission-driven enterprises needing patient capital and protection from acquisition. Indigenous ownership is appropriate for land-based resources requiring intergenerational stewardship, territories with treaty obligations, and enterprises where traditional ecological knowledge is essential.

There is no one-size-fits-all solution. The key is choosing a structure that aligns power with those who create value and are affected by outcomes.

Ownership as Kinship

The language of ownership in extractive economies is a language of separation: mine versus yours, individual versus collective, private versus public, owner versus owned. Clear boundaries. Exclusive control. The right to use, to profit from, to exclude others from, to extract from, to destroy if you choose.

But cooperative and Indigenous ownership models point toward something older: *ownership as kinship.*

You don't "own" your family—you belong to them and they belong to you. Not possession but relationship. Not control but responsibility. Not the right to extract but the obligation to care. The boundary isn't hard edge but permeable membrane—where you end and they begin is less clear, more fluid, constantly renegotiated through practice and attention.

This is what community land trusts recognize: The land doesn't belong to individual owners who happen to follow rules. The land belongs to the community, and the community belongs to the land, and the individuals are embedded within that mutual belonging. You can't sell your way out of kinship.

This is what worker cooperatives recognize: The enterprise doesn't belong to external shareholders who can liquidate at will. The enterprise belongs to those whose labor creates it, whose lives depend on it, whose future is bound up with its health. Ownership without kinship is extraction waiting to happen.

This is what Indigenous governance recognizes: You don't possess the forest—you're part of the forest, responsible to the forest, accountable to seven generations who will depend on what you leave. The question isn't "What's mine to use?" but "What am I part of, and how do I care for it?"

The legal structures explored in this chapter—cooperatives, land trusts, steward ownership, purpose trusts—are attempting to encode in law what many cultures never forgot: that ownership without relationship is violence, that property without reciprocity is theft, that justice isn't redistribution of possessions but restoration of kinship.

When we say "ownership as justice," we don't mean fairer division of private property. We mean recovering the understanding that we belong to each other, to the land, to the future—and that belonging, not possession, is what makes us human.

From Ownership to Belonging

In the previous section, we distinguished ownership (control) from belonging (relationship).

The ownership models explored here move us toward belonging by including stakeholders in governance so they have voice rather than just use rights, by distributing benefits so people share in the prosperity they help create, by protecting long-term relationships through structures that resist short-term extraction, and by embedding enterprises in place so ownership remains tied to community rather than abstracted from it.

When people belong to an enterprise—when it's genuinely theirs—behavior shifts. You don't extract from what you're part of. You steward it. This is why ownership reform is not just about equity. It's about *creating the conditions for regenerative behavior at scale*.

Conclusion: A Civilizational Choice

Ownership is not simply about property. It is about the moral blueprint of a society. We can design it to reproduce exclusion, or to embed belonging. We can allow it to accelerate extraction, or require it to sustain life.

The Impact Economy demands the latter. It asks us to see ownership as a form of guardianship—of land, of labor, of culture, of the future itself. And it reminds us that justice is not an aftermarket add-on; it is the operating system.

If we get ownership right, we can build an economy that does more than grow. We can build one that grounds—in place, in trust, in the shared inheritance of a planet worth keeping.

TOOL KIT: OWNERSHIP AS JUSTICE

Purpose: To design ownership structures that distribute power, repair historical harms, and embed long-term stewardship.

The journey from ownership as control to ownership as kinship requires more than conceptual understanding. It demands structural transformation. The tools that follow translate this chapter's core insight—that we belong to each other, to the land, to the future—into concrete design choices.

1. Name the Power

   Acknowledge that ownership determines who benefits, who decides, and who belongs. Map your current state: Who currently owns your enterprise? Who makes major decisions? Who benefits from value creation? Who bears the risks and costs?

2. Choose Stewardship over Extraction

   Explore models that distribute ownership: worker ownership (cooperatives, employee stock ownership plans), community ownership (land trusts, community development corporations), multistakeholder cooperatives, steward ownership (mission-locked governance), purpose trusts (ownership for mission, not individuals), or Indigenous governance (traditional structures, comanagement). Ask: Which model best aligns with our mission and stakeholders?

3. Embed Mission Permanence

   Use structures that prevent mission drift: legal forms (benefit corporation, cooperative, trust), governance provisions (stakeholder representation, mission-lock clauses), capital structures

(CONTINUED)

(patient investors, limited exit rights), and cultural practices (values recommitment, transparent accountability).

4. Design for Inclusion and Repair

   Address histories of exclusion. Ask: Who has been historically excluded from ownership in your sector or region? How could ownership structure actively repair that harm? Consider reserved ownership stakes for BIPOC founders and workers, community wealth building in disinvested areas, land-back agreements with Indigenous nations, and cooperative development funds for marginalized communities.

5. Distribute Decision-Making Power

   Move from concentrated to participatory governance through worker voice (board seats, councils, consensus processes), community representation (advisory boards, cogovernance), stakeholder participation (multistakeholder governance), and future generation proxy (board seat for long-term interests).

6. Ensure Benefit Distribution

   Design so value flows to those who create it through profit-sharing formulas, equity grants to workers, community dividend structures, reinvestment requirements, and pay equity ratios.

7. Build Governance Capacity

   Distributed ownership requires governance skills: training in democratic decision making, conflict resolution processes, transparent communication systems, and regular governance review and improvement.

8. Protect from Capture

   Build safeguards against future compromise through anti-acquisition provisions, supermajority requirements for mission

(CONTINUED)

changes, external oversight (community boards, certification), and cultural reinforcement (onboarding, rituals, storytelling).

9. Connect to Movement

   Join coalitions advancing ownership justice: cooperative development networks, land trust federations, steward-ownership associations, solidarity economy movements, and Indigenous sovereignty efforts.

Reflection Prompt

If ownership of your enterprise changed hands tomorrow, would the new owners be structurally compelled to continue your mission, or could they extract, sell, or redirect? What one ownership provision would make mission betrayal impossible?

Connects To

This tool kit builds on the enterprise design work in Chapter 3—ownership structure protects and enables regenerative design. For aligning capital with distributed ownership, see Chapter 5. For broader commons governance, see Chapter 15.

5

Capital as Custodian

The Lifeblood of Economic Life

If ownership is the skeleton of justice, then capital is its lifeblood—the force that animates, nourishes, and carries purpose through the body of the economy. Like blood, capital flows. And like blood, its flow is never neutral. It moves according to the architecture of the

Figure 13. Capital as Custodian—Two Paths

system it inhabits—channels carved by human design, stories, incentives, and power.

When we treat capital as a force of nature—impersonal, efficient, amoral—we forget that it is not a river springing from nowhere, but a current we have shaped. It rewards, disciplines, accelerates, and deprioritizes according to the values embedded in its design.

In an extractive economy, those values often serve concentration and speed—hoarding wealth, chasing volatility, demanding short-term yield. But in the Impact Economy, capital is reimagined as a *custodian*: patient, rooted, and answerable to more than profit alone (see figure 13).

Custodial capital aligns its returns with ecological cycles and social repair. It moves not to strip life from the systems it touches, but to return life to them—enduring like an old-growth forest rather than exhausting like a strip mine. It requires a cultural shift: from exit to endurance, from domination to stewardship, from speculation to belonging.

This chapter explores what custodial capital looks like, how it differs from extractive finance, and how to structure capital flows that serve regeneration rather than undermine it.

From Commodity to Custodianship

Conventional finance treats capital as a commodity: liquid, interchangeable, stripped of relationship. In this mindset, the "best" capital is that which moves fastest and multiplies most—regardless of what it leaves in its wake.

Custodial capital rejects this disconnection. It understands that money is never just money; it is condensed choice. Every dollar carries a set of commitments, whether explicit or hidden. Custodianship makes those commitments visible and intentional.

This shift requires both moral courage and structural innovation. It asks investors and entrepreneurs alike to redefine risk, not as the chance of losing money but as the possibility of betraying the future for short-term gain.

The Extractive Capital Pattern

Before we can design custodial alternatives, we must recognize the extractive pattern we're working against.

The pattern begins with *short-term horizons*—quarterly earnings pressure, three- to five-year fund cycles, exit-driven thinking that subordinates enterprise health to liquidity events. It continues with *asymmetric power*, where investors hold veto rights, board control, and liquidation preferences that can override mission whenever returns are threatened. *Misaligned incentives* reward speed and scale over depth and durability, growth over regeneration.

The pattern includes a *narrow stakeholder focus* where only shareholders matter—workers, communities, and ecosystems are treated as externalities. An *exit imperative* defines success as selling or going public, not building lasting enterprise. And *risk intolerance for mission* means any trade-off between profit and impact triggers investor pressure to compromise values.

This pattern doesn't emerge from malicious actors. It's structurally incentivized by fund structures with fixed timelines, fiduciary duty narrowly interpreted as shareholder primacy, compensation models tied to exits and multiples, and market competition favoring those who extract fastest.

Changing it requires redesigning the capital architecture itself.

What Custodial Capital Looks Like

Custodial capital is defined by seven core characteristics, each representing a departure from extractive norms:

- *Patient time horizons* measure returns in decades, not quarters. There is no artificial exit pressure; success is defined by enterprise vitality, not liquidity events. RSF Social Finance exemplifies this approach, providing ten- to twenty-year loans to mission-driven enterprises at below-market rates, with flexible repayment tied to cash flow rather than fixed schedules.[1]

- *Mission alignment* means investors who share values and understand that impact isn't a constraint on returns—it's the definition of returns. The Zebras Unite network connects entrepreneurs with investors who explicitly reject the unicorn-or-death mentality in favor of sustainable, equitable growth.[2]
- *Structural protections* embed mission permanence into capital terms: covenant agreements requiring impact alongside financial returns, anti-dilution provisions preventing mission drift, and governance protections ensuring no board control that could override values. Beneficial State Bank requires all loans to meet social and environmental criteria; borrowers cannot use funds in ways that contradict its mission.[3]
- *Shared risk and return* replaces asymmetric arrangements with revenue-sharing agreements, flexible repayment, and first-loss capital that absorbs early risks so others can participate. The steward-ownership model separates economic rights (which can be sold) from voting rights (held in trust), allowing patient capital returns while protecting governance.
- *Stakeholder accountability* makes capital providers answerable not just to limited partners but to workers, communities, and ecosystems affected by investments. Shared Capital Cooperative lends only to cooperatives, with borrower cooperatives electing board members—capital serves enterprises, not vice versa.
- *Place-based commitment* anchors capital in geographies, circulating locally, building regional ecosystems rather than extracting and exiting. Community development financial institutions like Self-Help Credit Union keep capital working in underserved communities for generations.[4]
- *Transparent impact measurement* requires regular, verified reporting on ESG outcomes, not just financial metrics. Triodos

Bank publishes detailed reports on every loan's and investment's environmental and social impact, demonstrating that transparency is operationally possible at scale.[5]

Designing the Capital Flows

Stewarding capital in the Impact Economy requires new financial architectures organized around three principles (see figure 14):

- **Patient capital structures:** These take several forms. *Perpetual purpose capital* deploys funds without fixed exit timelines, treating capital not as temporary allocation but as permanent stewardship, through evergreen funds, family offices with multigenerational mandates, or foundation program-related investments. *Revenue-based financing* ties repayment to actual revenue rather than fixed schedules, aligning investor returns with enterprise health through revenue share agreements, royalty financing, or flexible debt structures.
- **Risk-absorbing structures:** These unlock capital that would otherwise remain unavailable. *Catalytic capital*—first-loss, below-market-rate, or grant-like—absorbs early risks others won't take, enabling follow-on investment for marginalized communities or

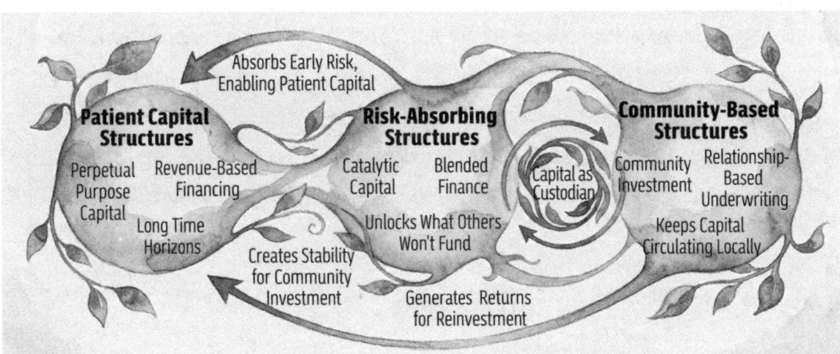

Figure 14. The Operating Architecture of Custodial Capital—How Regenerative Capital Flows

unproven models through guarantees, subordinated debt, forgivable loans, or recoverable grants. *Blended finance* braids public, private, and philanthropic funds to make regenerative investments viable, with each layer absorbing different risk/return profiles. Climate resilience projects, for example, might combine philanthropic grants for planning, concessional loans for construction, and market-rate bonds for operations.

- **Community-based structures:** These keep capital circulating where impact occurs. *Community investment* enables local ownership through community shares, bonds, and crowdfunding, such as when community-owned solar projects funded by local bonds return both clean energy and financial returns to residents. *Relationship-based underwriting* replaces algorithmic credit scores with trust-based assessment, character references, and community vouching—especially for those excluded from conventional finance. Grameen Bank's group lending model, where borrower circles provide mutual accountability, pioneered this approach.

The Patience Premium

Patience is often framed as sacrifice—accepting lower returns for moral satisfaction. But in the Impact Economy, patience is a competitive advantage. Enterprises backed by aligned, enduring capital are freer to innovate, to adapt, and to deepen trust with their stakeholders. They can measure success in soil health, restored watersheds, and community resilience—outcomes that compound in ways quarterly reports cannot capture, but that translate into more resilient returns over time.

Case Study: RSF Social Finance

RSF Social Finance demonstrates custodial capital at scale.

As a nonprofit financial services organization, RSF provides loans, equity, and donor-advised funds with all capital directed to enterprises advancing ecological, social, or cultural renewal. What distinguishes RSF is not just where the money goes but how it flows.

RSF staff know borrowers personally, visiting operations and understanding context. Loan structures adapt to enterprise cash flows rather than imposing rigid schedules. The organization accepts below-market rates, trading lower financial returns for higher impact returns. Pricing is transparent—borrowers and investors see how rates are set and where money flows. Annual gatherings bring together borrowers, investors, and RSF staff for learning and relationship building.

The outcomes speak for themselves: over $400 million deployed since 1984, with an extremely low default rate, including a 100 percent repayment rate in the Social Investment Fund—evidence that relationship-based underwriting works. Portfolio enterprises show stronger mission adherence and community impact than conventionally financed peers. Investors, who accept returns of 0–3 percent, report high satisfaction with impact outcomes.

The key insight: Patient, relational capital creates different incentives throughout the system. Borrowers can focus on mission rather than growth at all costs. Investors build meaningful relationships. Impact deepens because pressure for quick returns is removed.

Capital as Moral Actor

There is no such thing as value-free investment. The question is never whether capital will have an impact, but what kind of impact it will have, and on whom.

This is where custodial capital steps beyond mechanics into philosophy. It treats capital as a *moral actor*—one that must be held accountable for the consequences of its movement.

Custodial investors ask different questions: Who will be more resilient because of this capital? Whose agency will be restored? What systems will be healthier in twenty years because of this decision? Are we extracting wealth from this place or these people, or building capacity? Could this capital do more good deployed differently?

These are not "soft" questions. They are the deepest form of due diligence in an economy seeking to regenerate rather than extract.

This moral dimension of capital points to something deeper. There's a word that doesn't appear in conventional finance textbooks but that runs through every example of custodial capital: *devotion*. Not in the religious sense, necessarily, but in its root meaning—to dedicate, to pledge, to bind oneself in service to something larger. Patient capital requires devotion. Mission-aligned investing requires devotion. Structural protections that survive leadership transitions require devotion.

This isn't sentiment—it's the difference between capital that flows toward whatever offers highest return this quarter and capital that commits itself to healing a community over generations. The financial innovations we've explored are really technologies of devotion—ways of encoding long-term commitment so it can outlast individual mood and market pressure. They turn capital from wanderer into ancestor.

The Infrastructure of Custodial Capital

Building the Impact Economy requires capital infrastructure—institutions, networks, and standards that make custodial capital accessible and scalable.

Impact investment networks connect aligned investors with enterprises in need of capital, sharing deal flow, coinvesting, and building field knowledge. Organizations like Toniic, ANDE, and Investors Circle and regional impact investing networks like SWAN Impact serve this function.[6]

Community development financial institutions (CDFIs) are mission-driven lenders serving communities excluded from conventional finance, keeping capital circulating locally. Self-Help Credit Union and members of the Opportunity Finance Network exemplify this model.

Values-aligned banks offer full-service banking with explicit social and environmental missions, refusing to fund extraction. Beneficial State

Bank and Amalgamated Bank in the United States and Triodos Bank in Europe demonstrate that commercial banking and mission alignment are compatible.

Impact measurement standards provide shared frameworks for assessing and reporting impact, enabling comparison and accountability. IRIS+ metrics, B Analytics, GIIRS ratings, and Sustainable Development Goals (SDG) alignment tools are making impact as measurable as financial return.

Legal infrastructure includes enabling legislation for mission-locked structures, tax incentives for patient capital, and fiduciary duty clarification. Benefit corporation statutes, program-related investment regulations, and Opportunity Zone frameworks are examples, though much more is needed.

Capital and Power: The Critical Question

At its core, capital structure determines power dynamics.

Who controls the board? Capital providers often hold disproportionate board seats or veto rights, allowing them to override mission when returns are threatened. Who benefits from value creation? Waterfall structures, liquidation preferences, and equity distributions often ensure investors extract wealth before workers, communities, or ecosystems benefit. Who bears risk? Enterprises and communities often bear downside risk while investors hold upside guarantees and exit options.

Custodial capital redesigns these dynamics. Governance rights become proportional to mission alignment, not just capital contributed. Benefit distribution includes workers and communities. Shared risk means capital providers absorb first losses. Limited exit rights prevent destabilizing withdrawals.

The question every impact entrepreneur must answer is: *Do our capital terms entrench power, or share it?*

Because capital terms aren't just financial—they're governance decisions with decades of consequences.

Conclusion: From More to Enough

The Impact Economy will rise or fall on the integrity of its capital flows. If they replicate the impatience, volatility, and detachment of the old economy, they will erode the very systems they seek to serve.

But when capital becomes a custodian—patient, purposeful, and rooted in relationship—it can act as the bloodstream of regeneration, carrying nourishment to where it is most needed and ensuring that the body of the economy grows in balance and health, not in cancerous excess.

True wealth is not accumulation. It is the capacity to steward—to hold capital in trust for future generations, to deploy it in service of life, and to measure returns in resilience, beauty, and belonging.

The shift is as cultural as it is financial: from the restless hunger for more to the grounded sufficiency of enough.

And in making that shift, we do not just change how money moves. We change what it means to be wealthy.

TOOL KIT: CAPITAL AS CUSTODIAN

Purpose: To deploy capital in ways that align with ecological cycles, social repair, and intergenerational stewardship.

1. Redefine Return

   Measure success not only in financial yield, but in community well-being (employment, ownership, capacity), ecosystem health (restoration, biodiversity, soil and water quality), systemic resilience (reduced vulnerability, increased adaptability), and cultural vitality (knowledge preserved, traditions strengthened).

2. Align Capital with Time Horizons

   Match capital structure to impact timeline. Use patient or catalytic capital to allow impact to mature. Resist pressures

(CONTINUED)

for premature exits. Structure repayment around enterprise rhythms, not investor calendars. Consider perpetual or evergreen structures for long-term stewardship.

3. Design Protective Structures

   Guard mission through capital terms: limit investor board control and require stakeholder representation in governance; include impact requirements in loan and equity agreements through covenants; prevent mission drift through future fundraising with anti-dilution provisions; limit who can acquire or when investors can exit. Tools include perpetual purpose trusts, steward-ownership structures, blended finance with mission-aligned lead investors, and community investment with local governance.

4. Source-Aligned Capital

   Custodial capital can be found through impact-first investors and funds, family offices with multigenerational mandates, community development financial institutions, values-aligned banks, foundation program-related investments, patient individual investors, and community shares or bonds. Screen potential partners by asking: What is your investment time horizon? How do you measure success beyond financial returns? What governance rights do you require? How do you respond when mission and returns conflict?

5. Structure for Shared Risk

   Move beyond asymmetric risk and return by implementing first-loss capital from mission-aligned sources, revenue sharing rather than fixed debt service, profit sharing that includes workers and community, and downside protection for the enterprise rather than just investors.

(CONTINUED)

6. Build Transparent Accountability

   Report regularly on impact, not just finances: quarterly stakeholder updates, annual third-party impact verification, public dashboards showing outcomes, and honest communication about challenges and trade-offs.

7. Invest in Regenerative Multipliers

   Prioritize investments that replenish resources faster than they consume, restore trust and relationships, expand community capacity and ownership, strengthen ecosystems, and build the knowledge commons.

8. Practice Relationship-Based Capital

   Get to know your capital partners through site visits and direct relationships, understanding context and community, long-term partnerships rather than transactional deals, and mutual learning and adaptation.

9. Connect to Capital Infrastructure

   Participate in networks: join impact investing networks, connect with CDFIs and mission-aligned banks, share deal flow and coinvest, and contribute to field building through standards, tools, and knowledge.

10. Guard Against Capital's Distorting Influence

    Watch for mission drift pressures: investor demand for faster growth, board composition shifting toward finance over mission, metrics emphasizing financial over impact outcomes, exit timelines forcing compromise decisions. Build safeguards through mission-lock provisions in governance, regular values alignment audits, stakeholder voice in capital decisions, and a culture that can resist pressure.

(CONTINUED)

Reflection Prompt

If your capital partners disappeared tomorrow and you had to replace them, what terms would you refuse to accept—and what does that tell you about the capital you currently have?

Connects To

This tool kit provides the financing architecture for the enterprise design (Chapter 3) and ownership structures (Chapter 4) you have developed. Capital terms either enable or constrain regenerative work. For the market infrastructure that shapes capital flows, see Chapter 6.

6

Markets That Reflect What Matters

When we think of "the market," we often imagine an abstract force—supply meeting demand, prices finding equilibrium, the invisible hand allocating resources efficiently. But markets are not natural phenomena. They are designed systems, built on rules, platforms, standards, and power relationships that determine who can participate, what gets traded, how value is measured, and which outcomes are rewarded.

Every market is a set of choices about what matters.

The farmer's market that requires local sourcing is making different choices than the commodity exchange trading futures. The B Corp certification system is making different choices than the stock market valuing quarterly earnings. The platform cooperative governed by users is making different choices than the algorithm-driven monopoly extracting data.

In the extractive economy, markets were designed to optimize for speed, volume, and financial return—regardless of ecological cost, social harm, or long-term sustainability. Externalities were literally external to the market's accounting. What couldn't be monetized didn't count.

The Impact Economy requires redesigning markets themselves—not just asking enterprises to behave better within broken markets, but changing the architecture so that markets reward regeneration, penalize extraction, and make visible what has been rendered invisible.

This chapter explores how markets can be structured to reflect what actually matters: ecological health, social equity, community resilience, and intergenerational well-being.

This isn't a new insight. It's a recovered one.

The Moral Economist

I was twenty years old when I went looking for Adam Smith.

It was autumn 1985, my junior year abroad, and I'd been in Edinburgh for six weeks—long enough to find my way through the wynds and closes of the Old Town, to learn that the wind off the Firth could cut through any jacket I owned, to sit in pubs where the conversation turned easily to politics and philosophy in ways that felt foreign to an American undergraduate. Scotland in the mid-1980s was caught between UK Prime Minister Margaret Thatcher's market triumphalism and something older, a stubborn communitarian streak that resisted the notion that society was, as she'd famously declared, a fiction.[1] I didn't know it then, but that tension was about to snap. Just a year later, the Transport Act would deregulate the very buses I saw lining Princes Street, turning the orderly public network into a cutthroat free-market brawl. But in 1985, the uneasy truce still held.

I was studying English literature, Russian novels, Indian religion and philosophy—not economics. My interest in Smith was cultural, not disciplinary. Scotland had produced an astonishing concentration of literary and intellectual giants—Burns, Scott, Stevenson, Hume, Smith—and I wanted to understand the ground that had shaped them. But there was something more personal pulling me toward that ground. My maternal grandfather, Lionel Howarth Lee Kirby, was Scottish through and through, his lineage braiding Highland and Lowland, the Robertson clan from the north and the House of Sandilands from the south. Walking these streets, I was not just a visiting student. I was, in some sense I couldn't quite articulate, coming home.

Smith's name was everywhere that autumn. His face hung in university buildings, his ideas invoked as the foundation of modern economics, the proof that self-interest, left alone, would produce collective good. The invisible hand. I'd encountered the famous phrases. I thought I understood what they meant.

Then I took the train to Kirkcaldy. I rode in one of the old diesel "rattlers"—a Class 101 with fabric bench seats and heavy slam-doors that you had to open yourself by reaching out the window. The carriage shook violently as we crossed the Forth Bridge, the rhythmic clack-clack over the rails seeming to count down the centuries, carrying me away from the polished seminars of Edinburgh into something grittier.

It was a pilgrimage of sorts, though I wouldn't have called it that. Kirkcaldy sits on the Fife coast, just across the Firth of Forth from Edinburgh—close enough to see on a clear day, far enough to feel like another world. Smith had lived there with his mother for six years in the 1760s and 1770s, writing the book that would remake economic thought. I wanted to see what he'd seen, to walk where he'd walked, to understand this man who'd become such a towering figure not as an abstraction but as someone shaped by a particular place.

Stepping off the train, the first thing to hit me was not a view but a smell. The queer odor of linseed oil and cork—the hallmark of the town's linoleum factories—hung thick in the damp air, an olfactory border announcing arrival in the industrial heart of Fife. The High Street was bustling: shoppers crowding into Marks & Spencer and Littlewoods, the modern Mercat Shopping Centre drawing foot traffic away from older storefronts. If I'd come looking for heritage, I found commerce instead.

There was no Adam Smith Heritage Centre then—just a modest plaque on the wall at 220 High Street, marking where his house had stood before it was demolished and replaced. The close—a narrow passageway that would later be renamed Adam Smith Close—was still Halkett's

Close, a narrow functional vennel rather than a celebrated timeline. The garden where Smith had paced and dictated to his amanuensis was a private patch behind high walls, inaccessible to a curious student.

To see what Smith saw, I had to look past the 1980s storefronts.

The Old Kirk still dominated the skyline—the stout 15th-century tower where Smith had been baptized, a rough-hewn survivor (see figure 15). I walked the long concrete esplanade along the waterfront and stood where he must have stood. The wind was biting, whipping the Firth into cold, gray iron. I watched a tanker moving slowly toward the open sea—a singular point of commerce on a vast, indifferent expanse. Smith had looked at these same waters and seen a web of connection, a "great society" of exchange. But standing there in the chill of the 1980s, I struggled to see the sympathy he swore was there. I just saw the distance.

Still, something nagged at me. The Smith I kept hearing about—apostle of self-interest, father of laissez-faire—didn't match the Scotland I was experiencing, with its communal sensibility, its suspicion of pure individualism. Had this place really produced the man being quoted to justify Thatcher's dismantling of the social contract?

It would be years before I read *The Theory of Moral Sentiments*.

Figure 15. Kirkcaldy Esplanade—The Invisible Hand Needs a Visible Heart

Smith published that philosophical work in 1759, seventeen years before *The Wealth of Nations*. It was the book that made his reputation, the foundation on which everything else rested—and it had almost nothing to do with self-interest. It was about sympathy. About how human beings come to understand each other, to judge actions as right or wrong, to build the moral frameworks that make society possible.

"How selfish soever man may be supposed," Smith wrote in its opening lines, "there are evidently some principles in his nature, which interest him in the fortune of others, and render their happiness necessary to him, though he derives nothing from it except the pleasure of seeing it."[2]

This was not the Smith I'd been taught. This was a philosopher who understood that economic life is embedded in moral life—that markets function only within a web of trust, sympathy, and shared understanding. The "invisible hand" appears in *The Theory of Moral Sentiments* too, but not as a mechanism for transmuting greed into good. It appears in a passage about how the rich, despite their selfishness, end up distributing resources more widely than they intend—not because self-interest is virtuous, but because it operates within constraints that sympathy and social judgment impose.

Smith wasn't celebrating self-interest. He was explaining how it could be contained.

Standing on that esplanade in 1985, I didn't know any of this. I was a twenty-year-old who thought he understood something about markets because he'd absorbed the conventional wisdom—a Smith stripped of moral philosophy, reduced to a slogan, deployed in service of an ideology he would have found bewildering.

The extractive economy needed that caricature. It needed markets imagined as natural forces rather than human constructions. It needed self-interest sanctified rather than constrained. It needed Smith's moral foundations quietly removed so that his economic observations could stand alone, unmoored from the ethical framework that gave them meaning.

What I learned, eventually, was that Smith had been hijacked.

The man who wrote that concern for others is built into human nature, that we cannot help but imagine ourselves into the situations of those around us, that moral judgment arises from this sympathetic imagination—that man had been turned into a prophet of pure self-interest. The philosopher who understood markets as human institutions, shaped by law and custom and moral expectation, had been recast as proof that markets need no shaping at all.

Every market is a set of choices about what matters. Smith knew this. He spent his life trying to understand how those choices are made—not just economically, but morally, socially, psychologically. He was not an impact economist—he couldn't have been; he was working two centuries before the concept existed, in a world that hadn't yet learned what unconstrained extraction could destroy. But he understood something we've been forced to relearn: that we cannot separate what we exchange from how we live together, that economic systems are expressions of deeper values, that the invisible hand requires a moral architecture to function.

The Impact Economy isn't inventing this insight. It's recovering it—reclaiming a tradition that was deliberately obscured because it stood in the way of extraction without limit.

I think about that young man on the Kirkcaldy esplanade sometimes—a literature student on ancestral ground, looking for a writer he thought he understood. He didn't find what he was looking for, not that day. But the question that brought him there turned out to be the right one.

What did Adam Smith actually see, looking out at those gray waters?

He saw an economy that could only function because people cared about more than themselves. He saw markets that required moral infrastructure to survive. He saw, two centuries before we had language for it, that the invisible hand needs a visible heart.

Markets Are Technologies, Not Laws of Nature

The most dangerous myth about markets is that they're inevitable—natural systems we must accept and adapt to.

The truth is that markets are human inventions, and every aspect of them is designed. The rules of exchange determine who can buy and sell, what can be traded, and under what conditions. The platforms establish where exchange happens, who controls access, and what information is visible. The metrics define how value is measured and what gets counted versus ignored. The standards create certifications, verification systems, and transparency requirements. The enforcement mechanisms determine how rules are monitored and what happens when they're violated.

These design choices shape outcomes as surely as enterprise structure or capital terms. And if they were designed, they can be redesigned.

What Current Markets Hide

Extractive markets systematically hide their true costs through several mechanisms.

Externalization is the biggest trick: treating ecological degradation, social harm, and future costs as "external" to market transactions. The result is that prices lie. A $5 hamburger doesn't include the cost of methane emissions accelerating climate change, antibiotic resistance from factory farming, water pollution from manure runoff, worker exploitation in meatpacking, or topsoil depletion undermining future food security. The market says it's cheap. The actual cost—borne by communities, ecosystems, and future generations—is far higher.

Information asymmetry means sellers know far more than buyers about supply chains, labor conditions, and environmental impacts. Complex global networks make transparency nearly impossible. The result is that consumers can't make informed choices even if they want to, and "ethical consumption" becomes a privilege of those with time, money, and access to information.

Monopoly and concentration allow few actors to control markets and set terms, driving down supplier prices, extracting data, preventing competition, capturing regulators. Markets stop being competitive and become extractive. The fiction of "choice" masks structural coercion.

Short-term optimization rewards quarterly earnings in public markets and demands exits within three to seven years in private markets.

Long-term value creation is structurally penalized, and enterprises that could build durably are pressured to grow fast and exit, regardless of impact on stakeholders or ecosystems.

Commodification of the uncommodifiable treats everything—land, water, knowledge, care, attention—as tradeable commodities, stripping them of context, relationship, and sacred value. What cannot be priced is destroyed. What should not be traded is enclosed.

Designing Markets for Regeneration

What would markets look like if designed to reward what actually sustains life? The transformation from extractive to regenerative markets requires intervention at multiple levels simultaneously.

Internalized externalities make ecological and social costs visible in prices through structure. Mechanisms include carbon pricing, polluter-pays regulations, extended producer responsibility, and true-cost accounting. Interface Carpets shifted to a circular model partly because regulation made disposal costly—regenerative design became profitable when externalities were internalized. Carbon markets illustrate both promise and peril: The EU Emissions Trading System has reduced emissions by approximately 50 percent since 2005, while voluntary offset markets often enable continued extraction through cheap, unverified offsets.[3] The lesson is that market mechanisms work when mandatory, verified, and coupled with absolute reduction requirements.

Transparent supply chains make production visible so markets can reward good practices through mandatory disclosure, blockchain traceability, open data standards, and worker voice platforms. Fashion Revolution's "Who Made My Clothes?" campaign pressures brands for factory lists, enabling accountability that was previously impossible.[4]

Certification and verification systems provide third-party standards signaling regenerative practices, such as B Corp, Fairtrade, Regenerative Organic, and Living Wage certification. These systems have drawbacks to address: costs exclude small producers, standards can be gamed, and verifiers may be captured. Design must prevent these failures.

Platform cooperatives and democratic marketplaces create markets governed by participants rather than extractive intermediaries—artist-owned photo platforms, worker-owned cleaning services, driver-owned rideshares. These models, explored in detail in the upcoming section on digital markets section, prove that platform governance can serve users rather than extract from them.

Regenerative procurement uses the purchasing power of large institutional buyers to reward regenerative practices through impact-weighted criteria, local preference provisions, and cooperative purchasing networks. Oakland Unified School District's Good Food Purchasing Policy commits the district to sourcing food locally and sustainably, with purchasing evaluated across five values: local economies, environmental sustainability, animal welfare, valued workforce, and nutrition.[5]

Alternative currencies and exchange systems redesign money to reward different behaviors through local currencies, time banking, mutual credit systems, and carbon-backed currencies. BerkShares in the Berkshires and the Brixton Pound in the UK circulate locally, strengthening the community economy.[6]

Impact-weighted stock markets price in ESG performance through dual-class reporting (financial plus impact), impact indices, long-term holding incentives, and stakeholder representation requirements. The Long-Term Stock Exchange requires stakeholder metrics and ties voting rights to holding periods.[7]

No single mechanism is sufficient—carbon pricing alone won't fix markets, nor will transparency or certification in isolation. But when deployed together, these seven interconnected interventions create reinforcing feedback loops that shift the entire market architecture. Each makes the others more effective: transparency enables certification, certification guides procurement, procurement drives demand for alternative platforms, platforms enable new currencies, and regulation provides the baseline that prevents backsliding.

Case Study: The B Corp Marketplace Effect

B Corp certification demonstrates how market infrastructure can shift behavior at scale.

The certification process requires enterprises to complete a verified assessment of social and environmental performance, meeting minimum standards across stakeholders, governance, community, and environment. Mission protection must be included in governance documents, and recertification every three years maintains standards over time.

The market effects have been transformative. The certification provides an information signal that allows buyers to identify values-aligned companies. Network effects among over ten thousand Certified B Corps create an ecosystem where companies share practices and coinvest.[8] The certification drives talent attraction, as workers seek out B Corps for meaningful work. Investor interest grows as impact funds preferentially deploy capital to certified companies. The movement has generated policy influence, catalyzing the benefit corporation legal structure now available in more than forty US states and multiple countries. And certified companies create supply chain pressure, pushing suppliers to meet standards and expanding impact.

The results are measurable: B Corps grow faster on average than conventional competitors, demonstrate higher worker satisfaction and retention, show better resilience through economic crises, and prove that mission-driven enterprises can outperform extraction.

Key insight: Certification creates market infrastructure that makes impact visible, measurable, and valuable—shifting incentives throughout the system.

Case Study: Fairphone and Market Transformation

Fairphone, whose integrity-driven design we explored in Chapter 3, demonstrates how one enterprise can create market effects disproportionate to its market share.

Mainstream consumers learned about electronics supply chain harms for the first time. Competitor pressure mounted as other manufacturers faced the question: "Why can't you do what Fairphone does?" EU Right to Repair legislation was partly inspired by Fairphone's demonstration that repair-friendly design is possible. Impact funds began seeing electronics as an investable impact sector. Engineers increasingly sought work on ethical hardware.

While Fairphone remains small, it shifted the industry conversation and regulatory landscape, demonstrating how market infrastructure changes when one enterprise makes extraction visible and proves alternatives are viable.

The Role of Regulation in Market Design

Markets don't regulate themselves. They require rules to prevent race-to-the-bottom dynamics.

Regulation serves several essential functions. *Baseline standards* establish minimum environmental, labor, and safety requirements that prevent competitive advantage through harm. *Transparency requirements* mandate disclosure of impacts, ownership, lobbying, and supply chains. *Antitrust enforcement* prevents monopoly concentration that eliminates genuine choice. *Liability and enforcement* create consequences for violations that make compliance cheaper than extraction. *Enabling frameworks* provide legal structures for cooperatives, benefit corporations, and land trusts, along with tax treatment favoring regenerative practices.

Examples of regulatory success demonstrate what's possible. The EU's General Data Protection Regulation (GDPR) forced global tech companies to respect data privacy by imposing fines for violations of up to 4 percent of global revenue, making privacy by design standard practice worldwide. Germany's Renewable Energy Act guaranteed long-term contracts for renewable energy producers, driving costs down globally through scale. The Montreal Protocol led to a near-complete global phase-out of ozone-depleting substances such as chlorofluorocarbons

(CFCs) among signatories, proving global coordination is possible. Denmark's bottle deposit system achieves return rates of over 90 percent, providing a model of a circular economy approach for beverage containers.[9] In India, Kerala's Kudumbashree Program, supporting a network of over 4.8 million women members, helped eradicate extreme poverty in the state by 2025.[10]

The truth is, there is no such thing as "free markets." All markets have rules. The question is whether those rules serve extraction or regeneration, concentration or distribution, short-term gain or long-term thriving.

Markets and the Commons

Markets exist within and depend upon commons—the shared resources that make exchange possible. These include *ecological commons* like clean air, water, soil, stable climate, and biodiversity; *social commons* like trust, rule of law, education, public health, and infrastructure; and *knowledge commons* like scientific research, cultural traditions, and open-source code.

When markets erode commons, they undermine their own foundations.

Markets that reflect what matters must price in commons degradation to make harm expensive, fund commons regeneration to make restoration profitable, prevent commons enclosure to keep shared resources accessible, and recognize commons governance by respecting community and Indigenous stewardship.

Digital Markets and Platform Power

The fastest-growing markets are digital—and they pose unique challenges and opportunities.

The extractive digital market pattern has several components. *Surveillance capitalism* extracts behavioral data, predicts and manipulates behavior, and sells access to attention. *Network effects plus monopoly* create winner-takes-all dynamics that produce extractive giants like Amazon, Google, and Facebook. *Algorithmic opacity* leads to black-box systems that make bias, manipulation, and harm invisible. *Labor precarity* emerges when gig platforms classify workers as contractors, avoiding labor protections.

Regenerative digital market alternatives are emerging.

Platform cooperatives like Stocksy United, Resonate, and Fairbnb are user-owned and democratically governed. *Data trusts* enable community governance of data rather than corporate ownership. *Algorithmic transparency* creates open-source, auditable systems. *Portable identity and data* give users control of their information across platforms. *Interoperability requirements* prevent lock-in and enable competition. The Mastodon/Fediverse demonstrates decentralized social media where no single entity controls the network—users can move between instances while maintaining connections.

Functioning platform cooperatives prove that platform governance can serve participants rather than extract from them. Stocksy United, a photographer-owned stock photo platform, pays artists 50–75 percent of sales, compared to 15–20 percent on conventional platforms. Up & Go, a cleaner-owned platform in New York City, gives workers 95 percent of booking fees and control over platform governance. Fairbnb directs 50 percent of platform fees to local community projects, preventing extractive tourism while strengthening neighborhoods. The Drivers Cooperative, also based in New York City, pays drivers 10–25 percent more per trip than ridehailing services like Uber and Lyft and gives them ownership of the platform they work through.[11]

We don't need to accept surveillance capitalism as inevitable.

From Competition to Coordination

Extractive markets assume competition as natural and healthy. But many challenges require coordination.

Climate change, pandemic response, inequality—these demand collective action markets weren't designed to enable.

Markets that reflect what matters must enable precompetitive collaboration, where enterprises share research, standards, and infrastructure, on challenges no single actor can solve. They must enable sectoral bargaining through industry-wide agreements on labor standards and sustainability baselines. And they must enable commons-based production through open-source development, knowledge sharing, and collective stewardship.

This doesn't eliminate markets—it redesigns them to reward cooperation when it's strategically essential.

Scaling Impact Through Market Architecture

Individual enterprises can be regenerative, but systemic change requires market-level intervention.

Consider the progression: At the enterprise level, Patagonia operates regeneratively. At the market level, the Outdoor Industry Association adopts Patagonia's standards sector-wide. At the regulatory level, government requires all apparel to meet labor and environmental standards. Each successive level multiplies the impact.

Impact entrepreneurs must work at all three levels: building regenerative enterprises as proofs of concept; organizing market infrastructure through coalitions, standards, and platforms; and advocating for enabling regulation through policy change.

Conclusion: Markets as Choice, Not Fate

The question is not whether markets work—they clearly do, for some. The question is: What do we want them to work for?

If we design markets to reward speed, volume, and extraction, we get speed, volume, and extraction. If we design markets to reward regeneration, equity, and resilience, we get regeneration, equity, and resilience.

The architecture determines the outcome. And the architecture is in our hands—through enterprise choices, investment decisions, platform governance, certification systems, procurement policies, and regulatory advocacy.

Markets that reflect what matters are not a distant dream. They're being built now—in B Corp networks, platform cooperatives, impact exchanges, regenerative supply chains, and policy reforms worldwide. The work is to scale what works, weave isolated experiments into coherent infrastructure, and shift the default from extraction to regeneration.

When that happens, markets become what they were always meant to be: tools for coordinating collective well-being, not engines of extraction dressed up as inevitability.

TOOL KIT: MARKETS THAT REFLECT WHAT MATTERS

Purpose: To help you participate in designing and strengthening market infrastructure that rewards regeneration.

1. Map Your Market Position

   Understand the markets you participate in. What exchanges, platforms, or networks connect you to customers and suppliers? Who controls these markets, and what are their incentives? What gets measured and rewarded, and what's invisible? Where do externalities hide? What information is transparent versus opaque?

2. Internalize Your Externalities

   Make your true costs visible by calculating full lifecycle impacts (ecological and social), pricing in costs currently externalized, adjusting pricing to reflect true cost where possible, and advocating for regulation that requires industry-wide internalization.

3. Demand Transparency

   Throughout your supply chain, publish supplier lists, verify labor conditions, trace materials to source, share honestly about

(CONTINUED)

challenges and failures, and use or build blockchain and digital verification systems.

4. Join or Build Certification Systems

   Signal your values to the market by pursuing B Corp, Fairtrade, Regenerative Organic, or similar certification. If existing certifications are inadequate, organize peers to create better ones. Support third-party verification infrastructure and advocate for standards that matter, not just easy-to-game metrics.

5. Participate in Regenerative Platforms

   Source from cooperative or mission-aligned platforms, sell through values-aligned marketplaces, invest in platform cooperatives, and support democratic governance of exchange infrastructure.

6. Use Procurement Power

   If you're a buyer, weigh impact alongside price in purchasing decisions, give preference to certified regenerative suppliers, pool demand with aligned buyers to support small regenerative producers, and publish procurement criteria to shift supplier behavior.

7. Advocate for Market Redesign

   Support carbon pricing, polluter-pays, and extended producer responsibility policies. Advocate for transparency requirements. Push for antitrust enforcement against monopolies. Support enabling legislation for cooperatives, benefit corporations, and land trusts.

8. Build Alternative Exchange Systems

   Start or join local currency networks, participate in time banks or mutual credit systems, create buyer and seller cooperatives, and support platform cooperative development.

(CONTINUED)

9. Measure and Share Impact

   Make regeneration visible by tracking and reporting social and environmental outcomes, using standardized frameworks like B Impact Assessment, IRIS+, or SDG alignment, sharing data openly to enable comparison and contributing to the commons of impact knowledge.

10. Connect Isolated Efforts

    Market infrastructure requires networks. Join trade associations or coalitions advancing regenerative markets. Share best practices, failures, and innovations. Coinvest in shared infrastructure, including platforms, standards, and verification systems. Build political power to shift regulation.

Reflection Prompt

If every enterprise in your sector operated like yours, would the market infrastructure support or resist that? What one change to market rules, platforms, or standards would make regenerative behavior the easiest path rather than the hardest?

Connects To

This tool kit completes the structural architecture of Part II—markets are the context within which enterprises (Chapter 3), ownership (Chapter 4), and capital (Chapter 5) operate. For protecting this infrastructure from systemic threats, see Part III. For the cultural conditions that shape markets, see Part IV.

Part III

Protection

The Five Pillars of Real Security

This section is written for anyone who allocates resources toward security—whether through governance, philanthropy, investment, enterprise, or community organizing. The leaders, founders, funders, and practitioners who read these pages face a common question: What does genuine protection actually require? The argument that follows applies whether you control billions or coordinate volunteers—because genuine protection comes not from fortification but from foundations, not from accumulating gold but from cultivating health. It comes from the living systems, institutions, and relationships that make collective flourishing possible. I learned this not in policy papers but on stages with poets, watching audiences confront what they didn't want to know.

I want to tell what the forests were like.
I will have to speak in a forgotten language.
—W. S. MERWIN, "WITNESS"[1]

Middlebury, Vermont, October 1993. My alma mater in peak autumn—the maples blazing orange and red against impossible blue sky, the Green Mountains shouldering up behind the campus, students crossing the quad in sweaters and flannel (figure 16). I stood outside the chapel where we'd hold the evening's event, watching leaves spiral down, and felt the weight of return. This place had shaped how I saw the world. Now I was bringing back language for what that world was becoming.

This was the Forgotten Language Tour in its second year—a program I'd launched as director of The Orion Society, taking its name from Merwin's poem.[2] The concept was simple, almost medieval: Travel to communities across North America like troubadours, bringing environmental writers and poets to town halls, universities, churches, anywhere people gathered. Not to lecture but to bear witness. To speak in the language we were forgetting—the language of connection to place, to nature, to the living world that sustained us.

Bill McKibben was with us that night. His *The End of Nature* had been published several years earlier, but in 1993, climate change was still abstract to most people, still debatable, still something that might be happening but wasn't yet *here*.[3] The tour's purpose was to make ecological threats immediate, personal, felt—to translate atmospheric science into human terms, to help people understand that the crisis wasn't just

Figure 16. Middlebury College in Autumn

environmental but existential, that it required not only technical solutions but a fundamental reimagining of how we lived.

What I didn't yet understand was that it also required reimagining what protection means.

Bill spoke that night about carbon concentrations and feedback loops, about the fundamental alterations we'd made to the planet's systems. His words were precise, careful, devastating in their clarity. The students listened with fierce attention—it was their mountains, their forests, their winters that were changing. But I watched the faces of the older alumni and community members scattered throughout the audience, and I saw something I hadn't anticipated.

Not disbelief. Not denial. Not even disagreement.

Fear. And the defensive posture fear produces.

During the Q&A, a man in his fifties—successful by his clothing, confident by his bearing—stood and said: "What you're describing—if it's true—means everything I've worked for is threatened. My business. My investments. The future I've built for my family. So what am I supposed to do? Just give all that up?"

Bill answered thoughtfully, talking about renewable energy, about new economic opportunities, about building rather than abandoning. But the man shook his head and sat down, unconvinced.

What he'd heard wasn't "Here's information about atmospheric carbon."

What he'd heard was: "Your model of security doesn't work anymore."

Between 1992 and 2003, the Forgotten Language Tour traveled to every region of the United States—from New England to the Pacific Northwest, from the upper Midwest to the Deep South, from the Southwest deserts to the Rocky Mountain states. We brought writers and poets to dozens of communities; progressive bastions and conservative strongholds. Each place different in culture and landscape, but similar in the pattern we encountered.

The writers we brought spoke in that forgotten language Merwin had named. They read poems about rivers. They told stories about wolves and salmon and old-growth forests. They tried to communicate something that Western industrial culture had systematically erased: the understanding that we *are* nature, not separate from it, that there is no "away," no outside, no fortress we can build against our own impacts.

We thought our task was education; we slowly realized it was paradigm shift. Because the resistance we encountered—which grew more organized as the decade progressed—wasn't about lacking facts. By the late 1990s, the science was clear. The evidence was accumulating. The early impacts were visible. People who wanted to understand could understand.

The resistance was about protecting a worldview. And more specifically, protecting an economic model built on that worldview.

I remember another stop on the tour. A man distributed pamphlets before our public reading—slick materials with graphs and citations, all arguing that climate concern was overblown, that warming would be modest and manageable, that economic growth must continue unimpeded. The pamphlets didn't list their funding source, but the rhetoric was familiar. We'd started seeing it everywhere: in op-eds, in speeches, in policy debates. The language of doubt, manufactured with the precision of any industrial product.[4]

What struck me wasn't that he disagreed. It was that he was *defending* something. His stance, his language, his entire posture was protective. Not seeking truth but fortifying position.

I thought: This is what security looks like when it's threatened.

And I wondered: What would security look like if it wasn't based on defending against threat but on addressing its root causes?

The 2000s brought the tour to its final communities, and the world closer to reckoning. Katrina. Unprecedented fires. Arctic ice disappearing faster than models predicted. The evidence moved from abstract to visceral, from future to present, from elsewhere to here.

The defensive campaigns intensified accordingly.

I watched foundation money, extracted from fossil fuel fortunes, flow into think tanks that produced doubt. I watched politicians adopt talking points designed not to convince but to delay. I watched the machinery of defense mobilize: lawyers, lobbyists, PR firms, all working to protect the extractive economy not by proving it was right but by making it impossible to act on the alternative.

This was security as we'd built it for centuries. Individual security through wealth accumulation. Corporate security through market dominance. National security through resource control. All of it based on the same logic: Take yours before someone else takes theirs. Build walls. Defend territory. Trust no one.

Climate change revealed that logic as suicide.

Because you cannot wall yourself off from atmospheric carbon. You cannot insure against systemic collapse. You cannot defend militarily against rising seas. You cannot compete your way to safety when the entire system is failing.

The planet doesn't recognize fortresses.

The greatest threat we faced was collective, systemic, and global. It could only be addressed collectively, systemically, and globally.

Which meant everything we thought we knew about protection was wrong.

•

I return to ecotones—those edges where two ecosystems meet. Forest and prairie. River and ocean. The places of maximum turbulence and maximum fertility, where neither system's rules fully apply, where new forms emerge.

The gulf between extractive economy and Impact Economy is an ecotone. And climate change is the rising tide that makes the boundary visible, undeniable, impossible to ignore.

On one side: The old model of security. Individual accumulation. Competitive advantage. Defensive fortification. The illusion that you can make yourself safe by making yourself separate, by building higher walls, by amassing more wealth, by projecting more force.

On the other side: Something that doesn't yet have adequate language. A form of security that isn't about separation but connection. Not about dominance but mutualism. Not about defending against the future but cultivating the conditions for a future worth inhabiting.

The forgotten language Merwin named turns out to be the language of genuine security. The vocabulary of reciprocity, of interdependence, of the sacred in the everyday—this isn't just poetry. It's the operating manual for survival.

What keeps us safe isn't walls. It's watersheds. It's public health systems that catch pandemics before they cascade. It's economic arrangements that prevent the desperation driving conflict. It's democratic institutions that channel grievance into dialogue rather than violence. It's communities woven tight enough to catch those who fall and mobilize when crisis hits.

Real security rests on foundations, not fortifications.

This insight crystallized for me into a framework I call the *Five Pillars of Real Security*—the interdependent systems that actually generate safety in an age of complexity:

1. **Ecological stability:** Healthy ecosystems are the original security infrastructure. They regulate climate, purify water, regenerate soil, buffer storms, and support the biodiversity upon which all life depends. When ecosystems degrade, security collapses.
2. **Public health capacity:** Pandemics, antimicrobial resistance, mental health crises—these are not "health issues" separate from security. They are security threats that kill more people and cost more economically than most conventional conflicts.
3. **Economic equity and resilience:** Inequality is a threat multiplier. When economic systems concentrate wealth and opportunity narrowly, they generate desperation, resentment, and fragmentation—conditions ripe for conflict, extremism, and institutional collapse.
4. **Democratic infrastructure:** Democracy is not a luxury; it is a security technology. When people trust that their voices matter, that institutions are accountable, and that conflicts can be resolved through dialogue rather than violence, stability deepens.

5. **Community cohesion and mutual aid:** Community cohesion is the social fabric that holds people together: the relationships of trust, reciprocity, and shared identity that allow for collective action. When communities are strong, they can organize mutual aid during crises, resist authoritarian capture, and hold institutions accountable.

Weaken any one pillar, and the entire system becomes brittle. Strengthen all five, and you create conditions where threats are less likely to emerge and easier to absorb when they do.

This is not abstract theory. Every dollar invested in these foundations generates measurable returns—what I call the *Prevention Dividend*. As you'll see in Chapter 7, for every dollar invested, disaster preparedness returns $4–$7 in emergency response and recovery, ecosystem restoration generates $7–$30 in economic returns, and early childhood education returns $7–$13 in reduced social costs. The evidence is overwhelming: Prevention is cheaper, more effective, and more durable than reaction.

And yet, we continue to pour trillions into militarized defense while starving the systems that actually keep us safe.

Globally, nations spend $2.7 trillion annually on military preparedness, fortifying borders, modernizing arsenals, projecting force.[5] Yet many of the crises that actually destabilize societies and end lives arrive not as invading forces but as cascading system failures: pandemics that expose healthcare fragility, climate disasters that overwhelm emergency response, supply chain breakdowns that empty shelves, disinformation campaigns that corrode civic trust from within.

We have constructed an enormous apparatus to defend against the wars of the last century while leaving ourselves dangerously exposed to the defining vulnerabilities of this one.

This is not an argument against all traditional defense. It is an argument about allocation, priority, and paradigm. The question is not whether nations need security capacity—they do. The question is: *What kind of security does this moment demand, and are we building it?*

The answer, increasingly, is no.

We defend territory while watersheds collapse. We guard financial markets while food systems become brittle. We harden digital perimeters while the social fabric that holds communities together unravels. We have mistaken the symbols of strength for the structures of resilience.

The cost of this misalignment is catastrophic. Every dollar spent preparing for the wrong threat is a dollar not spent building the capacities that would prevent crises from cascading in the first place.

You cannot defend your way out of atmospheric carbon. You cannot wall yourself off from pandemic. You cannot fortify your way to food security when the systems that produce food are collapsing. You can only cooperate your way toward livable futures.

The forests Merwin wanted to tell about aren't just the ones that were lost. They're the ones we must grow—the new ecosystems of protection that make mutualism normal and fortification obsolete.

What Follows

The chapters ahead translate this reckoning into architecture, examining what genuine security requires, who already provides it (though we rarely recognize them as guardians), why mutualism outperforms fortification, and how Defense as a Service can operationalize prevention at scale.

The forgotten language was never really forgotten. It was waiting for us to build an economy that remembers—that fortresses fail, but foundations endure.

7

The Misallocation of Defense

Every society is defined not just by what it protects, but by what it leaves unguarded. We protect borders, but not the rivers that feed us. We protect patents, but not the knowledge commons that could ensure our survival. We protect financial markets from volatility, but not our children from hunger or our elders from isolation.

The logic is consistent, if tragic: Our systems defend what is already capitalized, even when doing so undermines the very foundations of life. This is the great misallocation of our age—a security apparatus designed for yesterday's threats while tomorrow's crises compound unchecked.

The Mismatch Between Threat and Response

The nearly $3 trillion annual mismatch identified in this part's introduction reveals a fundamental disconnect: We have built enormous capacity for short-term, high-intensity conflict while leaving our long-term resilience systems underfunded, understaffed, and structurally weak.

It's like spending your entire household budget on reinforcing the front door while the roof rots, the water supply becomes poisoned, and the foundation cracks beneath your feet.

The threats most likely to destabilize economies, end lives, and unravel social cohesion in the 21st century rarely arrive as armies crossing borders. They arrive as ecological collapse—droughts that trigger mass migration, floods that overwhelm cities, soil depletion that undermines food security, biodiversity loss that destabilizes entire ecosystems. They arrive as public health failures—pandemics that expose healthcare fragility, antimicrobial resistance that renders common infections deadly, mental health crises that erode community fabric. They arrive as economic brittleness—supply chains optimized for efficiency but vulnerable to single-point failures, wealth concentration that fragments societies, automation that displaces workers faster than economies can adapt. They arrive as democratic erosion—disinformation that corrodes civic trust, polarization that prevents collective action, institutional capture that serves narrow interests over public good. And they arrive as social fragmentation—loss of community cohesion, erosion of mutual aid networks, breakdown of intergenerational knowledge transfer.

These are not hypothetical dangers. They are happening now, compounding and accelerating. And yet, the dominant security paradigm continues to allocate resources as if the primary threat were territorial invasion rather than systemic collapse.

The Iron Law of Misplaced Defense

Misallocated defense creates a self-reinforcing cycle (see figure 17). First, resources flow toward what's already protected—military budgets expand while public health, ecological restoration, and civic infrastructure struggle for funding. Second, what's protected gains political influence—defense contractors, fossil fuel interests, and concentrated wealth shape policy to preserve their position. Third, influence reinforces protection—lobbying ensures that outdated priorities continue to receive disproportionate resources, further starving the systems that provide

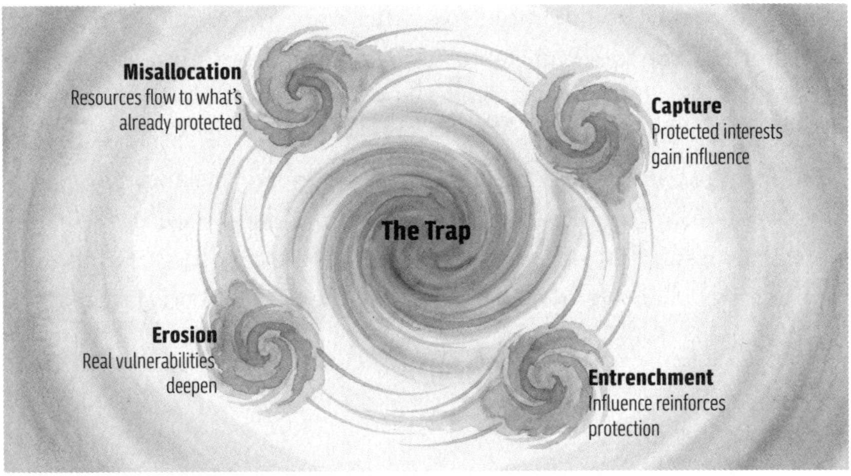

Figure 17. The Iron Law of Misplaced Defense

actual security. Fourth, real vulnerabilities deepen—while attention and capital flow toward symbolic threats, genuine risks go unaddressed until crisis forces a reactive, costly response.

This is not conspiracy. It is structural inertia—the enormous gravitational pull of legacy systems, legacy thinking, and legacy power.

The Hidden Costs

The opportunity cost of misallocated defense is staggering. Economically, every dollar spent on weapons systems that will never be used is a dollar not invested in renewable energy infrastructure, regenerative agriculture, or community health systems. Redirecting approximately 10 percent of global military spending—around $270 billion annually—could make decisive progress toward eliminating extreme poverty and hunger by 2030, according to UN and SIPRI analyses.[1]

Ecologically, military operations are among the largest consumers of fossil fuels and generators of emissions—yet they are often exempt from climate agreements, while ecosystem restoration, which provides natural disaster mitigation worth trillions, receives a fraction of defense budgets. Socially, communities lose trust when governments can fund wars but not schools, can deploy troops abroad but not ensure clean water at home, can bail out banks but not protect workers from economic dislocation. Strategically, perhaps most perversely, overinvestment in militarized security often creates the very instability it claims to prevent—arms proliferation triggers regional escalation, surveillance states breed mistrust and resistance, resource extraction to fund military expansion accelerates the climate and ecological crises that drive conflict.

Defense as Delay

Much of what passes for defense does not actually protect us—it buys time. And sometimes, not even that. We reinforce levees instead of restoring wetlands that would naturally buffer storm surges. We expand police budgets while starving the social services, mental health systems, and economic opportunities that prevent crime. We develop new weapons faster than we dismantle the reasons for war.

This is defense as symptom management, addressing surface manifestations while root causes deepen. It is expensive, exhausting, and ultimately futile. Delay becomes a design flaw when budgets prioritize short-term stabilization over long-term repair, when political cycles reward visible action now rather than durable outcomes later, when metrics measure "threat neutralized" instead of "threat prevented," when success is defined by incident response rather than by reducing the likelihood of incidents occurring.

The result: We defend yesterday's priorities with tomorrow's resources, while the foundations of genuine security erode beneath our feet.

The Comfort—and Danger—of Misplaced Defense

Misplaced defense has an emotional and political logic that makes it surprisingly resilient to reform. It is visible and dramatic—military parades, police presence, and border walls create the appearance of strength and action, while prevention infrastructure is largely invisible until it fails. It avoids uncomfortable redistributions—investing in root-cause prevention requires confronting structural inequalities, colonial legacies, and concentrated power, while reactive defense allows elites to avoid these thorny issues. It creates concentrated economic interests—defense contractors, surveillance technology firms, and private security companies have powerful lobbying capacity, while the constituencies for clean water, mental health services, and ecosystem restoration are diffuse and underfunded. And it serves short-term political incentives—politicians can claim to be "tough on security" by increasing military or police budgets, while long-term prevention investments pay off beyond election cycles and are harder to claim credit for.

But this comfort is illusory. Every year we delay the transition from reactive defense to proactive resilience, the costs compound. Climate tipping points approach. Social trust erodes. Democratic institutions weaken. And when the crises finally arrive—and they will—reactive defense will prove catastrophically inadequate.

Case Study: The Pandemic as Dress Rehearsal

COVID-19 offered a brutal preview of what happens when societies prioritize militarized security over genuine resilience. Nations with massive military budgets found themselves unable to produce enough masks, ventilators, or vaccines. Supply chains optimized for cost efficiency collapsed under strain. Public health systems, chronically underfunded, were overwhelmed within weeks. Misinformation spread faster than the virus itself, revealing profound vulnerabilities in our information ecosystems.

The pandemic killed millions and cost the global economy over tens of trillions of dollars—orders of magnitude more than the cost of the preparedness infrastructure that could have prevented or mitigated it.[2] And yet, even in the aftermath, military spending continued to rise while public health budgets remained stagnant or declined. The lesson was clear; we had not yet learned it.

This is the predictable outcome of defending the wrong things: When real threats arrive, we are unprepared—not because we lacked resources, but because we allocated them badly.

A Web, Not a Fortress

If misallocated defense is the diagnosis, what does genuine security infrastructure actually look like?

The answer lies in recognizing that real security is not a fortress. It is a web. It is not built from walls and weapons, but from the interwoven systems that make collective life possible: the health of ecosystems that buffer disasters, the strength of public institutions that maintain trust, the equity of economic systems that prevent desperation, the resilience of communities that care for their own.

These are not abstract ideals. They are material infrastructures with measurable impacts on survival, stability, and flourishing. And they are dramatically underfunded relative to their strategic importance.

What we fail to protect is precisely what we need to build.

The Five Pillars of Real Security

Security, properly understood, rests on the five interdependent pillars (see figure 18). Weaken any one, and the entire system becomes brittle. Strengthen all five, and you create conditions where threats are less likely to emerge and easier to absorb when they do.

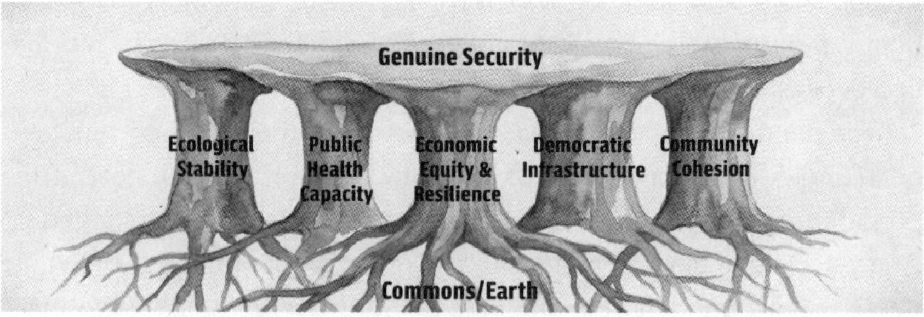

Figure 18. The Five Pillars of Real Security

Ecological Stability

Healthy ecosystems are the original security infrastructure. They regulate climate, purify water, regenerate soil, provide food, buffer against storms, and support the biodiversity upon which all life depends. When ecosystems degrade, security collapses—drought triggers resource conflicts and mass migration, deforestation increases flood risk and disease transmission, ocean acidification threatens food security for billions, soil depletion undermines agricultural stability.

Ecological security requires ecosystem restoration at scale—wetlands, forests, coral reefs, grasslands. It requires regenerative agriculture that rebuilds soil health, protection of biodiversity hotspots and migration corridors, climate adaptation infrastructure designed with nature rather than against it, and water security through watershed management and aquifer protection.

The return on investment is extraordinary. Every dollar invested in ecosystem restoration generates \$7–\$30 in economic returns through disaster prevention, food security, and climate regulation.[3] Coastal wetlands are estimated to have prevented over \$625 million in property damages in the United States during a single event, 2012's Hurricane Sandy.[4] By investing \$1.5 billion to protect its Catskill watershed—a "natural infrastructure" solution—New York City avoided the \$8–\$10 billion construction cost of a new water filtration plant and saves an additional \$300–\$500 million every year in operational costs.[5]

Public Health Capacity

Pandemics, antimicrobial resistance, mental health crises, chronic disease—these are not "health issues" separate from security. They are security threats that kill more people and cost more economically than most conventional conflicts.

Public health security requires universal healthcare access that treats prevention as infrastructure, surge capacity in hospitals and supply chains and trained personnel, early warning systems for disease outbreaks, mental health and addiction services integrated into communities, research infrastructure for vaccines and therapeutics and diagnostics, and health equity that addresses social determinants of disease.

The return on investment is compelling. The World Health Organization (WHO) estimates that every dollar invested in pandemic preparedness saves $5–$10 in outbreak response costs.[6] Universal healthcare reduces economic insecurity, increases productivity, and prevents the desperation that fuels instability. Thailand's landmark Universal Coverage Scheme successfully protected millions from medical-driven poverty, cutting the rate of households bankrupted by health costs in half in its first few years and providing a foundation for national economic productivity.[7]

Economic Equity and Resilience

Inequality is a threat multiplier. When economic systems concentrate wealth and opportunity narrowly, they generate desperation, resentment, and fragmentation—conditions ripe for conflict, extremism, and institutional collapse.

This is not new knowledge. We met W. E. B. Du Bois in Part II through a different lens—his Berkshires roots, his face on the BerkShares currency, what Randy Weinstein called his capacity to see that "everything connects." Here we encounter Du Bois the economic analyst.

Writing nearly a century ago about the failure of Reconstruction, he identified the broken promise at the heart of American insecurity: "So far as the Negroes were concerned, their demand for a reasonable part of the land on which they had worked for a quarter of a millennium was absolutely justified, and to give them anything less than this was an economic farce." He understood what genuine security required: "To have given each one of the million Negro free families a forty-acre freehold would have made a basis of real democracy in the United States that might easily have transformed the modern world."[8]

Du Bois saw what we're only now beginning to fully grasp—that security requires distributed ownership of productive assets, that democracy depends on economic foundation, that you cannot build stability on extraction and dispossession. The failure to distribute land after the Civil War created generations of concentrated wealth, entrenched inequality, and the structural insecurity we're still trying to address 160 years later.

Economic security is not about making everyone equally wealthy. It is about ensuring that everyone has access to dignified work, basic needs, and pathways to stability—what Du Bois called "a basis of real democracy." This requires living wages and worker ownership models, social safety nets that function as stabilizers rather than stigmas, local economic development that keeps wealth circulating in communities, access to affordable housing and education and childcare, distributed ownership of productive assets, and transition support for workers displaced by automation or climate adaptation.

The return on investment is clear. Societies with lower inequality have stronger social cohesion, higher trust, better health outcomes, and more stable governance. Every dollar invested in early childhood education returns $7–$13 through reduced crime, higher earnings, and lower social costs. The Perry Preschool Project—a landmark 1960s early childhood intervention study in Ypsilanti, Michigan—found that participants earned 42 percent more over their lifetimes and were 42 percent less likely to be arrested, generating $284,000 in societal benefit per child.[9]

Democratic Infrastructure

Democracy is not a luxury; it is a security technology. When people trust that their voices matter, that institutions are accountable, and that conflicts can be resolved through dialogue rather than violence, stability deepens. When democratic infrastructure erodes—through corruption, voter suppression, capture by concentrated interests, or information warfare—security unravels.

Democratic security requires civic education that builds media literacy and critical thinking, transparent and accountable governance at all levels, participatory decision-making mechanisms like citizen assemblies and participatory budgeting, campaign finance reform that reduces the influence of concentrated wealth, protection of press freedom and independent journalism, digital infrastructure designed for deliberation rather than manipulation, and conflict resolution mechanisms that address grievances before they escalate.

The return on investment is measurable. Democracies with high civic participation and institutional trust are more resilient to shocks, less prone to violent conflict, and better able to coordinate collective action on complex challenges like climate adaptation. Participatory budgeting—a pioneering Brazilian initiative originating in Porto Alegre in which citizens directly allocate portions of the municipal budget—has contributed to significant reductions in infant mortality across adopting municipalities. In Porto Alegre alone, it increased household access to water from 75 percent to 98 percent and dramatically expanded sanitation infrastructure, while strengthening democratic engagement.[10]

Community Cohesion and Mutual Aid

The final pillar is perhaps the most invisible—yet it is what activates all the others. Community cohesion is the social fabric that holds people together: the relationships of trust, reciprocity, and shared identity that allow for collective action. When communities are strong, they can organize mutual aid during crises, resist authoritarian capture, protect vulnerable members, and hold institutions accountable. When communities fragment, even the best-designed systems fail because there is no social substrate to sustain them.

Community security requires public spaces where people gather and build relationships, cultural institutions that preserve memory and foster belonging, support for community organizing and grassroots leadership, intergenerational connection and knowledge transfer, restorative justice systems that repair harm rather than merely punish, and local governance structures that distribute power.

The return on investment is profound. Strong communities have lower crime rates, better mental health outcomes, faster disaster recovery, and higher civic engagement. They are the connective tissue that makes all other security infrastructure functional. After Hurricane Katrina, the Vietnamese-American community in New Orleans East leveraged its dense mutual aid networks and strong social capital to rebuild far faster than the city average, with over half the neighborhood rebuilt and reopened in less than five months—all before most federal aid arrived.[11]

Australia, November 2019

I was there. November 2019. I had flown to Sydney for the Asia Pacific Impact Investing Summit, and afterward I gave myself two weeks to travel—to see the country I had heard so much about, to witness what I had only read about in reports and scientific papers.

I dove into the Coral Sea and snorkeled the Great Barrier Reef. Time seemed to stop as I drifted above that underwater cathedral—the branching corals, the darting fish, the impossible colors. I knew the Reef was stressed. I had read about the back-to-back bleaching events of 2016 and 2017.[12] But suspended in that water, watching a parrotfish graze on coral, I felt what no report could convey: this was not an abstraction called "biodiversity." It was a living world, intricate beyond comprehension, irreplaceable.

I traveled to Uluru, in the heart of Australian outback. For several days I stayed at that sacred site, entering what the Anangu people call *Tjukurpa*—Dreamtime—and sensing the Beings that shaped both that landscape and the Universe.[13] I watched the famous rock transform through the day: burnt sienna at dawn, yellow ochre as the sun rose, cadmium orange in the moments before sunset, Payne's grey in the shadows of approaching storms. That place, this world, is magic—if you simply stay still and pay attention. And dream.

Then I went south, to Kangaroo Island.

The island in November 2019 was a preserve of astonishing biological richness. Koalas dozed in eucalyptus trees. Mobs of Western gray kangaroos grazed in the golden light. Glossy black cockatoos called from the canopy. I visited the Flinders Chase National Park Visitors

Centre and spoke with one of the staff ecologists. She was proud of the diversity she helped protect—and she was worried. It was so dry. One lightning strike in the bush, she said, could set the park ablaze. She mentioned climate change several times in our conversation. She knew what was possible. She could feel it coming.

I left the island and made my way home.

It was just a few weeks later that the lightning strikes the ecologist feared arrived. Nearly half of Kangaroo Island went up in flames—48 percent of its total area, including much of Flinders Chase.[14] The loss of animal life was incalculable. Some estimates say that more than half of the koalas on the island—some twenty-five thousand—perished in the fires.

Of course, Kangaroo Island was only one area decimated during Australia's "Black Summer" of 2019–2020. Across the country, more than seventeen million hectares burned. Over three thousand homes were destroyed. Thirty-three people died during the fires; hundreds more from the smoke that blanketed cities for weeks. And the wildlife—WWF-Australia estimates that nearly *three billion* animals were killed or displaced. Three billion. The number is almost impossible to hold in the mind. Fifty million native rats and mice. Forty million possums and gliders. Five million kangaroos and wallabies. Sixty-one thousand koalas. A catalogue of loss that reads like an extinction event.[15]

Here one moment, gone the next.

And what was the Australian government doing while the continent burned? Expanding fossil fuel extraction. Approving new coal and gas developments. Pouring money into conventional military hardware. In 2019–2020, Australia's defense budget stood at A$38.7 billion—roughly 2 percent of GDP—with plans for a ten-year, A$270 billion investment in traditional defense capabilities: submarines, fighter jets, long-range missiles.[16] All the apparatus of security through force.

Meanwhile, the actual threat—the one that was *already* burning, bleaching, killing—received nothing like commensurate investment. The fires were not caused by a foreign adversary. They were caused by a destabilized climate system, by decades of accumulated emissions, by an economy that treated the atmosphere as a free dumping ground. No submarine could stop them. No missile defense system could protect the koalas sleeping in the trees of Flinders Chase.

This is what the misallocation of security looks like when it stops being abstract. It looks like an ecologist who knows what's coming and can do nothing to prevent it. It looks like three billion animals dead or displaced. It looks like the gulf between what we spend to project force across oceans and what we spend to stabilize the living systems that actually keep us safe.

I invoke these memories—I name these places, these animals, these colors of Uluru—because they are not distant abstractions. They are what genuine security is supposed to protect. And they are what we are failing to protect when we mistake fortification for foundation, when we invest in the weapons of yesterday's wars while tomorrow's threats burn unchecked across the landscape.

The Five Pillars we've just examined—ecological integrity, public health, economic equity, democratic resilience, social cohesion—are not academic categories. They are the difference between a world where the Great Barrier Reef survives and one where it doesn't. Between a future where Kangaroo Island's koala population recovers and one where it joins the growing list of what we've lost.

That ecologist at Flinders Chase—she was doing security work. She just wasn't recognized or resourced as such. And the system that should have protected what she was protecting was busy spending its billions elsewhere. What follows is the economic case for what I witnessed—the numbers that make prevention not just morally necessary but financially rational. The ecologist already knew this. The system still hasn't learned.

Security as Aliveness

The pillars we mapped—and the living world I had witnessed, now burning—reveal something profound: The infrastructure of real security is also the infrastructure of aliveness. Healthy ecosystems aren't just carbon sinks and water filters—they're the breathing, photosynthesizing, decomposing, regenerating web that makes Earth a living planet rather than a dead rock. Public health capacity isn't just pandemic response—it's the collective commitment that everybody matters, that nobody is disposable, that we're only as well as the most vulnerable among us. Economic equity isn't just fairness—it's the recognition that when some hoard while others lack, the whole community sickens. Democratic infrastructure isn't just governance—it's the practice of collective self-determination, the insistence that the future belongs to everyone, not just the powerful. And community cohesion isn't just social capital—it's what makes us human rather than isolated collections of atoms.

Security and aliveness, it turns out, are the same thing. You cannot be safe in a dead world.

The Prevention Dividend

One of the most consistent findings across security research is that prevention delivers a four to seven times return on investment compared to reaction (see figure 19). Every dollar invested in addressing root causes saves multiple dollars in crisis response. Disaster preparedness returns

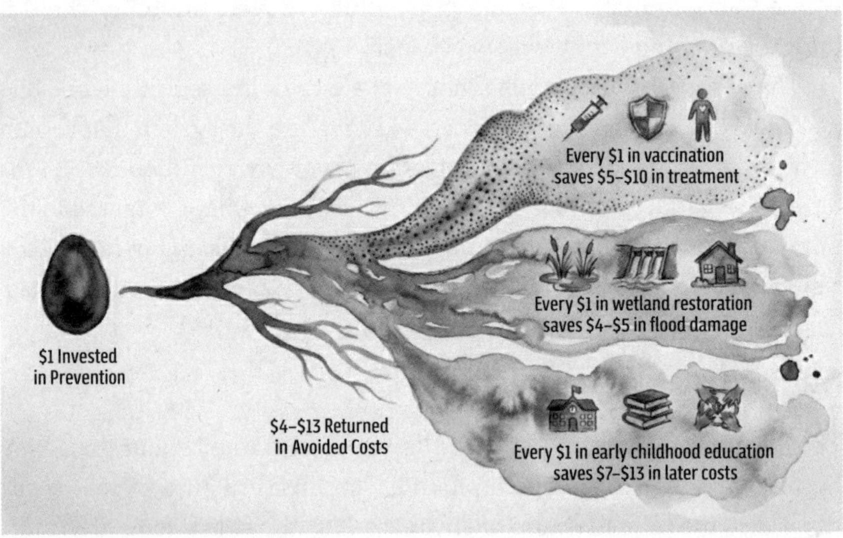

Figure 19. The Prevention Dividend—Investing in Causes, Not Symptoms

$4–$7 for every dollar invested.[17] Ecosystem restoration generates $7–$30 in economic returns.[18] Pandemic preparedness generates $1,102 in economic gain for every dollar spent.[19] Early childhood education returns $7–$13 in reduced social costs.[20] Conflict prevention saves $16 for every dollar invested in intervention costs.[21]

The evidence is overwhelming. So why does prevention infrastructure remain chronically underfunded?

The answer lies in political economy. Crises create urgency that unlocks emergency funding; prevention benefits are diffuse and long-term. Reactive response is visible and politically rewarding; prevention infrastructure is largely invisible until it fails. Industries built on reactive services—defense contractors, emergency response, insurance—have enormous lobbying power. And prevention requires confronting root causes like inequality and extraction, which powerful interests resist.

This is why shifting from reactive defense to proactive resilience is not just a technical adjustment; it is a political and cultural transformation. The task is to make prevention as visible, measurable, and politically compelling as reaction.

Redirecting Capital Flows

If we know prevention is more effective and costs less than reaction, how do we actually redirect capital at scale? This requires action across three domains:

- *Public investment reallocation* means governments shifting budget priorities: redirecting a percentage of military expenditure toward climate adaptation, public health, and ecosystem restoration; treating prevention infrastructure as nonnegotiable baseline spending rather than discretionary; establishing "resilience bonds" that finance long-term infrastructure with favorable terms; and creating cross-sector coordination so that defense, health, environment, and education budgets are seen as interconnected security investments.

- *Private capital realignment* means the Impact Economy building investment vehicles that reward prevention: catalytic capital that absorbs early risk for regenerative infrastructure; blended finance combining public, philanthropic, and private funds to make prevention investable; long-term patient capital aligned with generational time horizons rather than quarterly returns; impact-weighted accounting that prices in prevention benefits and externalities; and community investment funds that keep capital circulating locally.
- *Hybrid public–private models* recognize that the most effective security infrastructure often requires cooperation across sectors: public benefit corporations (PBC) delivering services with mission locked into governance; multistakeholder cooperatives where communities, workers, and investors share ownership; social impact bonds where private capital funds prevention programs and is repaid based on measurable outcomes; and community land trusts that hold infrastructure in perpetual trust.

Case Study: Costa Rica's Security Dividend

In 1948, following a brief civil war, Costa Rica made a radical choice: It abolished its military and redirected those resources toward health, education, and environmental protection.[22]

Three-quarters of a century later, the results are clear. Life expectancy exceeds that of the United States. The country has achieved nearly 100 percent literacy. More than 25 percent of its land is under environmental protection. Costa Rica ranks among the world's highest on happiness indices, enjoys political stability and democratic continuity rare in the region, and has built a thriving ecotourism economy on its preserved ecosystems.[23]

Costa Rica is not utopia—it faces challenges with inequality and crime. But it demonstrates that security can be achieved through investment in life systems rather than weapons systems, and that the dividends compound across generations. This is not a model every nation can or should replicate identically. But it proves that alternatives to militarized security are viable, strategic, and prosperity-generating.

Conclusion: From Infrastructure to Guardians

Mapping the infrastructure of real security is essential, but insufficient. The question is not just what we need, but who builds it, who maintains it, and who controls it.

In the next chapter, we will meet the people already doing this work—the nurses, teachers, watershed managers, community organizers, and regenerative practitioners who are the real security providers of our time. They are not waiting for permission or funding. They are building resilience from the ground up. And they deserve to be recognized, resourced, and celebrated as the guardians they are.

TOOL KIT: THE MISALLOCATION OF DEFENSE

Purpose: To help impact entrepreneurs, investors, and policymakers diagnose security misallocation, assess the Five Pillars in their context, and redirect resources toward genuine resilience.

1. Conduct a Defense Audit

   Map where your organization, community, or sector currently allocates "defensive" resources. What are you actively protecting—assets, markets, IP, reputation, territory? How much time, money, and energy goes into these defenses? Are they preserving something worth sustaining, or shielding something that should evolve? For each defensive expenditure, ask: What is *not*

(CONTINUED)

being funded because resources are locked in here? What preventive investments could reduce the need for this defense?

2. Distinguish Between Delay and Prevention

   Assess whether your security measures are delay mechanisms, buying time without addressing root causes (e.g., hardening infrastructure against climate impacts without reducing emissions), or prevention investments, addressing underlying conditions that create vulnerability (e.g., restoring watersheds that naturally buffer against floods). Map your current portfolio of security investments on this spectrum. Consider calculating your Prevention Ratio—the proportion of spending directed toward root-cause prevention versus symptom reaction—as a concrete diagnostic baseline (see Chapter 10 for the full framework).

3. Assess Your Five Pillars

   For your organization, community, or investment portfolio, evaluate the strength of each pillar on a scale of one to ten:

   Ecological stability: Are ecosystems in your context healthy or degraded? What restoration is needed?

   Public health capacity: Can the system absorb shocks? Is prevention prioritized?

   Economic equity: Are people secure in their livelihoods? Is wealth concentrated or distributed?

   Democratic infrastructure: Is governance transparent and accountable? Do people trust institutions?

   Community cohesion: Are relationships strong? Can people mobilize mutual aid?

   Any pillar you score below six is a critical vulnerability requiring immediate attention.

(CONTINUED)

4. Calculate Your Prevention Dividend

   For any proposed security investment, ask: Does this prevent harm or only respond to it? What is the measurable return on prevention? How does this compare to reactive alternatives? Also consider: If you could redirect 10 percent of your organization's or community's "defensive" resources toward prevention infrastructure, where would it go? What threats would that actually reduce more effectively than current expenditures?

5. Design for Resilience

   Once you've identified gaps, design investments that strengthen multiple pillars simultaneously. The most effective resilience infrastructure creates benefits across domains—ecosystem restoration that also creates jobs and builds community, healthcare investments that also strengthen democratic participation, economic development that also restores ecological function. Ask: How can this investment strengthen more than one pillar? Who needs to be at the table to design this well? What governance structures ensure benefits are distributed equitably?

Reflection Prompt

Which of the Five Pillars is weakest in your context, and what would it take to strengthen it by two points on the one-to-ten scale within the next year?

Connects To

This chapter establishes the diagnostic foundation and infrastructure framework for Part III. For the people who provide genuine security, see Chapter 8. For the strategic case for cooperation over competition, see Chapter 9. For operational implementation, see Chapter 10.

8

Who Really Keeps Us Safe

When we picture security, we tend to imagine uniforms, weapons, and fortified perimeters. We think of standing armies, intelligence agencies, border patrols—the visible apparatus of defense. But this picture is incomplete. And in many cases, it is misleading.

The truth is that much of what truly keeps us safe operates far from the spotlight, without parade grounds or press conferences. It is built not by force of arms, but by the quiet persistence of systems and people whose work makes violence less likely, disasters less devastating, and recovery more possible.

The real security providers are already among us. The public health nurse tracking disease outbreaks before they become epidemics. The regenerative farmer restoring soil that provides buffering against drought and flood. The teacher building critical thinking skills that inoculate against disinformation. The community organizer weaving networks of mutual aid that activate in crisis. The water engineer ensuring aquifers remain clean and abundant. The conflict mediator resolving disputes before they escalate into violence.

These are not peripheral actors in some adjacent domain called "social services." They are the foundation of security itself—the people who prevent the conditions that make reactive defense necessary. And yet, they are rarely recognized as such. They receive a fraction of the resources, prestige, and political support given to conventional defense. Their work is treated as expendable rather than essential, discretionary rather than strategic.

This chapter makes them visible. It names them as the guardians they are. And it asks: What would change if we funded, celebrated, and organized our societies around the people who actually keep us safe?

The Ecology of Safety

Think of a resilient community and trace the threads of what makes it secure. Real safety is not produced by a single institution or profession. It emerges from an *ecology of roles*, each essential, each interdependent (see figure 20).

The *ecological stewards* maintain the living systems that buffer us from disaster and sustain life itself. Foresters manage watersheds that

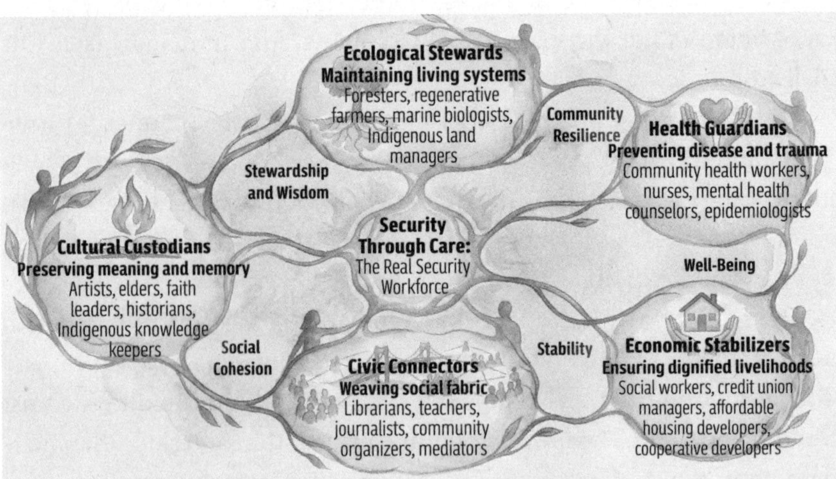

Figure 20. The Ecology of Safety—Who Really Keeps Us Safe

prevent floods and purify water. Farmers practice regenerative agriculture that sequesters carbon and builds soil health. Marine biologists protect coastal ecosystems that buffer storms. Park rangers maintain biodiversity that stabilizes food webs. Indigenous land managers apply traditional ecological knowledge developed over millennia. Their work is security work—they prevent the ecological collapse that triggers resource conflicts, mass migration, and societal destabilization.

The *health guardians* protect our bodies and minds from disease, trauma, and breakdown before crisis hits. Community health workers prevent disease through education and early intervention. Mental health counselors address trauma before it manifests as violence. Epidemiologists track patterns and build early warning systems. Nurses provide care that keeps minor issues from becoming emergencies. Public health administrators coordinate surge capacity. Their work is security work—they prevent the health crises that overwhelm systems, kill millions, and cost trillions.

The *economic stabilizers* ensure everyone has access to dignified livelihoods and basic material security. Social workers connect people to resources before desperation sets in. Credit union managers provide fair financial services that prevent predatory debt cycles. Job training coordinators help workers adapt to economic transitions. Affordable housing developers ensure people have stable shelter. Cooperative business developers distribute ownership and wealth. Their work is security work—they prevent the economic desperation that fuels conflict, extremism, and institutional collapse.

The *civic connectors* weave the social fabric that enables collective action and democratic resilience. Librarians provide information access and community gathering space. Teachers encourage critical thinking and build civic literacy. Journalists hold power accountable and expose corruption. Community organizers build networks of mutual aid and collective action. Mediators and facilitators resolve conflicts before they escalate. Election administrators ensure democratic integrity. Their work is security work—they prevent the democratic erosion and social fragmentation that make societies vulnerable to authoritarianism and collapse.

The *cultural custodians* maintain the stories, practices, and wisdom that give communities meaning and continuity. Artists preserve and create culture. Elders pass down knowledge and maintain intergenerational connection. Faith leaders build moral communities and provide pastoral care. Historians document memory so that lessons endure. Indigenous knowledge keepers maintain cosmologies of reciprocity and stewardship. Their work is security work—they preserve the cultural coherence that allows communities to act collectively, resist manipulation, and maintain identity through crisis.

Each of these roles prevents harm, builds resilience, or enables recovery. Together, they create the conditions in which violent conflict, social collapse, and cascading crises become less likely—and ensure that when they do occur, communities are better able to weather them and adapt. This is what an actual security workforce looks like. Not an army, but an ecology.

Why We Don't See Them

If these are the real security providers, why are they invisible? Several factors converge:

- **The visibility bias:** Military and police forces are designed to be visible. Uniforms, ceremonies, displays of force—all signal strength and generate political support. Prevention infrastructure is largely invisible until it fails. We notice the water system only when it breaks, the teacher only when literacy rates drop, the ecosystem only when it collapses.
- **The immediacy trap:** Reactive defense addresses immediate, visible threats—a virus is spreading, deploy medical response; a border is contested, send troops. Prevention addresses slow-moving, diffuse risks that don't generate the same urgency. Soil depletion, declining civic trust, eroding biodiversity—these threats compound quietly, until suddenly they cascade.

- **The prestige hierarchy:** Societies confer status on those who "protect" through force, not those who prevent harm through care. Warriors receive medals; nurses receive applause (briefly, during a pandemic). Generals become public figures; watershed managers remain anonymous. This prestige gap has material consequences: lower pay, less political influence, weaker institutional support.
- **The gendered and racialized nature of care work:** Much of the real security workforce is disproportionately composed of women, people of color, and immigrants—groups historically undervalued in labor markets. Care work, teaching, community organizing, and environmental stewardship have been systematically devalued precisely because they are associated with these groups. Making security providers visible requires confronting these inequities directly.

Real Guardians in Action

The real guardians of security are already at work. Here are some of them in action:

- **Grameen Shakti (Bangladesh):** The solar energy enterprise we met in Chapter 3 employs thousands of technicians, trainers, and community liaisons—mostly women—who bring power to rural households one installation at a time. These workers are security providers: Each solar panel they install reduces resource competition, builds local economic capacity, and prevents the desperation that fuels instability. Yet they are categorized as "development workers," not security personnel.
- **Community health workers (global):** In regions from rural India to urban Baltimore, community health workers prevent disease through education, early intervention, and connection to care.[1] During COVID-19, they were often the first line of defense,

yet they received a fraction of the resources given to militarized pandemic response.

- **The Civilian Conservation Corps (1933–1942, United States):** During the Great Depression, the Civilian Conservation Corps (CCC) employed millions to restore forests, build trails, prevent erosion, and create parks. It was framed as economic relief, but it was also security infrastructure—preventing ecological collapse, reducing desperation, and constructing the natural buffers that protect communities today.[2]
- **Agroecology networks (Latin America):** Farmer-to-farmer networks across Latin America teach regenerative agriculture that restores soil, increases yields, and reduces dependence on expensive chemical inputs.[3] This is food security, climate adaptation, and economic stability—all dimensions of genuine defense—delivered through peer education, not top-down programs.
- **Restorative justice practitioners (global):** In communities from New Zealand to Oakland, restorative justice facilitators address harm by bringing together those affected to repair relationships and prevent recurrence. This approach reduces recidivism more effectively than incarceration, strengthens community cohesion, and prevents cycles of violence.[4] It is conflict prevention infrastructure.

The Economics of Invisible Labor

One of the great economic distortions of our time is that we systematically undervalue—and underpay—the work that actually generates security and well-being.

Care work—childcare, eldercare, nursing—is essential to human development and resilience, yet it pays near-poverty wages in many countries. Teaching shapes the cognitive and civic capacities of entire generations, yet teachers are chronically underpaid and politically scapegoated. Environmental restoration prevents disasters and saves trillions, yet restoration workers often earn less than those in extractive industries that create the damage. Community organizing builds the social fabric that allows democracy to function, yet it is done largely by volunteers or underfunded nonprofits.

This is not an accident. It reflects a deep cultural and economic logic that values extraction over regeneration, control over care, and dominance over stewardship. Revaluing this work is not charity. It is strategic necessity. If we want societies capable of navigating the polycrisis, we must pay the people who build resilience as much as—or more than—those who manage reaction.

From Recognition to Resourcing

Making security providers visible is the first step. The second is resourcing them at a scale commensurate with their strategic importance.

Policy changes must reclassify prevention as security spending—integrating public health, ecosystem restoration, education, and community development into national security budgets, not as auxiliary programs but as core defense infrastructure. Funding for care, education, health, and the environment must be protected from political capture, treated as nonnegotiable baseline investment rather than subject to ideological budget cuts.

Cultural shifts must build career pathways and prestige for prevention workers—professional development, leadership opportunities, and public recognition for care workers, teachers, environmental stewards, and community organizers. We must celebrate prevention heroes the way we celebrate warriors, telling their stories, creating awards, and developing media coverage and cultural representations that honor their contributions.

Material support must invest in the systems these workers need to succeed: surge capacity in hospitals and clinics, professional development for teachers, equipment and resources for ecosystem restoration, space and support for community organizing.

The Regenerative Security Workforce

This chapter reveals what a regenerative security workforce actually looks like. It is not a new bureaucracy to be built from scratch. It is a recognition and reorientation of the people already doing security work—and an investment in expanding their capacity.

When we shift from reactive defense to proactive resilience, we shift from a military-centric workforce to an ecology of care: from soldiers to stewards, from weapons operators to watershed managers, from intelligence analysts to community organizers, from border guards to public health workers.

Importantly, this shift doesn't require starting from scratch or abandoning existing security personnel. Many current military and police roles contain the seeds of this transformation. Military engineering corps already possess skills for large-scale ecosystem restoration and disaster-resilient infrastructure. Intelligence analysts trained in pattern recognition could track disease outbreaks or ecological tipping points. Police officers with deep community knowledge could transition into conflict mediation and restorative justice facilitation. Veterans with logistics expertise could coordinate mutual aid networks and emergency preparedness.

The question isn't whether people in traditional security roles have value—they do. It's how best to redirect their skills, discipline, and service ethic toward preventing harm rather than only responding to it. This is not about eliminating traditional defense roles—there will always be a need for some reactive capacity. It is about rebalancing so that the vast majority of security resources flow toward the people and systems that build safety proactively rather than manage crisis reactively.

Conclusion: From Guardians to Systems

The previous chapter showed what genuine security infrastructure looks like, and this chapter revealed who actually builds and maintains it. But these systems and people exist within a larger context—one still dominated by militarized logics of competition, dominance, and zero-sum thinking.

In the next chapter, we will examine that context directly, exploring the gravitational pull of militarization and how mutualism offers a more strategic, cost-effective, and durable alternative. Resisting that pull is essential, because until we shift the paradigm from "security through dominance" to "security through cooperation," even the best prevention infrastructure will struggle to take root and endure.

TOOL KIT: WHO REALLY KEEPS US SAFE

Purpose: To help impact entrepreneurs, investors, and communities identify, support, and resource the people who generate real security through prevention and care.

1. Map Your Real Security Workforce

   Identify who in your community or organization is actually doing security work: ecological stewards who maintain the natural systems you depend on, health guardians who prevent illness and build wellness, economic stabilizers who ensure people have dignified livelihoods, civic connectors who build trust and enable collective action, and cultural custodians who maintain memory, meaning, and belonging. For each category, name specific people and institutions. Where are the gaps?

2. Assess Resource Allocation

   Compare what your organization, community, or sector spends on reactive defense (security systems, insurance, emergency response) versus prevention infrastructure (health, education, ecological restoration, community building). Is the ratio aligned with actual impact on safety and resilience? As part of this assessment, examine compensation: Are care workers, teachers, and community

(CONTINUED)

organizers in your ecosystem paid living wages? Do they have benefits, professional development, and career pathways?

3. Build Visibility and Prestige

   Create recognition systems that celebrate prevention work: awards for community health workers, teachers, and ecological stewards; storytelling campaigns that make their work visible; leadership pathways that give them voice in strategic decisions. Challenge cultural narratives that equate security with force—in communications, center stories of prevention and care; in hiring, prioritize relational skills alongside technical expertise; in leadership development, cultivate stewardship over dominance.

4. Protect and Invest

   Structure funding so prevention work is not vulnerable to budget cuts or political capture: long-term contracts and endowments, legal protections for essential services, multistakeholder governance that distributes power. Invest in the infrastructure these workers need: training and professional development, tools and technology and resources, peer networks and communities of practice.

Reflection Prompt

Who is one person in your community doing essential security work that goes unrecognized—and how could you resource or celebrate them this month?

Connects To

This chapter identifies the actors and institutions that provide genuine security, building on the infrastructure mapped in Chapter 7. For the strategic case for cooperation over competition, see Chapter 9. For operational implementation, see Chapter 10.

9

From Militarization to Mutualism

The Strategic Case for Cooperation

The converted coach barn sat at the edge of the Rockefeller estate, its massive timber beams holding a century of history. Through tall windows, the early November light fell across a long table where two dozen of us had gathered—writers, activists, wisdom keepers—to discuss what felt like the fate of the world (figure 21).

It was 2003. I was serving as executive director of The Orion Society, and we had partnered with Rockefeller Brothers Fund Board Chair Steven Rockefeller and Priscilla Lewis of RBF's Peace and Security program to convene this multiday summit at the Pocantico Center in Tarrytown, New York. Our goal was ambitious: to envision a new framework for US global relations, one that moved beyond the Cold War hangover and addressed the emerging planetary crisis.

That ambition had been building for two years. In the weeks after September 11, 2001, as the United States lurched toward a security posture defined by surveillance, militarism, and the curtailment of civil liberties, I had recognized that the question The Orion Society had been

Figure 21. The Crossroads at Pocantico—Fortress World or Great Transition

circling for a decade—*What makes human systems durable?*—had acquired a new and urgent dimension. The ecological and cultural work we had been doing was not separate from the security crisis unfolding around us. It was, I came to believe, the answer to it.

That conviction became *The New Patriotism*, a book series I conceived and launched through The Orion Society in the immediate aftermath of the attacks. As Series Editor, I commissioned and wrote introductions for works by some of the country's finest writers—voices who understood that genuine security could not be built on fear, exclusion, or the suppression of dissent. The series opened with Wendell Berry's *In the Presence of Fear*, published in those raw first months. Berry's argument was deceptively simple and, in retrospect, prophetic: that the nation's rush toward militarized security was itself a form of vulnerability; that a society dependent on centralized systems and fossil energy was structurally fragile; and that no amount of military spending could remedy a fragility rooted in design. There followed works by Berry and David James Duncan on moral courage as a form of national defense; by Barry Lopez, Richard Nelson, and Terry Tempest Williams reframing patriotism from allegiance to power toward stewardship of place; and by Williams alone, making explicit what the series had been building toward: that democratic practice—the messy, demanding work of civic engagement—is itself a security infrastructure. Berry and Duncan's *Citizens Dissent: Security, Morality, and Leadership in an Age of Terror* received the American Library Association's Intellectual Freedom Award, a recognition that this work was engaging not at the margins of the security debate but at its democratic core.[1]

The summit at Pocantico grew directly from this body of work. These grounds—overlooking the Hudson Valley, where the river bends wide toward the Tappan Zee—had hosted such conversations before, seen generations of deliberation about the shape of the world. Now the trees were turning gold and rust, and we were asking whether a different shape was still possible. Steven Rockefeller had recently shepherded the Earth Charter to completion—a remarkable document years in the making, articulating ethical principles for a just, sustainable, and peaceful global society. At Orion, we had published a special issue of our magazine on the Charter and marshaled our network to secure endorsements. The document represented a kind of hope: that humanity might choose, deliberately and collectively, a path of ecological integrity and mutual care. But whether that choice would be made—whether it *could* be made—remained an open question.

Around the table sat several of the writers who had given their best language to The New Patriotism—Berry, Williams, Lopez—voices readers of this book have already met, whose contributions to the series had challenged the prevailing security paradigm. Alongside them were Bill McKibben and Peter Matthiessen, longtime Orion advisors who had been thinking deeply about the intersection of ecology, culture, and security for years. We are also joined by David Orr, who had spent years articulating what ecological intelligence would require of education and design, and Oren Lyons, Faithkeeper of the Turtle Clan of the Onondaga Nation, who carried the Haudenosaunee teaching that every decision must be made with the seventh generation to come in mind.

The presentation that defined the weekend—and which haunts me still—came from Paul Raskin of the Tellus Institute. Raskin presented the findings of the Global Scenario Group, outlining two distinct trajectories for humanity as we face the escalating pressures of climate change and inequality.

The first scenario he called "Fortress World." In this future, the global elite respond to environmental collapse and social unrest not by solving the root causes, but by retreating. They build metaphorical and literal walls to protect their enclaves of prosperity, managing resources through dominance and surveillance. Outside these fortresses, the majority of humanity navigates a chaotic, resource-scarce "barbarization." It was a chillingly plausible extrapolation of the militarized security mindset: safety as a zero-sum game, maintained by excluding the "threat."

The alternative was the "Great Transition." This future relied on a profound shift in values, from individualism and domination to solidarity and ecology. It envisioned a world where security was achieved through international cooperation, shared resilience, and the recognition of interdependence. Not fortress, but web. Not walls, but weaving.[2]

When Raskin finished, the silence was heavy. Outside, the November wind moved through the oaks. I looked around the table—at Wendell, whose life's work had been to stand for what he stood *on*; at Peter, whose stillness seemed to hold the whole room; at Bill, who had been documenting the unraveling for years and knew the data better than anyone; at Terry, whose witness to the dying Great Salt Lake had taught her that grief and action must move together.

We were staring at the precise fork in the road.

And then, in the conversation that followed, something shifted in me. Bill laid out the climate projections with the precision I had come to expect from him. Wendell spoke quietly about the agrarian roots of real security—the way genuine stability grows from the ground up, from communities that know how to feed themselves and care for their own. Terry brought her fierce attention to what was being lost and what might still be saved. We were discussing tipping points, the scale of transformation required—and I felt a wave of panic rise through my chest. The enormity of it. The inadequacy of our efforts against the forces arrayed. My face must have shown it, because across the table, Oren Lyons caught my eye.

He said something then—something quiet, something that felt directed at me across the long table, though everyone heard it. I cannot retrieve the exact words today; they live in me like the echo of thunder in distant hills, present but beyond precise recall. What I remember is this: His voice was utterly grounded and somehow also vast, as if the room had suddenly extended to include forests and rivers and ancestors and generations unborn. He spoke from a tradition that had faced civilizational threat before—and endured. He spoke of time differently than we usually speak of it. And something in what he said made me feel that I was home—not just in that room, but anywhere on Earth I might find myself. That the ground was trustworthy. That the work was worth doing regardless of outcome. That panic was understandable but not necessary.

I have carried that moment for two decades. I cannot quote it. I can only say that it changed something in the quality of my fear.

"Fortress World" is the ultimate expression of what I call *fortress thinking*. It assumes that if we just build the walls high enough and the weapons smart enough, we can isolate ourselves from the consequences of a breaking world. But as we discussed that weekend at Pocantico, the fortress is an illusion. In an age of airborne pathogens, atmospheric carbon, and economic contagion, there is no wall high enough to keep the world out. The defended enclave is not safer; it is merely lonelier, and ultimately just as doomed.

The "Great Transition" is not utopian fantasy; it is strategic necessity. It represents the mutualist path—the recognition that genuine security emerges from healthy systems and reciprocal relationships, not from the capacity to dominate.

The Five Pillars of Real Security we examined in Chapter 7—ecological stability, public health, economic equity, democratic infrastructure, community cohesion—are the architectural blueprints for that transition. This chapter makes the strategic case for choosing them: why mutualism outperforms militarization, why cooperation is more durable than competition, why the fortress, for all its apparent strength, is the path to collapse.

As we examine the case for mutualism, keep the image of the fortress in mind—not as a goal, but as a warning of what happens when we mistake dominance for safety. Keep Oren's voice in mind too: that grounded presence that could hold both the enormity of the crisis and the steadiness to act anyway.

We are still at the crossroads. The choice is still before us.

The Gravitational Pull of Militarization

Militarization has a gravitational pull. Once a society invests heavily in weapons, command structures, and security doctrines built on dominance, it tends to see more and more of life through that lens. Problems become "threats." Neighbors become "potential adversaries." Public resources are allocated first to defense postures and only later—if at all—to the infrastructures of peace.

In this way, militarization is not just a budgetary choice; it is a cultural frame. It defines what counts as "serious" policy, who is considered a protector, and which risks are seen as worth acting on. But this framing comes with costs—costs that compound over time and undermine the very security militarization claims to provide. By focusing on dominance and deterrence, militarization often sidelines the quieter, slower work that builds trust, strengthens reciprocity, and prevents conflict in the first place.

Mutualism is not idealism. It is the most cost-effective, durable, and strategic form of defense available. Cooperation does not mean weakness. It means recognizing that in an interconnected world, security is coproduced—and that societies that invest in mutual benefit and shared resilience consistently outperform those that rely on arms races and zero-sum competition.

The Limits and Costs of Militarized Security

Militarization is built on the logic of scarcity and competition. It assumes that safety is won through superiority—more troops, better weapons, faster strikes—and that every gain for one side is a loss for another. This zero-sum mindset creates self-fulfilling prophecies.

Arms races generate insecurity. When we arm in anticipation of attack, we often provoke others to do the same, and what begins as defensive preparation becomes an escalating cycle of mutual threat. The Cold War demonstrated this at global scale; regional arms buildups repeat the pattern today.

Militarization diverts resources from actual security—every dollar spent on weapons systems that may never be used is a dollar not invested in public health, climate adaptation, or economic stability, the systems that actually prevent the conditions that generate conflict. It erodes trust and legitimacy—heavy-handed security measures like surveillance, border militarization, and police occupation of communities often damage the social fabric they claim to protect, and when people feel occupied rather than served, security institutions lose legitimacy, making cooperation harder and resistance more likely. It is structurally brittle—militarized security depends on maintaining constant readiness for specific threat scenarios, and when different threats emerge, like pandemics, climate disasters, or economic collapse, the apparatus is often useless or counterproductive. And it creates perverse incentives—defense industries, private military contractors, and surveillance technology firms profit from insecurity and have enormous lobbying capacity and strong incentives to frame problems in ways that justify their services, even when those services don't actually make societies safer.

The Economic Logic of Peace

If violence is expensive, peace is economically strategic. The Institute for Economics and Peace estimates that violence costs the global economy $19.1 trillion annually—roughly 13.5 percent of global GDP. This includes direct military spending and security services, armed conflict and its destruction of infrastructure, homicide and violent crime, incarceration and policing, terrorism and its economic disruption, and lost productivity from fear, trauma, and displacement.[3] If violence were an industry, it would be one of the largest on Earth.

And yet, we rarely speak of *peace* as a growth sector—as an economic opportunity with massive returns on investment.

The peace dividend is real and measurable. Nations that reduce military spending and redirect resources toward health, education, and infrastructure see improvements in human development that compound across generations. Regions that establish cooperation agreements reduce the likelihood of conflict and increase trade, tourism, and investment. Communities that invest in conflict prevention—mediation, restorative justice, economic opportunity—see lower crime rates and higher social cohesion at a fraction of the cost of incarceration.

This is what the business of peace looks like: *investments that generate returns in stability, prosperity, and resilience.*

Mutualism as Strategic Advantage

Mutualism begins with a different premise than militarization: Security is coproduced. No single actor—not a state, not a corporation, not an army—can unilaterally guarantee stability in a complex, interconnected world. Security emerges when interdependent systems and communities agree to protect each other's well-being because it is in everyone's interest to do so. This is not naive. It is adaptive intelligence.

Mutualism changes the competitive dynamic. Instead of racing to accumulate more destructive capability, participants compete to become the most reliable, trustworthy, and value-adding partner in the network. This creates positive feedback loops: the more value you contribute, the more secure you become; the stronger the network becomes, the less attractive aggression becomes to any outside actor; trust compounds over time, reducing transaction costs and increasing coordination capacity.

Mutualism is more resilient. Distributed, cooperative systems are harder to destabilize than centralized, hierarchical ones. When security depends on a web of relationships rather than a single power center, the system can absorb shocks without collapsing.

Mutualism scales through pattern, not replication. You don't need identical governance structures everywhere. You need shared principles and interoperable protocols that allow diverse actors to cooperate while maintaining local autonomy.

The Architecture of Mutualism

What does mutualistic security look like in practice?

Cooperative infrastructure means that rather than each actor building redundant systems, mutualistic models pool resources: shared early warning systems, joint investment in resilience infrastructure, mutual aid networks, open-source knowledge platforms. The Nordic Civil Preparedness Networks exemplify this—Scandinavian countries integrate local volunteer organizations, civil defense, and social welfare systems into national security strategy, with mutual aid training, food security planning, and inclusive disaster simulations ensuring that communities can respond collectively, reducing dependence on centralized force while building social cohesion.[4]

Economic interdependence as stabilization recognizes that when economies are intertwined through fair trade, shared infrastructure, and mutual investment, conflict becomes economically irrational. This is different from exploitative or fragile interdependence—mutualistic interdependence is reciprocal, transparent, diversified, and regenerative. Community-owned renewable energy cooperatives across Germany, Denmark, and Scotland show how this works: Communities own shares in wind and solar installations, creating economic stake in energy stability, distributing wealth locally, and reducing dependence on centralized fossil fuel systems vulnerable to geopolitical disruption. Energy security becomes a function of cooperation, not control.[5]

Conflict prevention as core business means enterprises contribute to peace not through philanthropy but through design: supply chains that avoid exploitation and conflict minerals, fair labor practices and living wages, anchor jobs in post-conflict communities, trust-based trade relationships across political divides. Meru Herbs in Kenya—a worker-owned cooperative producing herbal teas and jams in a region once marked by drought-induced resource conflicts—links fair-trade markets abroad with sustainable water use at home, turning local stability into global value.[6] Peace becomes profitable for all parties.

From threat assessment to opportunity mapping shifts the focus from what could go wrong to what shared strengths could emerge. In militarized systems, risk analysis focuses exclusively on threats. In mutualistic systems, risk analysis pairs with opportunity mapping: Where do we have shared vulnerabilities that could become shared strengths? Which infrastructures would benefit most from cooperative stewardship? What incentives could lock in long-term collaboration? The African Risk Capacity initiative, where African Union member states pool financial resources for rapid payouts after disasters, demonstrates this logic—by sharing risk and response capacity, countries reduce the temptation to hoard resources, achieving stronger collective resilience at lower individual cost.[7]

The Felt Experience of Mutualism

There's a quality to militarized security that everyone who's experienced it recognizes: the constant vigilance, the assumption of threat, the exhaustion of maintaining defenses that can never fully be relaxed because danger might come from anywhere at any time. The airport security theater. The gated community. The alarm system. The surveillance cameras. The sense that you're safe only as long as you stay inside your fortress, maintain your advantage, keep potential threats at a distance.

It's exhausting. Even when you're wealthy enough or powerful enough to keep up the defenses, the posture itself drains life. You can't fully rest. You can't fully trust. You can't be vulnerable, which means you can't be fully human. The defended self is a diminished self—hard where it should be permeable, closed where it should be open, separate where it should be connected.

This is the cost of militarization that never appears in defense budgets: the atrophy of our capacity for relationships, for trust, for the vulnerability that makes deep connection possible. You can't simultaneously defend against everyone and belong to anyone. The logic of fortification is the logic of isolation.

Mutualism feels different. Profoundly, viscerally different.

I've seen this in communities that practice mutual aid—the way shoulders drop, breath deepens, faces soften. Not because threats disappear, but because they're faced together; because when crisis comes, you're not alone; because the question shifts from "How do I defend what's mine?" to "How do we care for what's ours?"

The Nordic countries, with their robust social safety nets, register highest on measures of happiness and social trust. That's not because they're naive about danger, but because they've built security through mutualism rather than militarization. When you know that sickness won't bankrupt you, that unemployment won't make you homeless, that education is accessible, that elder care is provided—when these are guaranteed through collective commitment rather than individual struggle—you can breathe.

You can be generous, because you're not operating from scarcity. You can take risks, because failure won't be fatal. You can trust, because the system is designed for mutual support rather than individual survival. You can be vulnerable, because vulnerability won't be exploited—it will be met with care.

This is what militarization steals: the possibility of this kind of aliveness. The defended life is a smaller life, a harder life, a lonelier life—even when, especially when, you "win" at individual security.

Mutualism isn't naive idealism. It's recognition that the defended fortress—no matter how well resourced—is still a prison. That the only security worth having is the kind that increases aliveness rather than protecting against it. That genuine safety comes not from being strong enough to stand alone but from being connected enough that you never have to.

The strategic case for mutualism is sound. The economic case is sound. But the *felt* case—the lived experience of what it means to move through the world trusting rather than defending—is what makes mutualism worth choosing even when militarization seems more immediately powerful.

Because power that isolates is a diminished power. Strength that requires constant defense is a fragile strength. Security that depends on others' insecurity is no security at all.

The mutually secured community isn't just more resilient than the defended fortress. It's more alive. And in the end, that's what we're building for—not just survival, but the conditions for human flourishing.

The Cultural Shift: From Fear to Reciprocity

Militarization thrives on fear—of loss, of the "other," of falling behind. Mutualism thrives on reciprocity—the recognition that our safety is intertwined, and that trust is cheaper to build than conflict is to resolve.

This cultural shift is as important as the structural one. It requires new narratives that celebrate cooperation as strength rather than weakness—stories of successful mutual aid, collaborative infrastructure, and peace-building enterprises need the same cultural prominence as war stories. It requires new metrics that measure security in terms of trust, interdependence, and shared resilience rather than military dominance or deterrence capacity. It requires new leadership models that reward those who build bridges, broker cooperation, and strengthen networks—not just those who project force or win zero-sum competitions. And it requires new education that teaches conflict transformation, systems thinking, and collaborative problem solving as core civic skills.

Peace as a Service Economy

If Chapter 8 revealed that the real security providers are care workers, teachers, and ecological stewards, this chapter reveals that peace itself can be structured as a service economy—one where enterprises, investors, and institutions compete to deliver the conditions for stability, not just profit from its absence.

What would it look like to operationalize this? Rather than waiting for governments to shift militarized budgets, we need market mechanisms that reward cooperation: resilience assessments that identify shared vulnerabilities and opportunities for collective infrastructure, peace-building procurement where organizations preferentially source from enterprises that reduce conflict drivers, mutual benefit protocols where participants commit to reciprocity agreements creating win-win incentives, and trust-building services that help communities and institutions navigate conflict without escalation. The next chapter introduces a framework for exactly this translation: from principle to practice.

This is peace not as an aspiration, but as a business model. And it's one that generates better returns—economic, social, and strategic—than the militarization it replaces.

The Choice Before Us

We are at a civilizational inflection point. We can continue down the path of militarization: competing to accumulate more destructive capability, defending the wrong things, and spending trillions preparing for wars that may never come while real crises cascade unchecked.

Or we can choose mutualism: building networks of cooperation that generate security through shared resilience, preventing conflict through economic interdependence, and investing in the quiet work of stewardship that keeps societies stable and alive.

The first path is familiar. The second is strategic.

And in an age of polycrisis—where climate, pandemic, inequality, and democratic erosion compound simultaneously—the societies that master mutualism will not only survive. They will flourish.

Conclusion: From Paradigm to Practice

We have now seen the problem (misallocated defense), the infrastructure (what real security requires), the people (who actually keeps us safe), and the paradigm (mutualism over militarization).

In Chapter 10, we will make all of this operational. We will explore exactly how Defense as a Service works: its governance model, service offerings, client types, and implementation pathways. This is where framework becomes practice and vision becomes tool kit.

TOOL KIT: FROM MILITARIZATION TO MUTUALISM

Purpose: To help leaders, entrepreneurs, and investors shift from security models rooted in control and force toward those grounded in cooperation, reciprocity, and shared resilience.

1. Identify Militarized Assumptions

   Audit your organization's strategies, policies, and culture for language and practices borrowed from militarized thinking. Do you talk about "competitors" as "enemies"? Is information treated as a zero-sum resource to be guarded? Are relationships transactional rather than relational? Does "winning" require someone else losing? Expand your definition of threat beyond adversaries to include ecological breakdown, economic inequality that generates instability, erosion of trust and social cohesion, and brittleness in supply chains or infrastructure. Ask: How could mutualism mitigate these better than competition?

2. Invest in Cooperative Infrastructure

   Support projects and systems that encourage resource sharing and distributed governance: renewable energy cooperatives, community land trusts, open-source technology platforms, regional mutual aid networks, cross-sector partnerships for resilience. Replace competitive scarcity with abundance logic—shift incentive structures so collaboration produces greater rewards than unilateral control through shared ownership models, revenue-sharing

(CONTINUED)

agreements, joint ventures with transparent terms, and procurement preferences for peace-building enterprises.

3. Build Trust as Strategic Infrastructure

   Treat trust building as essential security work: transparent governance and decision making, regular stakeholder engagement, conflict resolution mechanisms built into operations, long-term relationship investment over transactional efficiency. Build organizational capacity in skills that enable mutualism: active listening and empathy, mediation and conflict transformation, consensus building and participatory decision making, systems thinking and pattern recognition.

4. Celebrate Interdependence

   Make cooperation visible and culturally valued. Track indicators that reveal the health of cooperative relationships: trust levels among partners, frequency and quality of collaboration, shared benefits distribution, resilience to shocks, longevity of cooperative agreements. Publicly acknowledge partnerships and cocreated wins. Share credit generously. Tell stories of mutual aid and collaborative success. Create awards and recognition for bridge builders.

Reflection Prompt

What is one relationship in your work where shifting from competition to cooperation could generate better outcomes for all parties—and what first step could you take toward that this week?

Connects To

This chapter synthesizes the diagnosis (Chapter 7), infrastructure (Chapter 7), and actors (Chapter 8) into a paradigm framework. For comprehensive implementation guidance, see Chapter 10. The cultural shifts required connect to Part IV.

10

Defense as a Service

The Operating Model

The previous chapters established a radical reimagining: Security comes not from fortress thinking—the belief that safety means higher walls, bigger weapons, and isolated defenses—but from mutualism; not from defending against symptoms but from addressing root causes; not from concentrated force but from distributed resilience.

But how does a city council member translate security through ecosystem health into budget line items? How does a corporate board operationalize protection through stakeholder well-being? How does an impact investor evaluate whether capital is building genuine resilience or just performing sustainability theater?

This is the translation problem: moving from vision to practice, from framework to implementation, from "this should exist" to "here's how to build it."

Defense as a Service (DaaS) enables that translation. It's both a conceptual framework and a practical approach for embedding resilience, regeneration, and civic capacity directly into the economic and governance systems that shape our lives. This chapter shows how protection as mutualism becomes operational.

The Service Model: From Ownership to Access

Traditional defense operates on an ownership model. Nations own armies. Corporations own security departments. Wealthy individuals purchase private protection. Each actor builds isolated defenses, creating siloed, redundant, and often brittle infrastructure.

Defense as a Service applies service economy logic to security itself.

Think of cloud computing. Before Amazon Web Services and similar platforms, every organization maintained its own server infrastructure—expensive, redundant, requiring specialized expertise most of them didn't really have. The cloud changed everything: Instead of owning servers, organizations access computational capacity as needed. Instead of duplicating infrastructure, they share resources.

The result isn't just cheaper; it's more resilient. Distributed systems don't have single points of failure. Updates happen continuously rather than episodically. Small organizations gain sophisticated capabilities they could never build alone. Large institutions reduce costs while improving performance.

Defense as a Service does the same thing for security. Rather than each community, enterprise, or institution building isolated protective infrastructure, DaaS distributes capacity across networks of participants who share resources, intelligence, and response capabilities. Rather than reactive defenses, it provides preventive infrastructure. Rather than competition for scarce security, it creates mutual benefit through cooperation.

The practical advantages are immediate:

- **For communities:** Access to sophisticated resilience assessment, ecosystem restoration planning, democratic infrastructure strengthening, and emergency response coordination they couldn't afford to build independently.

- **For enterprises:** Supply chain resilience analysis, stakeholder governance frameworks, regenerative operational design, and collaborative risk sharing that reduces costs while improving outcomes.
- **For investors:** Portfolio-wide resilience integration, impact measurement frameworks, systemic risk assessment, and network effects that compound security across holdings.
- **For governments:** Evidence-based prevention infrastructure, cross-jurisdictional cooperation frameworks, budget reallocation strategies, and measurable outcomes that prove effectiveness.

But the deepest advantage isn't efficiency. It's the shift in logic itself: from protection as something you purchase individually to security as something we create collectively.

The Three Pillars of Defense as a Service

Defense as a Service rests on three foundational principles distinguishing it from conventional security: distributed capacity, preventive infrastructure, and mutual benefit protocols. These three operational principles describe how DaaS functions. They work across the Five Pillars of Real Security we examined in Chapter 7: ecological stability, public health, economic equity, democratic infrastructure, and community cohesion. Whereas the Five Pillars define *what* genuine security protects, these three principles define *how* protection is delivered.

Distributed Capacity

Security functions are embedded across networks, not concentrated in single institutions. Local communities, private enterprises, civil society, and government agencies each hold pieces. No single failure point exists; redundancy and diversity are built in. This results in decentralized decision making that enables rapid, context-appropriate response; specialized nodes with deep expertise in particular domains; interoperable protocols that allow coordination without central control; and resilient architecture that functions even if some nodes are compromised.

Practical implication: A coastal city facing climate risk accesses expertise from conservation organizations, mutual aid networks, engineering firms, and impact investors—all coordinated through shared frameworks rather than siloed in separate departments.

Preventive Infrastructure

DaaS prioritizes investments in root conditions of safety: stable ecosystems, equitable economies, robust public health, resilient democratic institutions. These *are* security. This shifts resources from reaction to prevention through early warning systems that identify vulnerabilities before they cascade, root-cause interventions that address conditions generating threats, regenerative design that leaves systems stronger after each engagement, and long-term stewardship rather than short-term fixes that create new problems.

Practical implication: Instead of spending billions on post-flood response, cities invest millions on wetland restoration, permeable surfaces, and distributed water management—preventing flooding while simultaneously improving air quality, biodiversity, and community amenities. "Security" investment pays multiple dividends.

One way to measure where any institution stands on this spectrum is what I call the *Prevention Ratio*—the proportion of security-related spending directed toward addressing root causes versus reacting to symptoms. Most organizations discover that their Prevention Ratio is dramatically skewed toward reaction, often with just 10 to 20 percent of spending dedicated to prevention. Simply making this ratio visible—naming it, measuring it, tracking it over time—shifts the conversation from abstract values to concrete allocation decisions. The Prevention Ratio complements the Prevention Dividend introduced in Chapter 7: whereas the Ratio diagnoses how resources are currently deployed, the Dividend quantifies the return available from shifting that deployment toward prevention.

Mutual Benefit Protocols

Participants commit to reciprocity agreements: sharing data, resources, and response capacity in ways that create positive cooperation incentives. These function like service level agreements (SLAs), defining expectations, accountability, and benefit sharing. Cooperation becomes self-reinforcing: The more value you contribute, the more secure you become; the stronger the network becomes, the less attractive defection becomes. Trust compounds over time, reducing transaction costs.

Practical implication: A regional food network shares resilience strategies and creates mutual aid where surplus buffers others, shares information freely, and uses collective negotiating power. Security becomes mutual, not competitive.

Translation Across Contexts

DaaS principles translate across radically different contexts. The following four scenarios—from municipal climate work to Indigenous sovereignty—demonstrate how the same underlying framework adapts to diverse challenges while maintaining its core logic of distributed capacity, preventive infrastructure, and mutual benefit.

Scenario 1: Municipal Climate Resilience

A mid-sized coastal city facing increasing flood risk, heat stress, and storm damage begins with assessment: mapping vulnerabilities including flood zones, infrastructure dependencies, vulnerable populations, and ecosystem degradation. It builds distributed capacity by engaging watershed organizations, community groups, engineering firms, health institutions, and mutual aid networks as partners rather than contractors. It designs preventive infrastructure including wetland restoration, permeable surfaces, green infrastructure, and distributed stormwater management—interventions that address root causes and create multiple benefits. It structures mutual benefit so that neighborhoods adopting green infrastructure see increased property values, better air quality, and community gathering spaces; businesses reduce insurance costs; and the city reduces disaster spending.

The outcome: Flood damage drops by 60 percent over five years. Five hundred green jobs are created. Air quality improves. Social cohesion strengthens through collaborative projects. The city becomes a model, attracting climate-conscious residents and regenerative businesses.

The Prevention Dividend: Every dollar shifted from reactive flood response to wetland restoration returns roughly $4–$5 in avoided emergency spending and insurance costs.

Scenario 2: Enterprise Supply Chain Transformation

A mid-sized consumer goods company facing supply disruptions and reputation risks begins with assessment: mapping supply chain failure points, geopolitical risks, climate vulnerabilities, and labor exploitation hotspots. It builds distributed capacity by partnering with regional suppliers, regenerative producers, worker cooperatives, and logistics providers committed to resilience. It designs preventive infrastructure by redesigning products for longevity and repair, building long-term supplier relationships, and investing in supplier capacity, worker well-being, and ecosystem health. It structures mutual benefit so that suppliers get stable long-term contracts, workers get better conditions and ownership stakes, communities see local economic development, and the company reduces disruption risk while building competitive advantage.

The outcome: Supply disruption risk drops by 40 percent. Emissions drop by 30 percent. Labor retention improves. Community relationships strengthen. Resilience becomes a brand differentiator that commands premium pricing.

The Prevention Dividend: Investments in supplier relationships and worker well-being generate returns exceeding 5:1 through avoided disruption, reduced turnover, and strengthened market position.

Scenario 3: Indigenous Sovereignty and Land Stewardship

An Indigenous nation seeking to restore sovereignty and traditional land management begins with assessment: mapping sacred sites and cultural resources, traditional ecological knowledge, threats to cultural continuity, legal vulnerabilities, and external dependencies that undermine sovereignty. It builds distributed capacity by creating alliances with conservation organizations that respect Indigenous leadership, legal advocates, academic researchers, and ethical businesses. It designs preventive infrastructure by restoring traditional land management practices, creating sustainable livelihoods through regenerative forestry and traditional food enterprises, and establishing cultural education programs. It structures mutual benefit so that partners gain access to traditional ecological knowledge, regional ecosystems benefit from Indigenous stewardship, regional economies gain from sustainable enterprises, and legal precedents strengthen Indigenous rights broadly.

The outcome: Fifty thousand acres are restored to traditional management. Cultural practices and language programs are preserved and expanded. Sustainable livelihoods replace extractive dependencies. Legal protections are strengthened. The nation becomes a model for Indigenous-led conservation globally. This pattern has real precedent: Menominee Tribal Enterprises in Wisconsin has practiced sustainable forestry for over a century and a half, harvesting more than 2.3 billion board feet from the tribe's 235,000 acres of timberland while actually increasing forest quality and biodiversity—a demonstration that over time, Indigenous stewardship generates both economic and ecological returns that extractive models cannot match.[1]

The Prevention Dividend: Traditional land management practices deliver ecosystem services—fire prevention, watershed protection, carbon sequestration—that would cost orders of magnitude more through technological substitutes.

Scenario 4: Impact Portfolio Resilience Integration

A $500 million impact fund seeking to integrate resilience across its portfolio begins with assessment: evaluating current holdings against genuine resilience criteria—distributed capacity, preventive infrastructure, mutual benefit. It builds distributed capacity by connecting portfolio companies to each other for knowledge sharing and resource pooling, constructing networks across holdings. It designs preventive infrastructure by prioritizing investments that address root causes—regenerative agriculture, democratic technology, worker ownership, ecosystem restoration. It structures mutual benefit so that portfolio companies benefit from network effects, communities where investments land see tangible improvement, and the fund achieves better long-term returns through reduced volatility.

The outcome: Forty percent of capital is redirected toward explicit resilience building. Returns improve through lower volatility and stronger community relationships. The fund demonstrates that mutualist security is strategically superior, attracting additional capital seeking similar approaches.

The Prevention Dividend: Portfolio companies report lower volatility and stronger community relationships, with prevention-oriented holdings outperforming reactive competitors by measurable margins over five-year horizons.

From Service to System

Defense as a Service isn't a single organization or product. It's an emergent system—a set of principles, practices, and protocols that anyone can adopt, adapt, and improve (see figure 22).

As more actors embody these principles, the logic spreads. Communities see other communities building resilience through ecosystem restoration and begin their own projects. Enterprises see competitors gaining advantage through supply chain mutualism and restructure their own relationships. Investors see funds achieving better returns

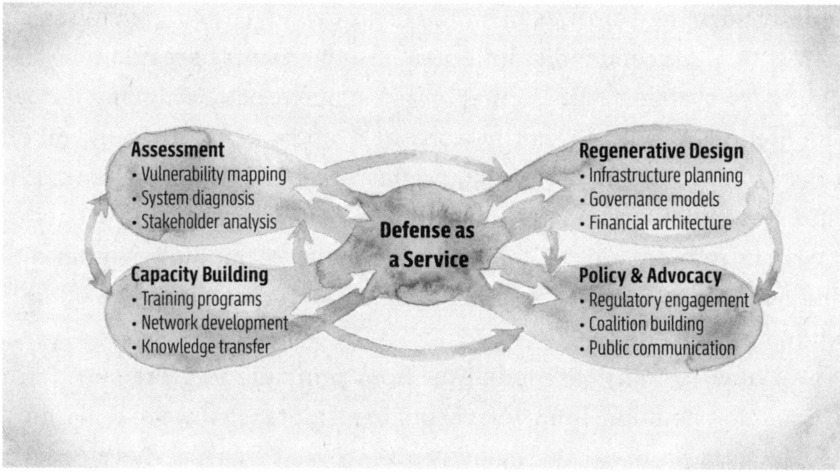

Figure 22. Defense as a Service—The Operating Model

through portfolio-wide resilience integration and redirect their own capital.

This is how paradigms shift: not through top-down mandate but through bottom-up demonstration. As the strategic advantages of cooperation over competition, prevention over reaction, and stewardship over extraction become evident through lived experience, the framework spreads.

The goal isn't for Defense as a Service to become a monopoly provider of security. The goal is to seed a movement where every actor sees themselves as both client and provider of security, where resilience is understood as shared responsibility, where conditions for collective flourishing are continuously cocreated.

This is defense reimagined—not as a fortress but as a garden, tended by many hands, nourished by reciprocity, growing more abundant the more it's shared.

Conclusion: Building What's Needed

In July 1944, while the old financial order was still collapsing around them, delegates gathered at Bretton Woods to architect something entirely new. They didn't wait for the crisis to end. They understood that moments of maximum disruption are also moments of maximum possibility for systemic transformation.[2] We face a parallel moment now. The Bretton Woods of security won't be a single conference—it will be a distributed process of paradigm construction, already beginning in cities redesigning resilience, enterprises restructuring supply chains, investors redirecting capital, and communities building mutual aid. The question is whether you'll help design it, or watch others build it without you.

It's time to translate mutualism from principle into practice, from vision into operation, from what should exist into what we're building.

The framework exists. The evidence proves it works. What's needed now is the will to build—city by city, institution by institution, partnership by partnership. Some will lead this transformation through government policy; others through investment allocation; still others through community organizing or enterprise design. Each approach strengthens the others.

The principles underlying Defense as a Service are meant to spread. The Five Pillars framework, the shift from fortress to foundation, the recognition that prevention generates returns—these ideas belong to the commons of regenerative practice. Any city, enterprise, or fund can implement prevention-first security, whether or not they ever engage with Impact Entrepreneur. I trademarked Defense as a Service, Prevention Dividend, and Prevention Ratio not to restrict the paradigm but to ensure quality and coherence as it scales—and to sustain the organization building the intellectual infrastructure, practitioner networks, benchmarking tools, and proof points that demonstrate regenerative security is not only morally right but strategically superior. This work needs many architects, many builders, many hands—and Impact Entrepreneur is here to support those ready to build.[3]

The forgotten language Merwin named—the language of reciprocity, interdependence, the sacred in the everyday—turns out to be the language of genuine security. Defense as a Service is simply the translation of that ancient wisdom into contemporary practice.

The forests we must tell about aren't gone. They're growing, right now, in every community that chooses mutualism over militarization, in every enterprise that builds for regeneration rather than extraction, in every investment that seeds resilience rather than defending decay.

TOOL KIT: DEFENSE AS A SERVICE

Purpose: To provide a practical guide for implementing Defense as a Service principles in your organization, community, or investment portfolio—translating protection as mutualism from concept into operation.

Quick Start: Your First Thirty Days

Week 1: Complete the self-assessment (step 1 below).
Week 2: Identify and reach out to three potential partners.
Week 3: Design one pilot project with clear metrics.
Week 4: Convene initial partners to create a mutual benefit agreement.

1. Assess Your Starting Point

   Begin with an honest inventory: What security and resilience capacities do you already have? What vulnerabilities are most pressing? What resources (time, capital, expertise) can you commit? Who are your potential partners and collaborators? Ask yourself: Do you spend more on reaction or prevention? Is your security infrastructure centralized or distributed? Do you measure only threats avoided or also conditions strengthened? Are those most affected by decisions included in decision making?

2. Choose One Entry Point and Build Your Network

   Select one domain where you can demonstrate results: assessment if you need to understand vulnerabilities, regenerative

(CONTINUED)

design if you know what needs fixing, capacity building if you have vision but lack internal expertise, or policy work if you need to change funding or regulatory structures. Start small and specific—one pilot project with clear success metrics is more valuable than diffuse efforts across many domains.

Identify potential partners: Who else faces similar vulnerabilities? Who has expertise you need? Who could benefit from collaboration? Who holds resources or authority you'll need to engage? Create mutual benefit agreements that specify what each party will contribute, what each needs in return, how decisions will be made, how conflicts will be resolved, and how success will be measured and shared.

3. Design for Participation and Aligned Incentives

   Ensure that those most affected have voice: include community members, workers, and frontline organizations in design; use participatory methods like community mapping, scenario planning, and consensus processes; build in feedback loops and adaptation mechanisms; create accountability structures that give stakeholders real power.

   Structure financing to reward resilience, not just activity: pay-for-success contracts tied to measurable outcomes, shared savings agreements where efficiency gains fund further investment, community ownership models that ensure benefits stay local, and impact bonds where returns depend on resilience metrics.

4. Measure, Iterate, and Scale

   Track both outputs (projects completed, people trained, investments made) and outcomes (ecosystems restored, communities strengthened, crises prevented, trust built, systems transformed). Use mixed methods: quantitative data on health indicators, ecosystem metrics, and economic measures; qualitative assessment

(CONTINUED)

through stories, case studies, and lived experience; participatory evaluation using community-defined success criteria.

Build learning into your process through regular reflection and adjustment cycles, transparent documentation of what works and what doesn't, sharing lessons with network partners, and willingness to change course based on evidence. Scale through pattern, not replication—identify core principles that work in your context, share those principles with others facing similar challenges, support others in adapting to their unique conditions, and build infrastructure for knowledge exchange and peer learning.

5. Protect Your Mission and Celebrate Success

   Lock in regenerative intent through legal structures that prevent mission drift, governance that distributes power among stakeholders, transparent accountability mechanisms, and long-term funding that doesn't depend on short-term political cycles. Make success visible by documenting and sharing your journey, celebrating milestones and learning moments, acknowledging partners and collaborators, and contributing your insights back to the commons.

Reflection Prompt

If you were to implement one element of Defense as a Service in your work within the next ninety days, what would have the highest impact—and what is the first concrete step you could take tomorrow?

Connects To

This tool kit integrates all of Part III into an actionable framework. It protects the structural innovations of Part II (Chapters 3–6) from systemic threats. For the cultural infrastructure that sustains mutualist security, see Part IV—particularly Chapters 11 and 14.

Part IV

Integration

The Architecture of a Regenerative Economy

It happens with increasing regularity now, though each time still catches me by surprise. I'll be scrolling through LinkedIn—that strange digital commons where professional identity is performed, and reperformed, endlessly—when I pause on a profile. Not because I know the person. Often I don't. But because of what's written at the top, in that precious real estate where people announce who they are to the world.

Next to their name, in bold: **Impact Entrepreneur**.

Not their company name. Not their job title. Not "Founder" or "CEO" or any of the conventional markers of professional identity.

Impact Entrepreneur.

As if it were a profession. A calling. Not just what they do, but who they are.

I created that term in 2011. Deliberately. With intention.[1] With the explicit hope that it might become not just terminology but identity—a way for systems-minded changemakers to recognize themselves and each other, to claim a different stance toward economy and enterprise, to inhabit a role that didn't yet have a name.

Watching it claim its own life still moves me, every time.

There's something unsettling about watching a phrase you created take on life beyond your intention. Like releasing a child into the world—you shaped them, but you don't control them. They become themselves, make choices you didn't foresee, enter relationships you'll never know about, carry meaning you never intended.

"Impact entrepreneur" was never meant to be just mine. That was the point—to create an identity that people could claim, inhabit, and make their own. But I hadn't anticipated what it would feel like to watch it happen. To see the term in job titles, conference themes, university programs, investor portfolios, government initiatives. To realize that in thousands of conversations I would never be part of, in hundreds of communities I would never know, people were using this language to describe who they were.

It felt like conjuring. I'd put words together, given them particular meaning, sent them out into the world—and they'd become animate. Not metaphorically animate, but actually: moving, spreading, reproducing, evolving beyond my original intent. The phrase had become what Kevin Kelly calls a "technium"—a life-like system of ideas that evolves through culture rather than cells.[2]

Robin Wall Kimmerer writes about the power of naming in Indigenous cultures. She notes, for example, that "In some Native languages, the term for plants translates to 'those who take care of us.'"[3]

Her work illustrates a simple but radical idea: How we name the world determines what we see, and what we see determines how we act. This resonated deeply with my own experience. I'd named something—a way of being in the world, an identity, a practice—and by naming it, I'd made it visible. Once visible, it could be claimed. Once claimed, it could organize action. And once organizing action, it could shift reality.

This is the work of *cultural infrastructure*: creating language that makes new identities possible, new stories thinkable, new ways of being legitimate. It's not about controlling outcomes. It's more like planting seeds you'll never see fully grown, or speaking words that will echo in conversations you'll never hear. The magic—and there's no other word for it—is that once enough people claim an identity, it starts to create its own reality. "Impact entrepreneur" was aspirational in 2011. By 2018, it was operational. Not because the external world had changed that much, but because enough people were operating as if it were true—and in doing so, making it so.

This is how breakthrough works. You don't argue people into new systems. You don't force behavior change through policy alone. You create the conditions for new identities to emerge, give people language to claim those identities, and trust that identity will reshape action, action will reshape culture, and culture will eventually reshape systems. It's slow magic—patient, invitational, collective. The kind that works not through control but through conditions, not through force but through invitation, not through individual will but through collective becoming. And it's already working. Not the structural innovations I've helped develop. Not the capital models or governance frameworks. Something more fundamental than structure.

Culture worked. Story worked. Identity worked—the infrastructure beneath all the other infrastructure.

•

I've spent thirty-five years building cultural infrastructure for economic transformation, though I didn't always call it that.

In the 1990s, as director of The Orion Society, I'd organized the Forgotten Language Tour, which I spoke about in Part III.[4] We thought we were doing environmental education, but we were actually doing something more fundamental: teaching people to see themselves differently; to understand identity as connected to place rather than abstracted from it; to recognize that who you are is inseparable from where you are and what you care for.

During those years I was also working closely with Dr. John Elder at Middlebury College. In the mid-1990s, we decided we needed a name for the pedagogy we'd been developing. We'd been funding teacher fellowships, publishing books, running institutes—all focused on learning rooted in place. John was describing the principles: "holistic, interdisciplinary, creative, community-centric, place-based . . ."

I stopped him. "Place-based. Place-based education. That's it."[5]

The term stuck. Within a few years, it had spread across the field. Within a decade, it was standard terminology in education. Within two decades—here's what fascinates me—it had migrated entirely out of education and into finance.

By the 2010s, community foundations and impact investors were talking about "place-based investing." The Russell Family Foundation launched an initiative called Canopy to nurture "place-based impact investing" in the Pacific Northwest. The MacArthur Foundation created "Benefit Chicago" as a place-based investment strategy. The Rockefeller Foundation and Smart Growth America announced initiatives for "place-based, community-led approaches" to economic development.[6]

The cultural work we'd done in the 1990s—teaching people to understand identity through place—had created the conditions for structural financial innovation twenty years later. A shared story had primed a shared lens; the lens made new instruments legible.

That's what cultural infrastructure does. It makes the impossible thinkable. It makes the unimaginable inhabitable. It turns technical innovations into movements.

•

In 2004, I edited and published Terry Tempest Williams's book *The Open Space of Democracy*. In my foreword, I quoted Terry describing the stance we need: "In the open space of democracy, we are listening—ears alert—we are watching—eyes open—registering the patterns and possibilities for engagement. Some acts are private, some are public. Our oscillations between local, national, and global gestures map the full range of our movement."

That triadic oscillation—between local, national, and global, with each informing the others—became central to my thinking. You can't address systemic challenges from only one level. You need simultaneous deep-rootedness in place and sophisticated understanding of global patterns. You need to think like a monarch butterfly: profoundly local in its dependence on specific ecosystems, and profoundly international in its miraculous multigenerational migration.

But more than that, I was learning something about how transformation actually happens. It doesn't happen through policy alone, or technology alone, or even brilliant structural innovation alone. It happens when enough people can imagine themselves differently. When identity shifts. When the story changes.

Around that same time, in the early 2010s, I was executive director of Seven Pillars House of Wisdom, an organization founded by Sufi teacher Pir Zia Inayat-Khan. We worked with scholars and wisdom keepers from Christian, Jewish, Hindu, Buddhist, and Indigenous traditions on a question that obsessed me: How do spiritual and cultural traditions provide the foundation for ecological and social healing?

We produced a multimedia book called *Journey Toward Wisdom*, structured around seven pillars of human consciousness and responsibility. One of the core insights we articulated: "Wisdom arises where information, knowledge, experience, science, cosmology, faith and the arts collide, converge, and play with the unknown—with intuition, serendipity, and imagination."

But the passage that stayed with me most was this: "Stories have been used throughout the ages to connect us to place, to community, to self. These stories create a lens through which we see the world and through which we understand our relationship to place, to community, to self. Now we need a new story—one that honors the other stories and connects us to this planet as a whole."

A new story. Not just new policies. Not just new technologies. A new story that makes new identities possible.

•

In 2011, I founded Impact Entrepreneur.

I'd spent the previous decade building B Corporations, doing impact investing, working at the intersection of business and social change. One of the organizations I'd founded had become one of the first Certified B Corps in 2007. I'd seen how powerful it was when business had a vocabulary and legal structure for operating differently—triple bottom line instead of single bottom line, stakeholder value instead of shareholder primacy.

But I kept noticing something: The structural innovations existed. The legal frameworks, the capital models, the governance structures—they were all being developed. What was missing was the cultural infrastructure that would make them cohere into a movement. So I deliberately chose to create not a consulting firm, not an investment fund, not a policy organization, but something else: a platform for identity formation.

I defined "impact" as transformation, not incrementalism; "entrepreneur" as innovator across domains, not just company founder. An *impact entrepreneur*, then, was someone committed to transforming systems through innovation.

But more than that, I wanted it to be an identity. A way of being. A lens through which people saw themselves and their work.

I built Impact Entrepreneur explicitly as cultural infrastructure: a magazine to tell the stories, webinars to build shared understanding, summits to create community, a global network—now encompassing over seventy thousand people, and growing by the day—to provide the sense of collective identity that makes individual risk taking possible.

I wasn't trying to report on a movement. I wasn't trying to chronicle one, but to *conjure* it—by giving it a home, a name, a drumbeat. I was trying to create the conditions that would allow a movement to recognize itself.

•

What I've come to understand through all this work is something about how the mind itself must integrate for transformation to be possible.

The extractive economy depends on compartmentalization. It puts social concerns in one box, environmental concerns in another box, economic concerns in a third. It assigns them to different departments, different disciplines, different career paths. It makes sure the person managing environmental compliance never talks to the person managing community relations, who never talks to the person managing the investment portfolio.

This compartmentalization isn't just organizational. It's cognitive. It's literally how we've been trained to think—separate domains with separate logics, separate metrics, separate accountability.

The impact entrepreneur's mind works differently. The artificial barriers between social, environmental, and economic have broken down. Blood flow has returned to normal, enabling the kind of whole-brain work where analysis and imagination inform each other. The person who understands regenerative agriculture also understands capital structures, community governance, and ecosystem restoration—not because they're a polymath, but because they understand these as inseparable aspects of a single system.

This integrated thinking—the hallmark of what I call the *systems-minded changemaker*—is itself a form of identity. It's a way of being in the world where you cannot separate your economic decisions from your social commitments and your environmental values. They're not trade-offs to be managed. They're expressions of a unified worldview.

But this worldview, this identity, has to be cultivated. It doesn't emerge naturally from a culture that's spent centuries teaching compartmentalization. It requires deliberate effort—language that makes it legible, stories that show integration is possible, communities that demonstrate it works.

•

I think now about the Race Brook Lodge summit in 2018 I talked about in Part II, where forty leaders in systems change gathered to map the path toward an Impact Economy. We spent two days identifying the structural innovations needed—new capital models, new ownership structures, new governance frameworks.

But one working group focused on something different: *narrative*. How do we tell the story of this emerging economy in ways that inspire rather than alienate? How do we make the possible tangible? How do we give people permission to be different?

Because that's what narrative does. That's what identity does. That's what cultural infrastructure does.

Transformation isn't just structural—it's psychological. It depends on permission. Permission to imagine yourself as an impact entrepreneur even though that wasn't a career path when you were in school. Permission to deploy capital as stewardship and to structure ownership for stakeholder benefit, even when that's not the model you inherited.

Permission to measure success by triple bottom line even though a single bottom line is all the systems can currently track.

Without that permission—without the story that makes it thinkable, the identity that makes it inhabitable, the community that makes it sustainable—all the brilliant structural innovations in the world will remain marginal experiments.

With it, they become the new normal.

•

This is why Part IV matters as much as the previous three sections.

Parts I through III mapped the structural transformations: enterprises that heal rather than extract, ownership that distributes rather than concentrates, capital that serves rather than dominates, security through mutualism rather than fortification.

All of that is necessary. None of it is sufficient. Because structure requires culture. Models require stories. Innovations require identities.

You can have the perfect cooperative ownership structure, but if people can't imagine themselves as member-owners rather than employees or consumers, it won't scale.

You can have the perfect regenerative capital model, but if investors can't see themselves as stewards rather than extractors, it won't attract capital.

You can have the perfect governance framework for stakeholder accountability, but if leaders can't inhabit the identity of servant rather than sovereign, it won't function.

The cultural infrastructure that makes these structures legible, desirable, and inhabitable is as load-bearing as any financial architecture. Maybe more so.

•

I watch it happen in real time now, this work of identity formation.

A webinar where someone in the chat says: "I've been doing this work for years but didn't have a name for what I was. Now I know—I'm an impact entrepreneur." A conference where strangers recognize each other immediately: "Oh, you're Impact Economy people. Me too."

A LinkedIn message from someone I've never met: "I saw your profile and realized—that's what I am. Impact entrepreneur. It gave me permission to leave my corporate job and start building what I actually believe in."

A media story—not from *Impact Entrepreneur Magazine* but from mainstream business press—that uses the term naturally, without definition, assuming readers know what an impact entrepreneur is.

Each time, I feel that same surprise, that same recognition: The cultural infrastructure is working. The identity is taking hold. The story is spreading beyond my ability to control it.

Which means it's real. Which means it's sustainable. Which means the structural innovations now have the cultural foundation they need to scale.

•

There's a concept in ecology: *pioneer species*. The plants that colonize barren ground after a fire or a flood, that create the conditions for other species to follow, that build the soil that makes the forest possible.[7]

Cultural work is pioneer work: It prepares the ground, creates the conditions, makes the impossible thinkable and the thinkable doable and the doable normal.

Thirty-five years of this work—from teaching people to identify with place in the 1990s, to exploring how wisdom traditions provide cultural foundation in the 2000s, to deliberately creating identity for systems-minded changemakers in the 2010s—has taught me something essential: You cannot transform economic systems without transforming economic identity. You cannot change how capital flows without changing how people understand themselves in relationship to capital. You cannot restructure ownership without restructuring what people think ownership means.

The structural innovations are necessary. The cultural infrastructure that makes them inhabitable is what determines whether they transform systems or remain interesting experiments.

This is the work of Part IV. This is what integration means.

Not integrating different sectors—though that matters too. Integrating structure and culture. Integrating innovation and identity. Integrating the mechanical and the meaningful.

Building the story that makes the structure make sense. Building the identity that makes the innovation feel like coming home rather than jumping off a cliff. Building the attention—the sustained, deep, patient attention—that allows transformation to take root before the extractive economy's machinery of distraction can pull people back to business as usual.

•

I scroll through LinkedIn again today. Another profile. Another person announcing to the world: Impact Entrepreneur.

I don't know them. They don't know me. The term has spread far beyond my network, my influence, my ability to shape it.

Which means it worked.

Which means the structural innovations—all the brilliant models being built, all the capital being deployed, all the enterprises being designed, all the governance being reimagined—now have something essential that they lacked before: A cultural home. An identity to inhabit. A story to tell. Permission to be.

The work continues. The cultural infrastructure requires constant tending—new stories, new exemplars, new articulations of possibility. But the foundation is laid.

Impact entrepreneur isn't just a term anymore. It's an identity thousands of people claim as who they are. And in claiming it, they are making the Impact Economy real.

Identity is what ultimately enables capital, policy, and technology to *transform* systems.

Because people don't change systems. People who know who they are, who can imagine themselves differently, who have permission to inhabit that different identity—*those* people change systems.

The wings we built in the previous sections are structural.

This section is the wind that lets them fly.

The Architecture of a Regenerative Economy

The understanding that culture is the foundation beneath all other foundations brings us to the architecture of integration itself.

You can design the most elegant regenerative systems imaginable—B Corps with locked missions, DaaS networks preventing crises, circular supply chains, community land trusts. But if the surrounding culture does not support them, they will be slowly eroded, co-opted, or abandoned when pressure mounts. Technical solutions fail without cultural transformation.

Culture is the operating system—it determines what we notice and what we ignore, what we value and what we discard, which futures we can imagine and which we cannot even conceive.

Throughout the previous sections, an implicit question has been building: We know what needs to change structurally. But how do we create the conditions where those changes stick—where they become not just policy victories or market innovations, but the new normal?

The four chapters ahead answer that question by moving from broad to specific, from context to carrier (see figure 23). *Culture* is the medium—the water we swim in, often invisible until we try to change it. *Story* is the vehicle—the way culture travels, evolves, and shapes imagination. *Attention* is the substrate—the cognitive capacity that story

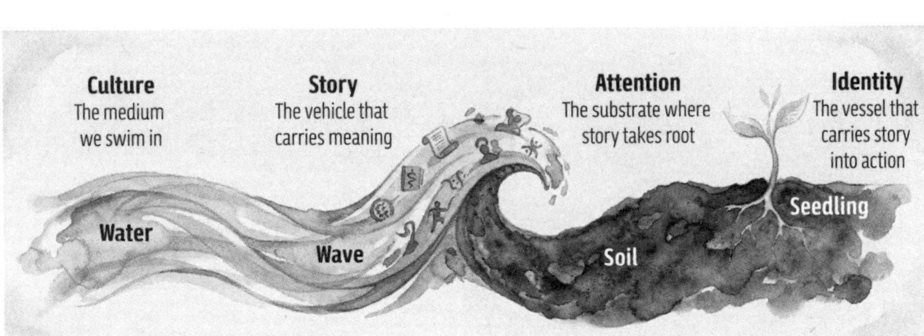

Figure 23. The Four Dimensions of Cultural Infrastructure

requires to be received and integrated. And *identity* is the vessel—the sense of self that carries story into decision and action.

Together, they form the cultural infrastructure without which technical infrastructure collapses back into the extractive default. Once culture shifts, everything downstream shifts with it.

11
The Culture We Keep Alive

When organizations fail to become more sustainable, more equitable, or more regenerative—despite good intentions, adequate resources, and technically sound plans—the problem is almost never the plan.

It's the culture.

Culture is the invisible architecture that shapes behavior, priorities, and possibility. It hums along like a computer's operating system (OS): mostly invisible, functioning in the background, determining which programs can run and which will crash. You can install the most elegant regenerative "software": B Corp certification, stakeholder governance, impact metrics, sustainability initiatives. But if the underlying cultural OS is still running *extraction.exe*, those programs will either fail to launch or be slowly corrupted back into business as usual.

This is why technical solutions fail without cultural transformation. And this is why the Impact Economy's success depends not just on redesigning enterprises, capital flows, and markets, but on cultivating the cultures that can sustain them. Culture is not decoration. It is infrastructure. And like all infrastructure, it can be designed, maintained, and regenerated—or allowed to degrade.

What Culture Actually Is

Culture is easy to sense but hard to define. We know it when we experience it—walking into an organization and feeling whether it's rigid or fluid, extractive or generative, fearful or trusting. But to work with culture intentionally, we need more precision.

Culture is the pattern of assumptions, values, and behaviors that shapes what gets noticed and what gets ignored, what's rewarded and what's punished, who has voice and who is silenced, what's considered professional or "serious," how conflict is handled, how time is structured, what questions can be asked, and how decisions get made—both formally and informally.[1]

Culture is transmitted through multiple channels. It doesn't live in mission statements. It lives in *stories* (what gets told and retold—successes, failures, origin myths, cautionary tales), *rituals* (regular practices that reinforce values—meetings, celebrations, transitions), *symbols* (physical artifacts, language, dress codes, office design), *relationships* (how people treat each other, power dynamics, trust levels), *rhythms* (how time is structured—urgency versus spaciousness, seasons, sabbaths), and *boundaries* (what's inside/outside, us/them, acceptable/unacceptable).

Culture is self-perpetuating until disrupted. People hire those who "fit" the existing culture. Behaviors that align with culture get rewarded; those that don't get punished or filtered out. Norms become "just how things are done." Questioning culture feels risky or taboo. This self-perpetuation is culture's greatest strength (stability, coherence) and greatest danger (resistance to needed change).

The Cultural Operating System: Extractive Versus Regenerative

Before we can cultivate regenerative culture, we must recognize the extractive pattern we're often working against.

The Extractive Culture Pattern

Extractive culture operates through six reinforcing patterns:

- *Short-termism* means quarterly thinking dominates long-term strategy. R&D budgets get cut to meet quarterly earnings targets, despite long-term innovation needs. A move to sustainable packaging that would pay off in three years gets rejected because it impacts this year's margins. Future costs are externalized or ignored, and "move fast and break things" becomes a virtue. Products launch before safety testing to beat competitors to market.
- *Hyperindividualism* rewards competition over collaboration. Sales teams compete for the same client rather than strategizing together. Bonuses are based on personal key performance indicators even when team goals aren't met. Employees keep crucial information in private files to remain "indispensable," and company success gets attributed to CEO genius while thousands of workers' contributions are ignored.
- *Scarcity mindset* creates zero-sum thinking where your gain is my loss. Departments fight over budget rather than finding creative shared solutions. Teams refuse to share tools or data that could help other departments. Managers withhold information to maintain power, and every project gets labeled "urgent" to justify overtime and prevent strategic thinking.
- *Hierarchy as control* means top-down decision making, where the C-suite makes workspace changes without consulting the people who use the space daily. Information flows upward while orders flow downward, and frontline workers' insights never reach decision makers who need them. Junior staff are afraid to point out obvious problems in executive proposals, and employees get labeled "not a team player" for suggesting alternative approaches.
- *Mechanistic thinking* treats people as "human resources" or "capital"; layoffs become "optimizing human capital allocation." Efficiency is prioritized over resilience, and "redundant" positions

get eliminated even though they provided crucial backup during emergencies. Optimization for single variables like production speed ignores worker injury rates, and "non-work conversations" get banned to increase productivity.

- *Performance culture* expects constant availability—praise for answering emails at 2 a.m. creates pressure for others to do the same. Working eighty-hour weeks becomes a bragging point, a sign of commitment. Rest is seen as weakness, and employees conceal medical appointments or work while sick. "Flexible" work means you're expected to check in even while on vacation.

These patterns don't emerge from individual bad actors. They're structurally incentivized by extractive economic systems. Quarterly earnings pressure creates short-termism. Winner-takes-all markets create hyper-individualism. Growth imperatives create scarcity mindsets.

Changing culture without changing structure is difficult. But changing structure without changing culture is impossible.

What Regenerative Culture Looks Like

Regenerative organizational culture has distinct patterns that contrast sharply with extraction:

- *Long-term orientation* means seven-generation thinking in strategic decisions—like investing in apprenticeship programs that won't show ROI for a decade. It means patient capital and patient decision making, taking the time that's needed to make a major decision with full stakeholder input. It means investment in relationships and capacity building, funding employee education even if employees might leave the company, and valuing intergenerational continuity through mentorship programs pairing senior workers with new hires.
- *Interdependence* defines success as collective, not just individual—bonuses are triggered only when the entire team meets goals,

not when individual quotas are met. Knowledge sharing and cross-pollination happen through regular "learning lunches" where departments teach each other their expertise. Transparent communication becomes the default, with financial statements shared with all employees rather than just executives. Collaboration and mutual aid are celebrated through public recognition for employees who help other teams meet deadlines.

- *Abundance mindset* actively seeks win-win solutions, such as by partnering with "competitors" on industry-wide sustainability standards. Resources are stewarded for multiplication rather than hoarding, and successful training programs get shared with other organizations. An open-source ethos publishes internal tools and methodologies for sector-wide benefit. Trust becomes the foundation rather than the exception, and unlimited vacation policies actually get used without guilt.
- *Distributed authority* pushes decision making to those most affected—frontline workers design their own safety protocols. The subsidiarity principle means decisions are made at the most local level possible, with individual stores setting hours based on community needs rather than corporate mandate. Psychological safety exists at all levels, so interns and new hires are comfortable challenging the CEO's ideas in meetings. Dissent and questioning are welcomed as health signals, with "devil's advocate" roles rotated in strategic planning sessions.
- *Systems thinking* sees people as whole beings—employees experiencing difficulty outside the workplace are supported even if it impacts productivity. Resilience is prioritized over brittle efficiency by maintaining "redundant" suppliers to ensure continuity during disruptions. Multiple stakeholders and long-term impacts are considered by including community members in expansion decisions. Feedback loops are built in and honored through quarterly reviews where employees evaluate leadership, not just vice versa.

- *Sustainable rhythms* build rest and reflection into structure through mandatory company-wide shutdown weeks for collective renewal. Boundaries between work and life are respected—email servers cache after-hours messages until the next business day. Burnout is prevented rather than managed through mandatory vacation minimums and workload redistribution during absences. Cycles of activity and renewal are normalized, with lower summer pace acknowledged rather than maintaining constant intensity.

Case Study: Patagonia's Cultural Architecture

We examined Patagonia in Chapter 3 through the lens of impact integrity—how its supply chain practices, product design, and accountability mechanisms align mission with operation. Here we explore the same company through a different lens: cultural architecture. How does Patagonia maintain regenerative values across thousands of employees and decades of growth?

The "Let My People Go Surfing" flex-time policy allows employees to leave during work hours when conditions are good for surfing, climbing, or other outdoor pursuits. This isn't a perk—it's a cultural statement: We trust you, we honor wholeness, connection to nature matters. It reinforces that people are not machines to be optimized.[2] Environmental internships allow employees to take up to two months of paid leave to work with environmental organizations, signaling that environmental stewardship is core mission rather than corporate social responsibility add-on. (As an added bonus, employees build external relationships and bring learning back.) The Worn Wear program actively encourages customers to repair rather than replace, with the countercultural "Don't Buy This Jacket" ad campaign, launched on Black Friday in 2011, signaling that the company values durability over growth.

Since 1985, long before it was common or expected, Patagonia has donated 1 percent of sales (not profits) to environmental organizations—a self-imposed cultural commitment. This program was formalized in 2002 as the 1% for the Planet scheme, which has grown into a global network with over eleven thousand partners.[3] Transparent supply chain practices mean that factory lists, audit reports, and details on working conditions are published openly, modeling accountability and continuous improvement—challenges, as well as successes, are shared publicly. And in 2022, ownership was transferred to a purpose trust, ensuring mission permanence beyond the founder's tenure and protecting cultural values in perpetuity.[4]

What makes this culture work is *alignment* (practices reinforce stated values), *consistency* (applied across all levels, not just frontline), *embeddedness* (built into operations, not bolt-on), *protection* (governance ensures culture outlives individuals), and *iteration* (evolves while maintaining core integrity).

The result: Patagonia attracts talent that's values-aligned, retains employees longer, builds customer loyalty that transcends product, and maintains profitability while advancing its environmental mission. This is culture as moral architecture, and as competitive advantage.

How Culture Degrades

Even well-designed cultures can erode. Understanding the mechanisms that drive this erosion helps prevent it.

Growth pressure requires rapid scaling and hiring faster than culture can be transmitted. New employees bring different assumptions, and short-term performance pressure overrides long-term values. Leadership turnover leads to cultural patterns being imported from previous contexts, creating misalignment between espoused and embodied values and loss of cultural memory and institutional knowledge. The success paradox attracts attention and investment from (or partnerships with) misaligned actors, creating pressure to professionalize, standardize, and "grow up," with the original culture seen as quaint or inefficient.

Crisis response creates permission to bypass normal practices: "Temporary" measures become permanent, and fear-based decision making replaces trust-based. Drift compounds small compromises:

"Just this once" becomes pattern, not through a single dramatic shift but through slow erosion—like metabolic syndrome, invisible until crisis. Capture happens when external actors (investors, board, partners) gain influence, their cultural assumptions gradually imported, with mission drift following cultural drift.

Preventing degradation requires vigilance, clear boundaries, and structural protection. Early warning signs include increasing cynicism about stated values, rising turnover among culture carriers, more time spent managing politics than doing work, decisions increasingly made in private, and "That's not how we used to do things" heard frequently.

Case Study: When Mission Meets Market Pressure

Consider the trajectory of a prominent sustainable food company (a composite of several real-world examples) that began as a worker cooperative in the early 2000s. Founded by former farmworkers, it initially embodied regenerative culture: consensus decision making, profit sharing, commitment to local organic suppliers, and deep community roots. The tagline, "Food as it should be," reflected genuine values alignment.

The cultural erosion began subtly. Rapid growth in 2015 brought venture capital and pressure to scale. New executives were hired for their consumer packaged goods experience, not cultural alignment. The weekly all-hands meetings became monthly, then quarterly, then disappeared. Consensus decision making was deemed "too slow" for market opportunities. The founder-workers, once equal voices, became minority stakeholders after successive funding rounds.

By 2018, the company had shifted from local organic suppliers to "industrial organic" farms offering better margins. Worker-ownership was diluted to under 5 percent. The cooperative structure was dissolved in favor of traditional corporate governance. When workers protested working conditions in 2019—ironically, the same issues the founders had originally organized against—management hired the same union-busting firm their original adversaries had used.

The company still uses sustainability language in its marketing. It still donates to food justice organizations. But the regenerative culture that made it distinctive has been completely metabolized by extractive logic. Former worker-owners describe it as "watching your child turn into everything you fought against."

The lesson: Culture without structural protection is vulnerable. Growth without cultural intentionality is erosion. And once extractive culture takes hold, it's nearly impossible to reverse—the people who formed and nurtured the original culture have usually already left, taking institutional memory with them.

Designing Culture Intentionally

Culture can be designed. Not controlled—culture is emergent and alive—but shaped through intentional choices about structure, practice, and boundary. The following practices help encode regenerative values into organizational DNA:

- **Name your cultural DNA:** Make explicit what's often implicit. What values are nonnegotiable? What behaviors exemplify those values? What stories capture your culture at its best? What would be lost if this culture disappeared? A cooperative might identify democratic participation as the core value, consensus decision making as a core behavior, the time members rejected a profitable contract because the process excluded workers as a key story, and the loss of community voice if it became investor-owned as what's at stake.
- **Encode culture in structure:** Culture needs architecture to survive. Governance determines who has decision rights over what, how conflicts are resolved, and what checks prevent cultural drift. Ownership determines who benefits from value creation, whether ownership can be sold to misaligned actors, and whether cultural values are legally protected. Hiring and onboarding processes determine how you assess cultural fit versus cultural add, what

the onboarding process is for cultural transmission, and how you prevent homogeneity while maintaining coherence. Compensation and incentives determine what behaviors get rewarded financially, what the ratio is between highest and lowest paid, and whether incentives are individual or collective.

- **Build cultural practices:** Rituals transmit and reinforce culture. Daily practices include check-ins that honor wholeness (not just task updates), gratitude or acknowledgment practices, and clear start/end boundaries to prevent work colonization. Weekly practices include all-hands meetings with distributed voice, learning sessions or skill-shares, and community meals or connection time. Monthly practices include reflection on alignment between values and actions, storytelling sessions, and external input from speakers and community partners. Quarterly practices include strategic reviews that incorporate culture assessment, celebration of milestones and contributions, and rest and renewal periods. Annual practices include culture audits, values recommitment or revision processes, and major rituals like retreats, anniversaries, and transitions.
- **Tend boundaries:** What you allow shapes culture as much as what you celebrate. Entry boundaries determine who can join, what alignment is required, and how you balance diversity with coherence. Behavioral boundaries name what behaviors are incompatible with the culture, how violations are addressed, and whether people can learn and repair or must exit. Partnership boundaries clarify who you can collaborate with without compromising culture, what partnerships require careful firewalls, and when misalignment becomes too costly.
- **Create feedback loops:** Culture needs sensing mechanisms. Formal mechanisms include regular surveys on psychological safety, alignment, and belonging; exit interviews that surface cultural issues; and third-party culture audits. Informal mechanisms

include leaders actively soliciting feedback, anonymous channels for concerns, and regular check-ins on culture health. Responsive mechanisms include clear processes for addressing cultural issues, transparency about what's changing and why, and accountability when culture is compromised.

Case Study: Mondragon Cooperative Corporation

In Chapter 4, we examined the ownership structure of Mondragon, the world's largest worker cooperative. But structure alone doesn't explain Mondragon's resilience across nearly seventy years and more than eighty thousand worker-owners. The deeper question is cultural: How do values persist when the founders are gone and the scale is vast?

The structural elements include democratic governance (one worker, one vote); pay ratios capped at 6:1 between highest and lowest paid (versus 300:1 or more in typical corporations); profits distributed 45 percent to reinvestment, 45 percent to workers, and 10 percent to local communities; and an internal solidarity fund for struggling cooperatives. The educational elements include Mondragon University (which trains the next generation in cooperative values), continuous education in cooperative principles, and integration of work, education, and community.[5] Boundary maintenance requires new cooperatives to align with core principles, includes regular assessment of cultural alignment, and provides support for those struggling while requiring exit for those incompatible.

The result: Mondragon has weathered economic crises, maintained cultural coherence, and demonstrated that large-scale cooperative organization is viable—precisely because culture is structurally protected.

Culture Work from Below: Influence Without Authority

Not everyone reading this has the power to redesign organizational culture. Many impact-minded people work within traditional corporations, government agencies, or established nonprofits where they lack formal authority to implement cultural change. This doesn't mean you're powerless. Here are some suggestions for influencing culture without formal authority, along with examples where I've seen them work in practice:

- **Model the alternative:** Embody regenerative practices in your own sphere—collaborative rather than competitive, transparent rather than secretive, whole-person rather than mechanistic. People notice, and some will be attracted to your approach and begin experimenting themselves. One middle manager started doing walking check-ins with her team, creating space for human connection; within six months, three other departments had adopted the practice.
- **Build informal networks:** Find others who share your values, regardless of their position, and create "underground" communities of practice—lunch groups, reading circles, skill-shares. These networks often outlast formal structures and can influence from within. A "sustainability coffee" group that started with three employees eventually influenced its company to create a formal sustainability officer role.
- **Use your unique leverage points:** Everyone has some sphere of influence—your team, your projects, your expertise. A procurement officer who couldn't change company policy started asking suppliers about their labor practices anyway, creating market pressure.
- **Frame changes in existing language:** Translate regenerative concepts into terms your organization already values. "Psychological safety" might not resonate, but "innovation enablement" might; "seven-generation thinking" might seem radical, but "long-term risk management" is prudent. An analyst got leadership to adopt stakeholder consultation by framing it as "market intelligence" rather than "community engagement."

Document and share small wins to make regenerative approaches visible when they work in your sphere—write case studies, share metrics, tell stories in meetings. Success creates permission for others to experiment.

Finally, know when to stay and when to go. Sometimes you can be effective as an inside catalyst, but other times your energy is better invested elsewhere. There's no shame in leaving a culture that consistently violates your values. Your well-being matters.

Remember: Culture is stubborn but not static. Every interaction either reinforces or challenges existing patterns. You may not be able to transform the entire organization, but you can create pockets of regenerative culture that serve as proof of possibility—and sometimes, that's how transformation begins.

Conclusion: Culture as the Commons of Meaning

In the previous chapters, we explored how to reclaim material commons—land, water, knowledge, democratic institutions. Culture is another commons: the shared field of meaning, value, and practice that makes collective life possible.

Like all commons, culture can be enclosed (captured by narrow interests), degraded (eroded through neglect or contamination), or regenerated (consciously tended and strengthened).

The cultures we keep alive will determine which futures become possible. Extractive culture will reproduce extraction, no matter how elegant the technical solutions layered on top. Regenerative culture will enable regeneration, creating the conditions where Impact Economy innovations can take root, spread, and endure.

The question is not whether culture matters. The question is: Are you tending it?

TOOL KIT: THE CULTURE WE KEEP ALIVE

Purpose: To help you diagnose, design, and tend regenerative culture in your organization or community.

1. Culture Audit

   Assess your current cultural patterns across five dimensions:

   Values versus reality: What values does your organization claim, and what behaviors actually get rewarded? Where is there alignment and where are there gaps?

   Power and voice: Who speaks in meetings? How are decisions actually made, and how does that compare to how they're supposed to be made?

   Time and rhythm: Is urgency constant or cyclical? Are rest and reflection valued?

   Relationships: Are interactions transactional or relational? Is vulnerability safe or risky?

   Boundaries: What's clearly inside/outside acceptable behavior, and how are violations addressed?

2. Identify Cultural Carriers

   Culture is transmitted by people and practices. Who are your culture keepers—not necessarily formal leaders, but often long-tenured members, ritual holders, and storytellers? What are your cultural rituals at daily, weekly, quarterly, and annual levels? Where does culture live—in stories told and retold, physical space design, language and symbols, decision-making processes?

3. Design Cultural Practices

   Create rituals that reinforce values. For connection: regular check-ins that include personal alongside professional,

(CONTINUED)

community meals, cross-team collaboration. For learning: skill-sharing sessions, postmortems that celebrate learning from failure, external speakers. For alignment: values reflection exercises, decision making that explicitly references principles, storytelling sessions. For rest: protected time off, sabbaticals, seasonal rhythms that honor cycles.

4. Encode Culture Structurally

   Protect culture with architecture. Governance should include stakeholder voice in major decisions and conflict resolution mechanisms. Ownership should use legal structures like purpose trusts, B Corp status, or steward ownership that prevent mission drift. Hiring and onboarding should include values assessment and robust cultural onboarding with mentorship for transmission. Compensation should include pay equity ratios and collective incentives alongside individual ones.

5. Monitor Culture Health

   Build sensing mechanisms through formal assessment (annual culture surveys, psychological safety audits, exit interviews), informal sensing (leadership regularly asking about culture health, anonymous feedback channels), and response protocols (clear processes when issues surface, accountability for addressing them, transparency about changes).

6. Culture Triage

   For organizations in crisis: Stop the bleeding by identifying the most damaging practices and halting them immediately. Stabilize by rebuilding psychological safety through listening sessions. Diagnose honestly how far the culture has drifted. Decide whether it can be regenerated or needs rebuilding. Act through either renovation (gradual shifts) or revolution (fundamental reset).

(CONTINUED)

Reflection Prompt

If someone shadowed your organization for a week, what culture would they actually experience—not the stated values, but the lived reality? What would need to shift for alignment?

Connects To

This tool kit provides the cultural foundation for all the structural work in Parts I–III—without regenerative culture, technical innovations collapse. For specific cultural tools, see Chapters 12–14.

12
The Stories That Shape the Possible

Before there is policy, there is narrative. Before there is a budget, there is a belief about what is worth funding. Before there is war, there is a story about who is dangerous and who must be defended.

We live inside the architecture of inherited stories—about what is possible, what is inevitable, and what is impossible to change. These stories are rarely told outright; they seep into the background of daily life, shaping the questions we ask and the futures we can imagine.

The Impact Economy cannot be sustained with technical fixes alone. It requires a deep renovation of our narrative infrastructure—the myths, metaphors, and mental models that make a regenerative future believable.

Narrative as the Deepest Leverage Point

In systems thinking, leverage points are the places where small shifts can create big change. Donella Meadows put it plainly: One of the most powerful leverage points is to change the mindset or paradigm out of which the system arises.[1] Narrative is how paradigms travel. It is the courier of worldview. Change the narrative, and the rules, goals, and feedback loops of a system can shift in response.

Narratives are not just entertainment. They are social blueprints. They legitimize structures of power—if people believe that billionaires are proof of merit, inequality becomes a moral virtue rather than a design flaw. They define the horizon of change—if people believe that "human nature" is inherently selfish, they will not support policies that depend on cooperation. They embed incentives in culture—if people believe that success means individual accumulation, they will design systems that reward hoarding.

Conversely, regenerative narratives legitimize cooperative ownership, support ambitious climate policy, and embed reciprocity into economic life.

Narrative Victories: When Stories Shift Systems

The most hopeful truth about narrative change is that it can happen faster than structural change—and once it shifts, structure often follows. Here are a few examples (see figure 24):

- **Marriage equality (1990s–2015):** Support for same-sex marriage more than doubled during this period, due to personal storytelling that made LGBTQ+ people visible as neighbors and family, reframing from "special rights" to "equal rights," cultural infiltration through TV and film, coalition building with unlikely allies, and decades of patient organizing.[2]

  The lesson for the Impact Economy: Personal stories of regenerative success make abstract concepts concrete.

- **Tobacco regulation (1960s–2000s):** Regulation was achieved through scientific communication about the health impacts, exposing industry manipulation, reframing the issue from one of

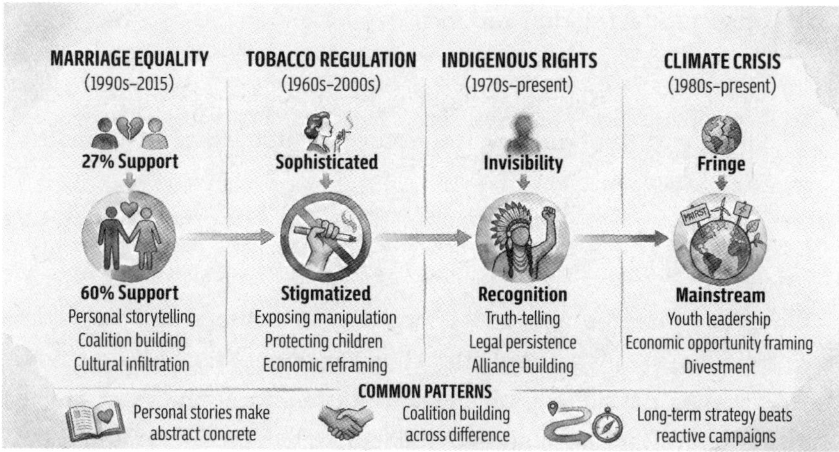

Figure 24. Narrative Victories: When Stories Shift Systems

individual freedom to one of collective responsibility, showing the economic costs to healthcare systems, and legal strategies forcing transparency.[3]

The lesson: Expose extractive business models' true costs, make externalities visible, protect future generations as a moral imperative.

- **Indigenous rights and Land Back (1970s–present):** Victories were achieved through historical truth-telling forcing acknowledgment of genocide and dispossession, legal persistence using colonizers' own systems, alliance building with environmental movements, cultural visibility through art and film, and direct action creating media moments like Standing Rock.[4]

  The lesson: Justice narratives are powerful when grounded in historical truth.

- **Climate crisis (1980s–present):** Attitudes to climate change have shifted due to youth leadership reframing inaction as intergenerational theft, youth climate lawsuits, extreme weather making abstract stories about the future concrete, economic opportunity framing around green jobs, and divestment campaigns making fossil fuels morally toxic. What hasn't worked: fear-only messaging without agency, perfectionism alienating allies, and treating it as an environmental rather than civilizational issue.

The lesson: Frame regeneration as opportunity, not just obligation.

Common patterns can be observed across successful shifts like these: personal stories make abstract concepts concrete, coalition building transcends predictable alliances, truth-telling about harm creates moral urgency, long-term strategy beats reactive campaigns, and cultural production amplifies policy change.

The Narrative Battleground

Understanding that narrative shifts systems is one thing. Actually winning the battle for shared imagination is another—especially when extractive interests have more resources and sophisticated strategies for narrative defense.

Reclaiming the Narrative Commons

Like land, water, and air, narrative is a commons—a shared resource that shapes the well-being of all. And like the material commons, it can be enclosed (when a small set of actors control dominant storytelling channels), polluted (when disinformation, propaganda, or manipulative framing crowds out truth), or depleted (when diverse voices are excluded, narrowing the range of possible futures we can imagine).

Protecting the narrative commons means democratizing who gets to tell the stories that shape public imagination, and ensuring those stories are grounded in integrity and multiplicity rather than manipulation and monologue.

Narrative Warfare: When Extractive Interests Fight Back

Shifting narratives is not neutral work. Extractive systems have enormous resources and sophisticated strategies for narrative defense (see figure 25):

- *Co-optation (greenwashing/impact-washing)* adopts the language of transformation while maintaining extractive practices—oil companies rebranding as "energy companies" with token renewables investments, "conscious capitalism" that's capitalism with better PR, ESG funds that exclude weapons but include fossil fuels.[5]

  Defense: Demand transparency and third-party verification, track actual outcomes, call out contradictions publicly, build certification systems with real teeth.

Figure 25. Narrative Warfare: Recognizing Extractive Tactics

- *Complexity manufacturing* makes issues seem too complicated for normal people—"the science isn't settled," "there are always trade-offs," "it's more nuanced than that."

  Defense: Simplify without dumbing down, use analogy and metaphor effectively, trust people's intelligence, name when complexity is genuine versus manufactured.

- *Both-sidesism* creates false equivalence—"jobs versus environment," "growth versus sustainability," "shareholder value versus stakeholder interests."

  Defense: Expose the false binary, show examples where both/and is possible, reframe as "short-term extraction versus long-term prosperity," make the status quo's costs visible.

- *Messenger assassination* attacks credibility rather than engaging with messages—"they're too young/old/inexperienced," "they're biased/ideological," "they're hypocrites who also use fossil fuels."

  Defense: Diversify messengers, shift focus from messenger to message, own complexity and imperfection, build coalitions with "unlikely" voices.

- *Hope deflation* makes alternatives seem impossible—"human nature won't change," "that's utopian," "we tried that and it failed."

  Defense: Show working examples at scale, reframe "realistic" as "limited imagination," celebrate small wins as proof of possibility.

- *Distraction and deflection* redirects attention to individual responsibility and away from systemic change—"calculate your carbon footprint," "vote with your dollar," "recycle more."

  Defense: Acknowledge individual action while emphasizing systemic change, show how individual and collective action reinforce each other, don't shame people for participating in systems they didn't design.

How to Win Narrative Battles When You're Outspent

The extractive economy has more money for messaging. The Impact Economy has something more powerful: *authenticity, community, and truth.* Here are some strategies you can employ when faced with a better-resourced opponent:

- *Narrative judo* uses the opponent's force against them—when fossil fuel companies claim to care about the climate, hold them accountable to that claim; when corporations tout stakeholder capitalism, demand stakeholder governance.
- *Make the invisible visible* by documenting and sharing true costs, making supply chains transparent, and showing who profits and who pays.
- *Decentralized storytelling* equips community members to tell their stories, uses social media for depth rather than just reach, creates shareable content that travels organically, and builds narrative infrastructure through tool kits and training.
- *Coalitions of the unlikely* transcend predictable alliances—business leaders for climate action, veterans for peace, faith communities for justice, rural communities for renewable energy. When "unexpected" voices speak, people listen.
- *Cultural production* supports artists, filmmakers, and musicians who embed regenerative narratives; creates entertainment that makes regeneration attractive; and uses humor, beauty, and joy rather than just fear and guilt.
- *Patience and repetition* repeats core messages in multiple forms, doesn't expect immediate conversion, celebrates small shifts, and plays the long game.

Remember: You're not trying to win every individual debate. You're trying to shift the default assumptions of the culture. That happens through accumulation, not single victories.

Conclusion: The Imagination We Defend

Narrative work is imagination work. If Part III asked us to defend what is physically essential to life, cultural transformation asks us to defend what is *psychically essential to possibility*.

The stories we keep alive will either anchor us to a dying system or carry us toward a regenerative one. The Impact Economy will endure only if it lives inside stories people want to tell—and retell—because those stories make life feel worth living.

TOOL KIT: THE STORIES THAT SHAPE THE POSSIBLE

Purpose: To equip impact entrepreneurs with tools for crafting and amplifying narratives that expand collective imagination and create fertile ground for regenerative change.

1. Identify and Challenge Dominant Stories

   Ask: What is the prevailing narrative in my sector or community that limits what people believe is possible? Name the assumptions embedded in that story about value, risk, success, or human nature. Be clear about why it needs replacing, not just resisting. Identify who benefits from the dominant story remaining unchallenged.

2. Craft the Alternative Narrative

   Define "the world you want to normalize" in vivid, concrete terms. Use emotionally resonant language connecting values with lived experience. Show, don't just tell—illustrate through real examples and relatable metaphors. Test: Does it inspire action or just agreement?

(CONTINUED)

3. Recognize and Defend Against Narrative Attacks

   Learn to identify common tactics: greenwashing/impact-washing, complexity manufacturing, both-sidesism, messenger assassination, hope deflation, and distraction/deflection. For each attack type, prepare your defense: demand transparency, simplify without dumbing down, expose false binaries, diversify messengers, show working examples, and acknowledge individual action while emphasizing systemic change.

4. Use Multiple Story Forms

   Combine data with human stories to appeal to both head and heart. Deploy origin stories (how we got here), vision stories (where we're going), and transformation stories (how change happens). Tailor the form to the audience—policymakers, funders, media, or community members. Make the story participatory by inviting stakeholders to contribute experiences and visions.

5. Build Narrative Infrastructure

   Move from individual storytelling to movement-level capacity: create tool kits, training resources, and templates others can use; build networks of aligned storytellers reinforcing shared narratives; invest in media infrastructure (publications, podcasts, documentaries) reaching beyond the converted. Ensure narrative integrity by aligning operations and governance with the story you tell—nothing undermines narrative power like hypocrisy.

Reflection Prompt

What is one story your enterprise is uniquely positioned to tell that, if widely believed, would transform the way your community or industry defines success?

(CONTINUED)

Connects To

This tool kit builds on the cultural framework in Chapter 11. Stories require attention to land (see Chapter 13). Stories shape identity (see Chapter 14). For protecting narrative infrastructure from capture, these defensive strategies complement the Five Pillars of Real Security (Part III).

13 The Attention Commons

Defending Cognitive Infrastructure

In the previous chapter, we explored how stories shape the possible—how narrative acts as the carrier wave for paradigm shifts. But there is a prior question: What happens when people cannot sustain the attention necessary to engage with complex stories at all?

This is the crisis of the *attention commons*: the systematic capture, fragmentation, and commodification of human cognitive capacity. And it poses an existential threat to the Impact Economy. Not because the ideas are wrong, but because the cognitive infrastructure necessary to understand, evaluate, and act on them is being deliberately eroded.

If stories are the architecture of change, attention is the foundation. And that foundation is cracking.

Attention as Infrastructure

We typically think of infrastructure as physical: roads, water systems, electrical grids. But attention is infrastructure too—the shared cognitive capacity that allows societies to identify complex problems, deliberate on solutions, coordinate collective action, maintain accountability over time, and distinguish truth from manipulation.

When attention infrastructure degrades, everything else becomes harder. Climate policy stalls because people cannot hold focus long enough to understand feedback loops. Democratic deliberation collapses into slogans. Long-term planning gives way to reactive crisis management. Complex systems thinking—the very skill the Impact Economy requires—becomes impossible.

This is not accidental. It is engineered.

I keep thinking about the story I shared in Part I: David Abram at Cape Cod in 1991, standing before a room of environmental writers, performing sleight of hand while explaining shamanic healing. The magic wasn't in the trick itself—making stones disappear and reappear—but in how it broke habitual perception, creating space for new ways of seeing. "What we think is solid and fixed," he said, "is actually fluid, participatory, alive with possibility."

The shamans he'd apprenticed with understood something the extractive economy works hard to obscure: that attention isn't passive reception but active participation in creating reality. Where we direct our awareness, how we hold our focus, what we allow into our perceptual field—these aren't neutral acts. They shape what becomes possible, what remains invisible, what gets normalized, what feels inevitable.

Reclaiming the attention commons isn't about individual discipline or digital detox. It's about recognizing attention as the participatory infrastructure that determines what kind of world becomes real.

The Assault on Attention

The attention economy doesn't just compete for our focus—it systematically degrades our capacity to think, deliberate, and act collectively. Understanding how this assault operates is the first step toward mounting an effective defense.

The Architecture of Distraction

The attention economy is a $600+ billion industry built on a simple premise: that human attention can be captured, predicted, and sold.[1]

The business model is elegant and devastating: platforms offer "free" services (search, social media, news, entertainment), users pay with attention and data, algorithms optimize for engagement (time spent, clicks, shares), advertisers pay to access that captured attention, and profits scale with the total volume of attention harvested.

The problem is that engagement does not equal value. What captures attention most effectively is not the content that builds understanding, fosters dialogue, or enables wise decision making. It is the content that triggers emotional reactivity: outrage, fear, tribal identification, novelty seeking, status anxiety.

In the relentless optimization for engagement, platforms have discovered that distraction is more profitable than depth, polarization more lucrative than synthesis, and manipulation more scalable than education.

Weapons of Mass Distraction

The tools of cognitive capture have become increasingly sophisticated (see figure 26).

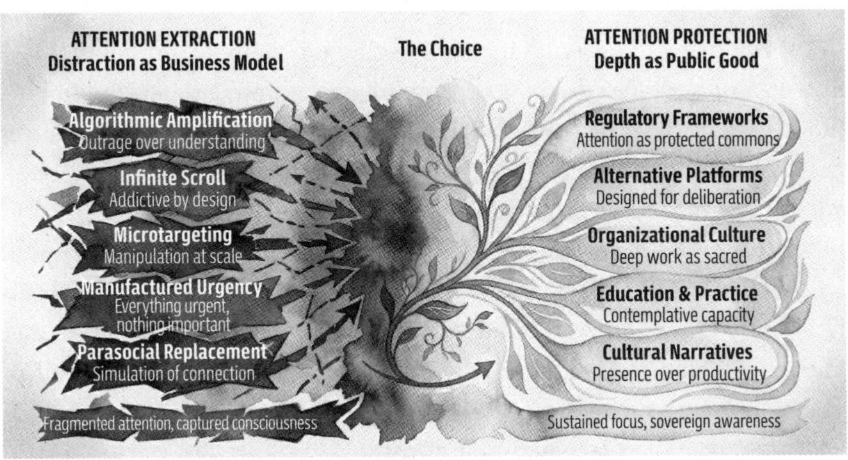

Figure 26. The Attention Commons—Two Futures

Algorithmic amplification means content is not presented neutrally. Algorithms prioritize what generates the strongest reactions, creating filter bubbles that reinforce existing beliefs and amplify extreme positions. The result: fragmented publics who cannot agree on basic facts, let alone complex solutions. A moderate climate policy discussion gets a hundred views, while "CLIMATE HOAX EXPOSED!" gets a hundred thousand.

Infinite scroll and variable rewards make platforms addictive, using the same psychological mechanisms as slot machines. The endless feed, the unpredictable reward of novelty, the social validation of likes—all engineered to maximize time spent, regardless of whether that time is meaningful or draining. Users report intending to check Instagram for five minutes but emerging two hours later, unable to recall most of what they saw.[2]

Microtargeting and behavioral prediction mean platforms know more about users than users know about themselves. They can predict behavior, trigger desired responses, and shape preferences at scale. This power is sold to the highest bidder—whether that's a shoe company or a disinformation campaign. Cambridge Analytica used Facebook data to build psychological profiles of an estimated eighty-seven million users, targeting them with personalized political manipulation.[3]

Manufactured urgency through notifications, breaking news alerts, and trending topics creates a sense that everything is urgent and nothing can wait. The average knowledge worker checks email every six minutes.[4] This crowds out the slow, sustained attention required for deep work, strategic thinking, or genuine relationship building.

Parasocial replacement means digital interaction increasingly substitutes for embodied community. This is not connection; it is the simulation of connection. And it leaves people more isolated, more anxious, and more vulnerable to manipulation. Teens report having hundreds of "friends" online but no one to call in a crisis; parasocial relationships with influencers replace actual friendships.

The Security Implications

In Part III, I argued that real security requires healthy ecosystems, robust public health, and democratic resilience. All of these depend on collective attention.

Without sustained focus, ecosystem collapse accelerates because people cannot hold the long time horizons required for regeneration, public health erodes because misinformation spreads faster than truth, and democracy fractures because citizens cannot deliberate, only react.

The attention economy is not a distraction from security work—it is a direct assault on the cognitive infrastructure that makes security possible. This is why cognitive security must be understood as a pillar of the Impact Economy. Without it, even the most brilliant regenerative designs will fail to scale, because the culture necessary to sustain them will have been eroded.

Reclaiming the Attention Commons

The attention economy treats cognitive capacity as a resource to be extracted. The Impact Economy must treat it as a commons to be protected and regenerated. This requires action at multiple levels.

Regulatory frameworks must treat attention as a public good, banning or severely limiting microtargeting and algorithmic manipulation, requiring transparency in content curation algorithms, holding platforms liable for harm caused by their design choices, establishing "right to disconnect" protections, and funding public media alternatives that prioritize depth over engagement.

Alternative platforms designed for deliberation rather than distraction must be built and supported: slow media cooperatives where members pay for fewer, better stories; civic dialogue platforms that reward listening and synthesis rather than volume and speed; knowledge commons structured for understanding rather than virality; and community-owned social infrastructure accountable to users rather than advertisers.

Organizational culture must become a steward of attention, limiting internal communication volume, protecting deep work time as sacred, modeling and rewarding sustained focus over constant availability, and building rhythms that honor human cognitive limits.

Education and practice must cultivate attention as a skill and discipline, teaching contemplative practices that strengthen focus, building media literacy from early childhood, creating rituals and spaces for collective deliberation, and normalizing "digital sabbaths" and other rhythms of disconnection.

Cultural narratives must shift what attention is for: from productivity metric to life quality, from infinite availability to bounded presence, from multitasking to deep engagement, from consumption to contemplation.

Case Study: Finland's Cognitive Defense

Finland offers a model of what cognitive security looks like in practice (see figure 27). Faced with sustained disinformation campaigns from a hostile neighbor, Finland integrated media literacy into its national

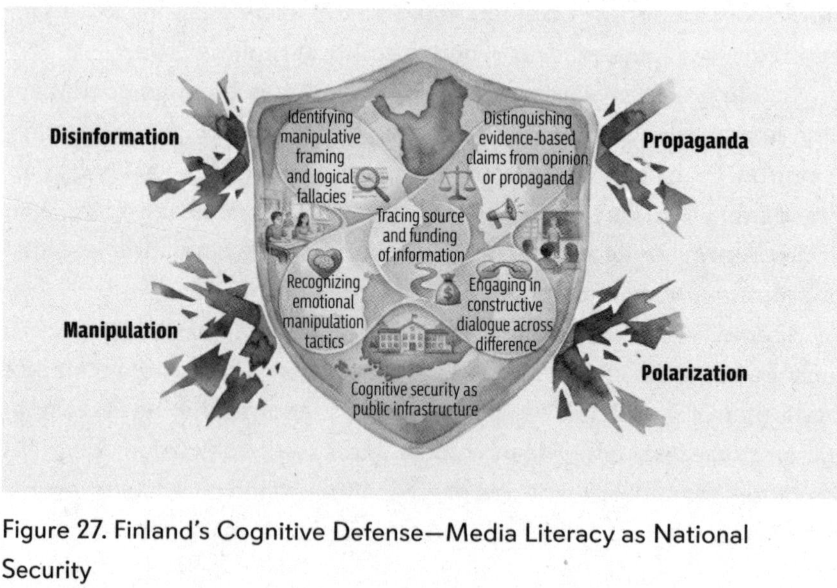

Figure 27. Finland's Cognitive Defense—Media Literacy as National Security

curriculum from primary school through university. Students learn to identify manipulative framing and logical fallacies, trace the source and funding of information, distinguish evidence-based claims from opinion or propaganda, recognize emotional manipulation tactics, and engage in constructive dialogue across difference.

The result: Finland consistently ranks as one of the most resilient democracies in the world when it comes to disinformation.[5] Its citizens are not immune to manipulation, but they have been equipped with the cognitive tools to resist it. This is *cognitive security as public infrastructure*—and it works.

Building Attention-Positive Alternatives

The attention economy's harms are clear. But critique without alternatives breeds despair. The good news: attention-positive models are emerging and succeeding.

Basecamp protects attention culture through "Library Rules" hours for focused work, asynchronous-first communication, and a "work can wait" ethos protecting boundaries. Patagonia reinforces that employees are whole people through "Let My People Go Surfing" flex-time, an email culture that doesn't expect instant responses, normalized sabbaticals and extended leave, and nature connection built into work rhythm. Mondragon cooperatives resist and reshape the pressures of the attention economy through worker ownership, intentionally slow democratic governance, long-term orientation reducing manufactured urgency, and community embeddedness creating natural boundaries.[6]

What they have in common: attention protection is structural rather than individual responsibility, culture explicitly values depth over speed, leadership models sustainable attention practices, and economic models don't depend on extraction of cognitive capacity.

Alternative digital platforms are gaining traction too. Substack (though still VC-funded and increasingly adding social features) makes long-form writing economically viable through direct writer-reader relationships without algorithmic mediation and subscription models aligning incentives with value rather than attention capture. Mastodon/Fediverse offers decentralized social media without engagement optimization through chronological feeds and community-governed instances with local norms. Are.na provides visual research designed for depth and connection through nonalgorithmic, user-curated collaborative knowledge building.

Regulatory victories have been seen in the European Union, with the GDPR giving users data rights, the Digital Services Act requiring algorithmic transparency, and proposals to ban microtargeting of minors; in France, with "right to disconnect" laws and school smartphone bans; and in the United States with state-level age-appropriate design codes and social media literacy requirements.[7] These are early steps, but they show regulatory approaches are possible.

Conclusion: Attention as an Act of Resistance and Creation

In an age of engineered distraction, sustained attention is an act of resistance. But it is also an act of creation—the cultivation of the cognitive capacity to imagine and build futures worth inhabiting.

The attention commons will not be reclaimed through individual willpower alone. It requires regulatory frameworks that treat attention as public good, alternative platforms designed for depth over engagement, organizational cultures that protect cognitive capacity, educational systems that build attention literacy, and social movements that make attention protection a justice issue.

The Impact Economy will rise or fall on whether we can protect and regenerate the attention commons—without the ability to think clearly, deliberate collectively, and hold focus across time, even the most elegant systems designs will collapse into reactive chaos.

The good news: When you protect attention, everything else becomes easier. Relationships deepen. Creativity flourishes. Complex problems become solvable. Meaning returns. The attention commons is the foundation. Everything else we build depends on it remaining intact.

TOOL KIT: THE ATTENTION COMMONS

Purpose: To help impact entrepreneurs and organizations protect and regenerate collective attention capacity.

1. Audit Your Attention Economy

   At the organizational level, consider: How many notifications do employees receive daily? What percentage of meetings could be emails, and what percentage of emails could be eliminated? Do you have protected time for deep work? Are people rewarded for thoughtful synthesis or rapid response?

   At the personal level, ask: How much of your day is reactive versus proactive? What percentage of your attention is self-directed versus algorithm-directed? When did you last sustain focus on a single task for ninety minutes or more?

2. Design for Depth, Not Distraction

   If you build products or platforms: Optimize for time well spent rather than time spent, eliminate infinite scrolling and autoplay, give users control over what they see and when, make transparency and consent the default, and measure success by user well-being rather than engagement metrics.

   If you lead organizations: Establish communication protocols that protect focus, create "no-meeting" blocks for deep work, default to asynchronous communication, and reward quality of thinking rather than speed of response.

3. Build Cognitive Security Capacity

   Media literacy programs should train teams to identify manipulation tactics, practice source evaluation and fact checking, and develop frameworks for assessing information quality. Contemplative practices should integrate mindfulness or other attention

(CONTINUED)

training, build rhythms of connection and disconnection, and create spaces for silence and reflection.

4. Set Boundaries and Norms

   Individual boundaries: Establish digital sabbaths or offline hours, delete apps that extract more than they give, curate information sources intentionally.

   Organizational norms: Implement right-to-disconnect policies, meeting-free days, and norms against after-hours communication.

   When your organization is already drowning: Declare an "attention emergency," implement immediate boundaries, identify and eliminate the worst attention drains, create one protected deep work session weekly (then expand), and measure improvement in output quality rather than quantity.

Reflection Prompt

What is one practice you could implement this week—personally or organizationally—to reclaim 10 percent more of your attention from algorithmic capture?

Connects To

This tool kit protects the cognitive infrastructure required for all other work. Without sustained attention, systemic intelligence (Chapter 2) becomes impossible, stories (Chapter 12) cannot land, and identity (Chapter 14) cannot develop. Attention is a commons requiring the governance principles outlined in Chapter 15.

14
Identities That Remember the Whole

Every economy is, at its root, a reflection of how we see ourselves. If we see ourselves as isolated units of production and consumption, we will build systems that reward isolation. If we see ourselves as threads in a shared fabric, we will weave systems that reward connection.

The Impact Economy is not just about shifting policies, markets, and technologies. It is about shifting the identities that animate them—moving from the myth of the separate self toward the lived reality of the interdependent self. This is not metaphor. It is the most practical work available. Identity determines behavior—not occasionally, but structurally. The stories we tell about who we are shape what we notice, what we value, what we believe is possible, and what we feel responsible for.

And right now, the dominant identity framework of our economic system is killing us.

The Fractured Self of the Extractive Economy

The market economy has cultivated a particular kind of identity: competitive, individualistic, self-maximizing, and deeply fractured. From childhood, we are trained to perform what we might call the "market self"—curating our résumés and personal brands, optimizing our performance metrics, measuring our worth in accumulation and status, treating relationships as transactions, and competing for scarce resources and opportunities.[1]

This self is not "natural." It is designed—shaped by advertising, education systems, corporate incentives, media narratives, and political ideologies that reward extraction and individualism over care and cooperation.

The fractures show up in three dimensions. *Ecological amnesia* means we forget that we are part of the biosphere, not apart from it. We treat nature as backdrop, resource, or recreational space—not as the living matrix that constitutes our bodies, regulates our climate, and makes every breath and meal possible. This amnesia allows us to destroy ecosystems while telling ourselves we're "succeeding." We externalize harm because we do not experience the natural world as *us*.

Social myopia reduces relationships to transactions. People become "human capital," "consumers," "users," "followers"—roles in an economic system rather than whole beings embedded in webs of reciprocity and care. This myopia allows us to tolerate profound inequality, because we do not experience others' suffering as connected to our well-being. Their deprivation doesn't register as *our* deprivation, because we do not see ourselves as part of the same whole.

Historical amnesia erases the lineages of exploitation that built current wealth and institutions—colonialism, slavery, Indigenous dispossession, gendered and racialized labor extraction. This amnesia allows us to treat present inequality as natural or earned, rather than inherited and structurally reproduced. We cannot repair what we do not remember.

These fractures are not personal failures. They are the predictable outcomes of an identity system optimized for extraction. A fractured self is easier to manipulate, easier to sell to, easier to mobilize for ends that undermine its own flourishing. The market self is lonely, anxious, perpetually inadequate—and therefore perpetually consuming.

The Cost of Fractured Identity

The psychological and social costs of this identity framework are staggering: epidemic loneliness even in densely populated areas, a meaning crisis with high rates of depression and anxiety despite material abundance, burnout from relentless self-optimization, moral injury from knowing one's work or consumption causes harm while feeling powerless to change, and fragile communities where individualized identity makes collective action nearly impossible.

But there is also an ecological and civilizational cost: fractured identities build fractured systems. They cannot hold the complexity, long time horizons, or reciprocal relationships that regenerative economies require.

You cannot care for what you do not experience as part of yourself. And you cannot build an economy based on interdependence when your identity is rooted in separation.

The Painting

There is a painting that hangs in my office (see figure 28). Those who have attended Impact Entrepreneur webinars over the years will recognize it—the framed canvas that sits over my shoulder in the Zoom frame, so much a part of the backdrop that I suspect most viewers have stopped seeing it. But I see it every day. And every day, it reminds me why this work matters.

I found the painting at the Hissar Historical and Cultural Reserve in Tajikistan, in the summer of 2005, halfway across the world from my home in the Berkshires.

I was there at the invitation of the Christensen Fund and the Aga Khan Trust for Culture to develop and lead a pioneering program introducing place-based education—and specifically place-based writing—to university professors in three Central Asian countries: Tajikistan, Kyrgyzstan, and Kazakhstan. These were educators who had spent their

Figure 28. The Displaced—a Tajik Painting (Based on Original Painting Acquired at Hissar, Tajikistan, 2005)

careers in a Soviet system that had deliberately severed people from their places, their traditions, their spiritual inheritance. They had no knowledge of this new pedagogy that my colleagues and I had spent a decade developing at Orion—the idea that attention to place, to the particular and the local, could be a pathway to both ecological and personal wholeness.

I brought with me to co-lead the weeklong instruction Robert Michael Pyle—Bob to those who know him—a world-class scientist, nature writer, lepidopterist, poet, and adventurer. Bob is a burly man with a shaggy white beard, often mistaken for either Jerry Garcia or Santa Claus, possessed of a grand intellect and a heart to match. We flew through Istanbul to reach Dushanbe, each leg of the journey taking us further from everything familiar.

Tajikistan is a country that defies easy comprehension. Ninety-three percent of its territory is mountainous—the Pamirs and the Alay ranges, including peaks above seven thousand meters that Victorian explorers called the "Roof of the World." The majority of the population is crowded into the remaining 7 percent, in the river valleys and lowlands, their lives shaped by landscapes they can see but cannot inhabit. It is a place of breathtaking beauty and brutal constraint.

When I arrived in 2005, the country was still recovering from a civil war that had ended less than a decade earlier. But the visible scars of that conflict were less striking to me than the invisible ones—the slow hemorrhaging of men from villages across the country, departing for Moscow and other Russian cities in search of work they could not find at home.[2] The official unemployment rate was perhaps 8 or 10 percent; the actual rate, in rural areas, was estimated at 40 to 60 percent. By that year, some 700,000 Tajik workers—in a country of only 6 million people—had migrated abroad, sending back remittances that constituted as much as half the nation's GDP. One in three households had lost a member to this economic diaspora. The women stayed behind to tend the fields and raise the children. The men worked construction in Moscow, sending money when they could, returning when they could, which was seldom. Divorce rates would double in the years that followed.

And beneath all of this lay an older, deeper dislocation. For seven decades, Soviet policy had attempted to eradicate Islam—suppressing mosques, killing clerics, converting religious observance into something furtive and hidden. The harshest campaigns came in the 1930s, but the pressure continued for generations. By 2005, a religious revival was underway—new mosques opening, new teachers emerging—but the tradition had been bent and fractured in ways that would take generations to heal. The Tajiks I met were people in search of something they could feel but not quite name: a coherence that had been taken from them, a sense of belonging that neither Soviet modernity nor post-Soviet chaos had been able to provide.

This, I came to understand, was the dissonance made visible. Not an abstraction. A lived reality.

Toward the end of our time in Dushanbe, Bob and I took a field trip to the Hissar Historical and Cultural Reserve, about thirty kilometers west of the city. The reserve encompasses the 16th-century Hisor Fortress, two madrasas, and several mosques—including the 8th-century Sangin Mosque, or "Stone Mosque," still standing after more than twelve centuries. The old madrasa had been converted into a museum and exhibition space, and when we arrived, it was hosting a show of contemporary Tajik art.

The paintings ranged from the derivative to the striking, but one canvas arrested me. I could not turn away.

The composition showed a group of men gathered in a humble interior—seated on the floor, draped in robes, their sandals removed. The palette was muted: ochres and grays, earth tones, the warm yellow of light falling on a bare floor. But what held me was the central figure: a man with dark, intense eyes, his face drawn with something between suffering and determination, his gaze directed outward as if he could see through the canvas and into whoever stood before it. To his right sat another figure, clad in white, his posture serene, almost beatific—a counterpoint to the anguish at the center of the composition.

I asked about the painting. I was told it was a scene familiar in Tajik art—a gathering of displaced persons, rendered in a style that echoed, without copying, the Christian tradition of the Last Supper. In that tradition, artists returned again and again to the same scene, finding in its tensions new meanings for new eras. This painting was titled, if I recall correctly, something like *Bexona*, "The Homeless." Or perhaps "The Displaced." The Tajik word escaped me the moment I heard it, but its meaning did not.

I purchased the painting and carried it home.

It hangs in my office now, two decades later, because it captures something I have spent my career trying to articulate—and trying to address. The figures in that painting are not merely without shelter. They are without place, without rootedness, without the web of relationships that make a life coherent. They are the human cost of systems that extract and dislocate and fragment. They are what happens when the threads that bind people to land—to community, to tradition, to meaning—are cut.

And they are not only in Tajikistan. They are everywhere. In the hollowed-out factory towns of the American Midwest. In the favelas of São Paulo and the refugee camps of the Mediterranean. In the boardrooms of companies that have lost any sense of purpose beyond quarterly returns. In the souls of people who have been told that efficiency and optimization are the highest goods, and who have discovered, too late, that those goods do not satisfy.

I have come to believe that the central crisis of our time is not climate change, or inequality, or democratic erosion—though all of these are urgent and real. The central crisis is the one that underlies them all: the systematic dismantling of the conditions that allow human beings to flourish in place. We have built an economy that treats rootedness as inefficiency, community as friction, and meaning as externality. We have optimized for throughput and called it progress. And we have produced, on a global scale, the faces in that painting—people who are materially surviving but spiritually adrift, economically participating but existentially homeless.

The Impact Economy is, at its heart, a response to this crisis. Not a complete answer—no single framework can heal wounds this deep—but a beginning. It starts from the premise that economies are not ends in themselves but means to human flourishing, and that flourishing cannot be reduced to consumption, productivity, or even income. It requires belonging. It requires purpose. It requires the kind of security that no amount of GDP growth can provide if the foundations of life are unstable.

This is why, in this book, I have returned again and again to the Five Pillars of Real Security that we examined in Part III. They are not abstract principles but responses to the precise dislocations I witnessed in Tajikistan and have seen replicated, in varied forms, across the world. *Ecological stability*—the assurance that the land, water, and air upon which all life depends will be sustained for generations. *Public health capacity*—systems that prevent disease and address trauma before they cascade into crisis. *Economic equity*—not merely jobs, but livelihoods that root people in place and purpose, wealth distributed rather than concentrated. *Democratic infrastructure*—governance that gives people voice, resolves conflict without violence, and remains accountable to those it serves. And *community cohesion*—the social bonds, mutual aid, and shared identity that hold societies together and transmit meaning across time.

These are not luxuries to be pursued after the "real" economic work is done. They are the foundation without which economic activity becomes extraction, growth becomes displacement, and progress becomes a euphemism for loss. The men in that painting lacked all five. And lacking them, they had nothing—even if, by some conventional measure, they were surviving.

When we speak of place-based thinking, of systems change, of regenerative enterprise, we are speaking of pathways back to integration—back to economies that root rather than extract, enterprises that regenerate rather than deplete, communities that hold their members rather than expel them. We are speaking of an economy in which the figures in that painting might find not only shelter but home. Not only income but livelihood. Not only survival but meaning.

The intense figure at the center of that painting stares at me every day. I take his gaze as a question: *What are you doing about this?*

I do not always have a satisfying answer. But I have never stopped trying to find one.

Remembering the Whole

If the fractured self is the problem, what does the alternative look like? And how do we get there? The journey from separation to interdependence is not abstract philosophy—it is a developmental path with recognizable stages, real challenges, and practices that work.

What Interdependent Identity Looks Like

What does it mean to hold an identity that "remembers the whole"? It means recognizing—cognitively, emotionally, somatically—that you exist in multiple dimensions of connection.

You are an *ecological* being. Your body is composed of elements cycled through ecosystems for billions of years. Every breath connects you to forests and phytoplankton. Your microbiome contains more non-human cells than human ones. Your survival depends on the health of soil, water, pollinators, and climate systems.

You are a *social* being. Your language, knowledge, and sense of self were shaped by others. Your well-being is inseparable from the well-being of your communities. Your wealth and opportunity rest on infrastructure built by generations before you. Your actions ripple through networks you cannot fully see.

You are a *historical* being. You carry inheritances—both gifts and debts—from those who came before. The systems you inhabit were built through specific histories of power, often involving harm. You have responsibility to repair what was broken, even if you did not break it. Your choices shape what future generations will inherit.

None of this diminishes individual agency or responsibility. *It clarifies them.* When you understand yourself as interdependent, you don't become passive. You become more responsive—able to act with fuller awareness of context, consequence, and relationship.

The Journey from Fractured to Whole: A Developmental Path

Moving from fractured to whole identity is not an intellectual exercise. It is a developmental journey—one that unfolds in stages and requires support, practice, and time (see figure 29).

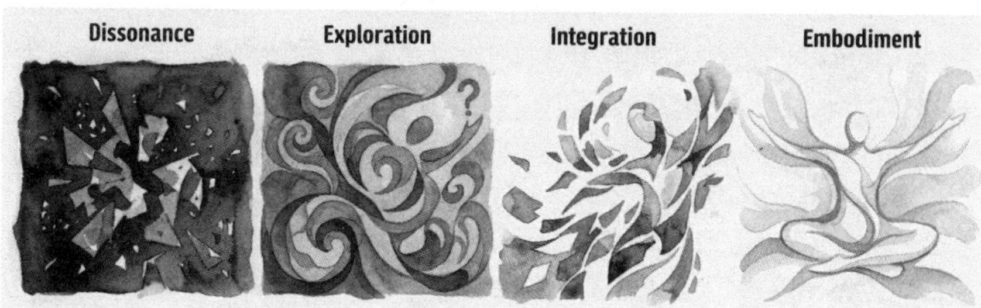

Figure 29. The Identity Development Journey

STAGE 1: DISSONANCE

Something breaks through the amnesia—perhaps an ecological crisis making your dependence on living systems visceral, a pandemic revealing how interconnected global systems are, a relationship showing you the poverty of transactional thinking, burnout forcing recognition that optimization is unsustainable, or injustice becoming impossible to ignore. You begin to feel the contradiction between the identity you've been performing and the reality of interdependence. This stage is uncomfortable—a necessary darkening, the decomposition of what no longer serves. Many people retreat back into the fractured self because wholeness feels overwhelming. This is where support matters most.

STAGE 2: EXPLORATION

You begin experimenting with different identity frameworks—reading Indigenous philosophy, systems theory, or ecological thought; practicing contemplation, embodiment work, or time in nature; joining communities organized around mutual aid or regeneration; engaging with histories you were taught to ignore; learning from elders, activists, or wisdom traditions. You start to *feel* connection, not just think about it—through grief for what's been lost, awe at the complexity and beauty of living systems, anger at structures enforcing separation, and joy in reciprocal relationship.

STAGE 3: INTEGRATION

Interdependent identity begins to stabilize. You make decisions informed by relationship, not just individual gain. You feel accountability to people and places you're connected to. You experience others' well-being as linked to your own. You can hold complexity and long time horizons. You find meaning in contribution rather than accumulation. This doesn't mean you're always selfless or enlightened—it means your default operating system has shifted, and you notice when you're slipping into fractured thinking and can course correct.

STAGE 4: EMBODIMENT

Interdependent identity becomes structural—not something you have to remember, but how you experience reality. Your work reflects reciprocity and stewardship. Your relationships are characterized by genuine care and accountability. You organize time around rhythms larger than yourself—seasons, generations, ecological cycles. You metabolize both grief and joy as part of being alive in a living world. You act with the confidence that comes from knowing your place in the whole.

This is not a linear progression. You will cycle through stages many times. Context matters—you might hold whole identity in one domain while remaining fractured in another. The goal is not perfection but direction.

The Shadow Side: When Wholeness Becomes Burden

There is a real risk in interdependent identity: *overwhelm*. When you begin to feel the connections, the responsibility can become crushing: "If I'm connected to everything, I'm responsible for everything." "The harm is so vast, what difference can I possibly make?" "I can't even buy groceries without participating in extraction."

This can lead to guilt and shame that paralyze rather than motivate, burnout from taking on responsibility beyond your capacity, cynicism or despair when change feels impossible, and moral purity spirals that alienate rather than build solidarity.

The antidote is not returning to the fractured self. It is learning to hold wholeness with boundaries.

Interdependent identity does *not* mean that you are personally responsible for fixing everything; that you must be perfect or pure; that you cannot have needs, limits, or prioritize self-care; or that individual action is all that matters. It *does* mean that you understand your actions have impacts and choose thoughtfully, you recognize you are one participant in a larger system, you do your part while trusting others to do theirs, you build power collectively rather than carrying everything alone, and you act from love and responsibility rather than guilt and shame.

Wholeness includes the wisdom of limits. You cannot tend the whole world, but you can tend your place in it.

Cultivating Whole Identity

Understanding interdependent identity is one thing. Actually developing it is another. This is not intellectual work alone—it requires practice, community, and sustained attention over time.

Practices for Cultivating Whole Identity

Identity work is not abstract. It requires practice—repeated, embodied, supported.

Ecological practices strengthen your felt sense of connection to living systems. Start with just one or two to rebuild your sensory connection to place: sit-spots (regular time in one outdoor place, observing changes across seasons), gratitude practices (daily acknowledgment of what sustains you—water, food, air), naturalist study (learning the names and relationships of species where you live), gardening or land tending (direct participation in ecological cycles), fasting or simplicity practices (experiencing dependence viscerally).

Social practices dissolve the transactional mindset by creating genuine experiences of reciprocity: mutual aid participation (giving and receiving support within networks), skill sharing (teaching what you know, learning from others), collective decision making (practicing consensus, dialogue, and listening), cross-cultural engagement (learning from communities with different identity frameworks), intergenerational connection (spending time with elders and youth).

Historical practices engage with the past not as burden but as teacher, acknowledging both inheritances and responsibilities. They include studying suppressed histories (colonialism, dispossession, extraction), reparations and repair work (contributing to healing historical harms), lineage acknowledgment (honoring those who built what you inherit), truth-telling (naming the systems that built current arrangements, and who benefits from them), and future ancestors practice (making decisions as if you'll be remembered).

Contemplative practices cultivate the inner spaciousness needed to hold complexity without fragmenting: meditation or prayer (quieting the performance self, accessing deeper awareness); somatic practices like yoga, dance, or martial arts (reconnecting mind and body); journaling (reflecting on identity patterns and shifts); therapy or spiritual direction (guided support for identity development); grief and celebration rituals (processing loss and honoring what endures).

Organizational practices transform institutional culture by embedding interdependence into structures and rhythms. These include land acknowledgment (not rote recitation but genuine relationship), stakeholder inclusion (governance representing the whole, not just shareholders), seven-generation thinking (evaluation criteria including long-term impacts), storytelling (sharing how identity shapes decisions and outcomes), and sabbaticals and sabbaths (rhythms honoring limits and regeneration).

Case Study: The Transition Towns Movement

Transition Towns offer a model of identity work at community scale. Started in Totnes, England, in 2006, the movement helps communities prepare for climate change and peak oil through relocalization (building local food, energy, and economic systems), skill sharing (reviving practical knowledge for resilience), psychological preparation (addressing grief, fear, and trauma), and new narratives (stories of adaptation and possibility rather than just collapse).[3]

What makes Transition distinctive is its explicit attention to *inner transition*—the identity work required for outer transition to succeed. Participants practice moving from consumer to producer identities, reconnecting with place and community, holding complexity and uncertainty without despair, and finding meaning in contribution rather than consumption.

The model has spread to over sixty countries, not because it offers perfect solutions, but because it offers *identity frameworks that make regenerative action feel coherent and meaningful* rather than overwhelming and impossible.

Identity and the Impact Economy

Everything explored in this book depends on identity. Enterprises that heal require leaders who see business as embedded in living systems, not extracting from them. Ownership as justice requires seeing wealth as inheritance to steward, not individual achievement to hoard. Capital as custodian requires investors who measure success in regeneration, not just returns. Defense as a Service requires redefining security as collective flourishing, not individual fortification. Cultural transformation (Chapters 11–14) shapes identity—and identity carries culture forward into action.

Without identity work, all the other work will eventually collapse back into extraction. Because when pressure mounts—and it will—people revert to their default identity. If that default is the fractured, competitive market self, they will choose short-term individual gain over long-term collective well-being. But if their identity is rooted in interdependence, they will choose differently—not because they are morally superior, but because the choice will be coherent with who they know themselves to be.

Conclusion: Identity as Homecoming

The shift from fractured to whole identity is often described as transformation. But it might be more accurate to call it *homecoming*. You are not becoming something alien or unnatural. You are remembering what you have always been: a participant in living systems, embedded in webs of relationship, carrying inheritances forward in time.

The fractured self is the aberration—a temporary construction of an economic system that required your amnesia to function. Whole identity is a return, not to some romanticized past, but to a more honest and embodied experience of reality.

And when enough people make that return—when interdependent identity becomes the norm rather than the exception—everything downstream shifts: the enterprises we build, the ownership models we choose, the capital flows we create, the security we pursue, the cultures we cultivate, and the futures we dare to imagine.

This is the final piece of integration. Not just technical systems or narrative shifts or attention protection, but identity itself, reconstituted around the truth of interdependence. The Impact Economy will rise or fall on whether we can cultivate identities capable of holding it.

The work begins with each of us. And it never ends.

TOOL KIT: IDENTITIES THAT REMEMBER THE WHOLE

Purpose: To support the developmental journey from fractured to interdependent identity—for yourself, your organization, and your community.

1. Assess Your Current Identity

   Self-reflection questions: When you think about "success," whose well-being do you include? How far into the future do your decisions typically consider? Do you experience nature as backdrop, resource, or living relation? When others suffer, do you feel implicated or separate? How do you respond to complexity—with reductionism or curiosity? What happens when your values conflict with your interests?

   Organizational reflection: What identities does your culture reward (competitor, optimizer, caretaker, steward)? Who is

(CONTINUED)

included in "we" and who is "they"? How are decisions evaluated—based on individual gain or collective impact?

2. Identify Your Developmental Stage

   Where are you in the journey? Dissonance (noticing contradictions, feeling uncomfortable), Exploration (experimenting with new frameworks and practices), Integration (interdependence becoming more stable), or Embodiment (whole identity as default operating system)? Don't rush the process—each stage has gifts. Honor where you are while moving forward.

3. Build Your Practice Ecosystem

   Choose two or three practices from different categories to start. For example:

   Ecological: Sit-spot (fifteen minutes weekly in one outdoor place), gratitude for what sustains you (daily), learn ten species where you live.

   Social: Join or start a mutual aid network, practice listening without fixing, engage across difference.

   Historical: Read one suppressed history, support reparations work, honor your lineage.

   Contemplative: Meditation or prayer (daily), somatic practice (weekly), journaling when needed.

   Organizational: Implement stakeholder voice in governance, practice seven-generation thinking, create rituals for grief and celebration.

4. Find Your Support Structure

   Identity work is hard to do alone. Build a community of practice with others also doing identity work through regular check-ins, shared practices, and mutual support. Find mentors and guides—people further along the path; wisdom from Indigenous

(CONTINUED)

elders, contemplatives, and activists; and therapists or spiritual directors if needed. Watch for overwhelm indicators like guilt, burnout, cynicism, or perfectionism, and address them through boundaries, rest, collective action over individual heroism, and self-compassion.

Reflection Prompt

What would change in your work, relationships, and sense of purpose if you fully embodied the identity of someone connected to—and responsible for—the larger systems you participate in?

Connects To

Identity is the foundation that makes all other work sustainable. Without interdependent identity, enterprises revert to extraction (Chapter 3), ownership concentrates (Chapter 4), capital extracts (Chapter 5), markets distort (Chapter 6), security militarizes (Part III), and culture fragments (Chapters 11–13).

This completes Part IV's integration work. Part V explores what we're integrating toward: the reclamation of commons and the work of civilizational renewal.

Part V

Reclamation

A Civilization Worth the Name

San Francisco, 2007. A conference room in a venture capital firm, polished table reflecting the city light coming through floor-to-ceiling windows. I'd come to pitch Hotfrog, the digital media platform I'd been building for the past year through my sustainability think tank, the Triad Institute. I was excited. The timing felt perfect. B Lab had just launched the B Corporation certification.[1] Investors Circle was pioneering something called "impact investing." Social Venture Network (SVN) was connecting mission-driven entrepreneurs.[2] The infrastructure for transformation was emerging from the think tanks into the public sphere. And Hotfrog—with its integration of social, environmental, and economic value creation—seemed positioned exactly right.

The venture capitalist listened to my pitch. I explained the business model, the market opportunity, the team. Then I mentioned that Hotfrog was becoming a "founding" Certified B Corporation—one of the first twenty-five Certified B Corps in the world. She stopped me. "What's a B Corp?" I explained: a third-party certification (with governance amendments) that requires companies to consider stakeholders—not just shareholders. That writes social and environmental responsibility into governance documents. That measures and reports on triple-bottom-line performance.

Her expression shifted. Not confusion anymore. Something else. Discomfort. "We could never fund something like that," she said. "You take too much into consideration."

She wanted to talk about ROI—only ROI. Returns, exit, shareholder value. The social and environmental value that defined Hotfrog wasn't merely irrelevant; it was a liability—too many variables, too much "noise," too many stakeholders "diluting focus."

I walked out of that meeting understanding something visceral I'd only known theoretically before: The infrastructure was emerging. The tools existed. B Corps, impact investing, triple-bottom-line measurement—they were real, they were operational, they were available.

But the culture to support them—the story that made them legible, the identity that made them desirable, the consciousness that made them valuable—barely existed at all.

The extractive economy's cognitive frame couldn't process what I was showing. Not wouldn't—couldn't.

•

I'd come to this work through a winding path. I'd spent fifteen years building cultural movements around place and sustainability—the Forgotten Language Tour, place-based education, the Orion Grassroots Network. I would spend several years at Seven Pillars House of Wisdom exploring how spiritual traditions provide foundation for ecological healing.

I'd become convinced that while governments and nonprofits were essential, it was the private sector—business and finance—that needed to transform most urgently. Because business and finance were the engines driving extraction, inequality, ecosystem destruction. And because they held the resources and reach that could, if redirected, actually build something different at scale.

I'd founded the Triad Institute to advance what I called "triadic thinking"—simultaneous deep-rootedness in place alongside sophisticated understanding of national and global systems. Like a monarch butterfly: profoundly local and profoundly international at once. Through the Institute, I'd started developing Hotfrog as a digital platform that would connect systems-minded changemakers globally. I assumed it would live in the nonprofit world, sustained by grant funding.

But then members of Social Venture Network pointed me toward something I hadn't known much about: mission-driven business. This new B Corporation structure. This emerging field called "impact investing." I attended an Investors Circle conference. I became a member of SVN. I went all in. Because here it was—the infrastructure I'd been waiting for. Ways to write stakeholder value into corporate DNA. Ways to measure and report triple-bottom-line performance. Ways to deploy capital toward social and environmental healing while generating financial returns. The tools existed. The frameworks were operational.

I pivoted. Instead of a nonprofit platform, Hotfrog would become one of the first B Corporations. Instead of grant funding alone, we'd raise impact investment. We'd model this new paradigm. The Christensen Fund had provided the catalytic grant funding, and their team, specifically the brilliant Ken Wilson and Gleb Raygorodetsky, rather remarkably had been enthusiastic about the project becoming a business.

And then I started meeting with investors. Meeting after meeting revealed the same pattern: confusion, discomfort, rejection. The infrastructure existed. But almost no one could see it, value it, use it.

•

Point Reyes, California, September 16, 2008. I drove up the coast to meet with an angel investor at her house overlooking the Pacific. She was a senior member of the Rockefeller family, known for her visionary "flow funding" models—patient capital deployed through unconventional structures to support transformational work. We sat in her living room looking out at the water (figure 30). Through the window, fog was rolling in from the Pacific, erasing the horizon. Sky, ocean, and coastline blurred into a single gray continuum. No edge between elements. No clear boundary between what was solid and what dissolved into mist.

Before we talked about Hotfrog, we talked about family. I told her about my father—a magazine industry entrepreneur, but also a chiropractor with a side homeopathic business. Someone who'd understood healing as requiring integration, not just symptom treatment.

Figure 30. Point Reyes Coastline, September 2008

"My great-grandfather was very interested in alternative medicine too," she said, meaning John D. Rockefeller. "He understood that health required looking at the whole system."

I thought about that. About systems. About health. About the financial system collapsing even as we sat there—Lehman Brothers had filed for bankruptcy the day before, the largest bankruptcy in US history. Bear Stearns had fallen in March. Merrill Lynch would be sold that weekend. AIG would be bailed out the next day. The system that preached infinite growth was revealing its own fragility.[3]

I thought about Hotfrog, struggling to find funding in a world where almost no one could see what we were building.

I've often described my work as "cultural acupuncture"—finding the precise points where small interventions can shift entire systems. Sitting there that day, the day after the old system began its spectacular collapse, felt like one of those points. An ecotone. A boundary where two systems meet, where neither's rules fully apply, where new forms can emerge. Like the fog outside, erasing the line between ocean and shore—everything threshold, everything breakthrough.

"How much do you need to keep going?" she asked.

And here, in this room overlooking the vanishing edge between ocean and sky, funding was materializing for a model based on different premises entirely. Not infinite growth, but regeneration. Not extraction, but reciprocity. Not shareholder primacy, but stakeholder well-being.

I walked out of her house with a half-million-dollar commitment.

The day after the financial crisis began, I'd secured funding for an alternative economic model.

Later, I would return to that image—the fog erasing boundaries, land and sea and air becoming one undifferentiated field. That's what thresholds feel like. You can't see clearly what's ending or what's beginning. You're between stories, between systems, between worlds. The old forms are dissolving, but the new ones aren't yet solid. Everything is mist and uncertainty and the sense that something fundamental is shifting.

That's where we were in 2008. That's where we are now.

The question isn't whether the extractive system is sustainable—it's already collapsing under its own weight. The question is what we're building in the spaces that open as it fails.

•

But she was an extreme rarity.

In 2008, almost no one knew the term "impact investor." The B Corporation certification was brand new. The infrastructure existed, but the ecosystem to support it—the community of practitioners, the shared understanding, the collective identity—barely existed at all.

Over the next two years, I tried to raise the additional capital needed to launch and scale Hotfrog. The 2008 crisis had turned off the funding tap. But more fundamentally, I kept encountering the same wall: investors who couldn't see value in what we'd built. Not because the business model was weak. Because their framework for evaluating businesses couldn't accommodate the additional dimensions we were measuring.

Hotfrog died. And with it, the illusion that architecture alone could animate a culture. I had built tools without story, structure without identity. The lesson was blunt: Ideas aren't enough until a community can *see* them.

It was the most challenging period in my thirty-year career, and the stress cascaded over my personal life. Everything I'd built seemed to collapse simultaneously—the company, my marriage, my financial stability, my sense of certainty about the path forward.

Failure is a threshold too. Different from the threshold between systems—this was the threshold between who I'd been and who I had to become. I'd built Hotfrog believing that if we just had the right structure—B Corp certification, stakeholder governance, triple-bottom-line measurement—transformation would follow. Structure would create culture. Infrastructure would generate movement. Build it and they will come.

But I'd built infrastructure without culture. Tools without story. Structure without identity. And it collapsed.

Not because the ideas were wrong. Because ideas alone aren't enough. You can have every structural innovation ready—benefit corporations, impact investing, regenerative business models—and they'll remain marginal curiosities if the culture can't receive them, if practitioners don't have identity and language and community, if there's no story making the new structure legible and desirable and necessary.

The shamans David Abram described that weekend at Cape Cod understood this. Healing requires shifting perception first.[4] You don't just treat the symptom—you change how the patient sees, experiences, participates in reality. Then new structures become possible, new behaviors natural, new ways of being obvious.

Hotfrog taught me that economic transformation is shamanic work. Not metaphorically—literally. You're not just building better businesses. You're shifting collective consciousness. You're creating new ways of seeing that make new ways of being possible. You're working with perception and identity and story and symbol—the deep infrastructure that determines what becomes real.

What I built next would be different. Not structure hoping culture would follow, but culture and structure built together, each reinforcing the other. The magazine telling stories that made the new identity visible. The network creating community where the identity could be claimed and practiced. The consulting helping organizations implement the structures. The educational programs training the next generation in both the tools and the consciousness.

Cultural infrastructure and technical infrastructure, woven together from the beginning.

Hotfrog's failure was the most valuable thing I built. Because it taught me what actually matters.

This was my mission. If I couldn't express it through Hotfrog, I would start something else. Something that addressed not just the structural gap but the cultural one.

•

June 2011. Sitting at my desk one morning, the phrase arrived complete: *Impact Entrepreneur.*

Not like I'd been searching for it. Not like I'd workshopped variations or tested alternatives. It simply appeared—whole, finished, with all its implications visible at once. The way poems sometimes arrive for writers, or melodies for composers, or mathematical proofs for physicists. The thing you've been circling around suddenly resolves into form, and you know it's right with a certainty that bypasses logic.

"Impact" meaning transformation, not incremental change. "Entrepreneur" meaning innovator across any domain, not just business founder. Impact entrepreneur: someone committed to transforming systems through innovation.

But more than that—an *identity*. Not a job title, not a company descriptor. An identity that people could claim, could inhabit, could recognize each other through. The way "artist" is an identity, or "parent," or "activist." Something that shapes how you move through the world, what you pay attention to, what you feel responsible for, who you understand yourself to be.

The phrase had the quality of remembering something you've always known rather than inventing something new. Like it had been waiting, and all I'd done was finally listen.

I understood immediately what it could do. I could see it spreading—claimed by entrepreneurs and investors and educators and policymakers and community organizers. I could see it becoming the center of gravity around which a movement could organize. I could see it providing the language that makes new possibilities thinkable, new identities legitimate, new collaborations imaginable.

I didn't know then that within three years it would be claimed by thousands. That within a decade it would be in university programs and conference themes and LinkedIn profiles and foundation strategies worldwide. That it would do exactly what I'd seen it could do in that moment of arrival.

But I knew it was right. The way you know when something clicks into place—not because you can prove it, but because every part of you recognizes truth.

Some transformations are built brick by brick, decision by decision, policy by policy. Others arrive whole, and your only job is to get out of the way and let them become what they already are.

•

As I built Impact Entrepreneur, I kept thinking about what made certain brands transformative rather than just successful.

Most brands work at the level of individual consciousness—rational choice, product features, price/performance trade-offs. Better brands reach individual subconsciousness—identity, aspiration, the emotional architecture of desire.

But truly transformative brands—the ones that shift culture, that change what's possible for everyone—reach the collective unconscious. They don't just sell products or inspire loyalty. They provide new archetypes, new stories, new ways of being that weren't available before.

Our logo crystallized this for me (see figure 31). I chose a frog—in part to honor Hotfrog, my earlier venture that had to die so Impact Entrepreneur could be born. Like the mythological phoenix, but more literal: Hotfrog didn't simply rise from its own ashes, it metamorphosed. The frog became a living reminder that transformation isn't resurrection of the same form—it's complete reorganization into something new. And

Figure 31. The Impact Entrepreneur Frog Logo—a Totemic Mandala

frogs themselves are threshold creatures—amphibious, living between water and land, between worlds. They are ancient symbols of transformation across cultures. Heqet, the Egyptian goddess of fertility and rebirth. Aztec rain bringers. Celtic indicators of healing. Chinese symbols of prosperity and yin energy. African trickster figures. Wherever humans watched the natural world closely enough to see transformation happening, frogs became sacred.

Because frogs are transformation made visible: not gradual improvement of the same form, but complete reorganization. Tadpole to frog isn't growth—it's metamorphosis. Gills to lungs. Tail absorbed into body.

Herbivore becoming carnivore. Water creature becoming land creature. The kind of change that requires everything to shift at once: a radical passage through a vulnerable, in-between state—half tadpole, half frog—that you can't remain in for long, on your way to becoming something you've never been before.

This is precisely the metamorphosis the Impact Economy demands—not reforming the extractive system but completely reorganizing it into something that has never existed at scale: an economy that regenerates rather than depletes, that distributes rather than concentrates, that remembers the whole rather than fragmenting into parts.

And there's the other frog story: the boiling frog. That apocryphal 19th-century experiment showing that a frog thrown into boiling water will jump out, but a frog in a slowly heating pot of water will sit there until it dies. The perfect metaphor for human inaction in the face of rising crisis—we don't respond to gradual danger, only sudden shock.

Our frog jumps. Before the water boils. While there's still time.

The logo became what I called a "totemic mandala"—a symbol operating on multiple levels of consciousness simultaneously, the way sacred symbols always have. Not decoration, but technology for shifting awareness.

The logo, like this book, operates on three levels simultaneously, each addressing a different dimension of how transformation happens.

At the level of *individual consciousness*, it offers what impact entrepreneurs *do*—specific practices, measurable outcomes, operational frameworks. The rational mind needs this: proof, evidence, replicability. Here are the tools; here is how they work; here is how to measure whether they're working.

At the level of *individual subconsciousness*, it offers who impact entrepreneurs *are*—an identity you can claim, permission to operate differently, belonging to a community of practice. The emotional and aspirational mind needs this: recognition, validation, the tribal marking that says *these are my people*. You are not alone in seeing what's broken; you are not naive in believing it can be rebuilt.

At the level of *collective unconscious*, it offers what impact entrepreneurs *represent*—transformation itself made into archetype. The human capacity to reorganize before collapse. The leap from one system to another. The refusal to boil. The mythic mind needs this: the hero's journey, the threshold guardian, the shapeshifter, the regeneration cycle. These patterns live deeper than argument; they are the stories our species tells itself about what we are capable of becoming.

A transformative symbol connects all three levels simultaneously—the triadic architecture of transformation. And transformation itself—economic, cultural, civilizational—requires engaging all three levels at once. You can't logic people into jumping (rational argument alone fails). You can't just inspire them to want to jump (aspiration without tools fails). You can't only invoke archetypal transformation (myth without practice fails).

You need the whole mandala spinning: practical tools + claimed identity + archetypal resonance = movement.

The frog wasn't decoration. It was encoding. It was invitation. It was a reminder that transformation is both ancient and urgent, both personal and collective, both practical and magical.

And like all good totems, it worked on people who never consciously thought about any of this. They just saw the frog—bright, alive, mid-leap—and something in them said, *Yes, that. I want to be that. I want to jump.*

•

Between 2011 and 2018, I watched the field mature.

More B Corporations. More impact investors. More tools for measurement, more frameworks for governance, more structures for accountability. Organizations like B Lab and the GIIN doing heroic work building infrastructure.[5] The UN Sustainable Development Goals launched.[6]

But also, more people claiming "impact entrepreneur" as their identity. More organizations using our frameworks. More communities of practice forming. More shared understanding emerging.

The culture was catching up to the structure.

By the time we convened at Race Brook Lodge in 2018, something had shifted. We weren't just mapping what infrastructure was needed. We were mapping how the existing infrastructure could be amplified, connected, made accessible.

The structural tools existed. The cultural foundation was forming. The question was becoming: How do we operationalize this at scale? How do we make these practices—triple-bottom-line measurement, stakeholder governance, regenerative capital deployment—not just possible but normal?

•

I think now about that 2007 meeting in San Francisco. The venture capitalist who couldn't fund a company that "took too much into consideration."

Her limitation wasn't moral. It was cognitive. She'd been trained in a framework where only one bottom line mattered, where fiduciary duty meant maximizing shareholder returns, where social and environmental considerations were externalities to be managed or ignored.

She couldn't see what I was showing her because she lacked the cognitive architecture to see it. The extractive economy had literally shaped her brain chemistry—compartmentalizing economic, social, and environmental into separate domains with separate logics, separate metrics, separate accountability.

What's emerged since 2007—slowly, unevenly, but persistently—is a different cognitive architecture. One where those artificial barriers have broken down. Where blood flows freely between hemispheres, where each domain informs the others, such that you cannot separate economic decisions from social commitments from environmental impacts.

The impact entrepreneur's integrated mind.

But that integration doesn't emerge spontaneously in a culture that's spent centuries teaching compartmentalization. It requires deliberate cultivation. Practices that reinforce integration. Tools that measure what matters across domains. Frameworks that make complexity navigable.

That's what this part maps: the practices that make transformation operational.

Not aspirational. Not theoretical. Operational.

Practices that turn values into outcomes. Metrics that drive behavior change. Governance structures that ensure accountability. Financial innovations that align incentives. Measurement frameworks that make impact as rigorous as profit.

The practices outlined in the following chapters work on all three levels simultaneously. At the *conscious level*, they demonstrate how to measure triple bottom line, structure stakeholder governance, deploy regenerative capital, ensure authentic accountability. At the *subconscious level*, using these practices reinforces identity—you are an impact entrepreneur when you operate this way, and the tools shape consciousness even as consciousness shapes the tools. The personal narratives throughout this book work the same register: not arguing but modeling, not instructing but giving permission. At the *collective level*, widespread adoption creates new normal. What was alternative becomes standard. What was complex becomes obvious. What required courage becomes common sense.

The failure of Hotfrog taught me something essential: Infrastructure without culture fails. But culture without infrastructure remains aspirational. Transformation requires both dissolution and reconstruction—breaking down what extraction built, reconstituting around regenerative logic. Structure and story. Tools and identity. Practices and permission.

The previous four parts established *why*. Part I showed we need systems thinking to see the whole. Part II showed possibility—enterprises, ownership, capital, markets reimagined. Part III showed protection requires mutualism, not militarization. Part IV showed integration requires cultural infrastructure.

This part—Part V—shows *how*.

Not as abstraction. As practice. As methods that work. As tools that have been tested and refined and proven effective.

The reclamation of economy from extraction. The reclamation of business from single-bottom-line thinking. The reclamation of capital from purely financial logic. The reclamation of measurement from narrow metrics.

Not reclamation through revolution. Reclamation through superior practice.

Because here's what I learned watching Hotfrog die and Impact Entrepreneur thrive: The extractive economy doesn't fall because we attack it. It falls because we build something that works better. That generates more value—economic, social, environmental—for more people over longer time horizons. That proves itself not through moral argument but through operational excellence.

The boiling frog sits in heating water until it dies because it doesn't have the sensory apparatus to recognize danger until it's fatal.

The impact entrepreneur jumps. Not from panic. From practice. From measuring what matters, from governance that ensures accountability, from capital deployed regeneratively, from frameworks that make complexity navigable.

From tools that turn transformation from aspiration into operation.

•

What follows in this section are those tools. The practices that make the Impact Economy real.

Not complete. Not final. The field continues evolving, continues learning, continues refining. But mature enough now, tested enough now, proven enough now to share as operational frameworks.

These are the practices that companies like Patagonia and Seventh Generation use daily. They work. Not in theory. In practice. Measured. Accountable. Replicable.

The infrastructure exists, thanks to heroic work by organizations like B Lab, RSF Social Finance, and dozens of others. The culture is forming. The practices are operational. The question isn't whether transformation is possible anymore. The question is: Will you use these tools to build it?

The frog is jumping.

The water's boiling.

Time to reclaim economy from extraction, business from narrow purpose, capital from short-term thinking, and measurement from what's merely easy to count.

Time to operationalize transformation.

A Civilization Worth the Name

This has been my journey—from the confidence that structure alone could transform, through the collapse that taught me otherwise, to the understanding that real transformation requires both infrastructure and culture, both tools and consciousness, both individual practice and collective movement.

But my story is only one thread in a much larger weaving. Across the world, millions are discovering the same truth through their own failures and breakthroughs. They are entrepreneurs reclaiming business from extraction, investors reclaiming capital from short-term thinking, communities reclaiming commons from enclosure, storytellers reclaiming narrative from the logic of separation.

Now we arrive at the work that gives all else meaning: reclamation. Not preservation, not nostalgic return—but the deliberate, disciplined work of restoring what has been degraded, reconnecting what has been severed, and making whole what has been fractured. Because transformation is not just about creating the new. It is about returning to communities and ecosystems what was taken from them—not as charity, but as justice.

The work of reclamation is not optional. It is not a preference or a lifestyle choice. It is the work of survival—for communities already on the front lines of climate chaos, for democratic institutions under authoritarian assault, for future generations who will inherit either a living world or a depleted one. But it is also the work of meaning—the work that connects us to something larger than ourselves, that allows us to become ancestors worth remembering.

The chapters ahead explore the commons we must reclaim and the daily practices that make reclamation real.

In the end, the Impact Economy will not be built by heroes or visionaries alone. It will be built by millions of people doing the unglamorous, essential work of reclamation—one enterprise, one investment, one commons, one story, one relationship at a time. This is that work. And it begins now.

15
Reclaiming the Commons
From Ownership to Belonging

There is a word that does not appear often enough in our conversations about the future: *belonging* (see figure 32). Not belonging as in ownership: "This belongs to me." Belonging as in relationship: "I

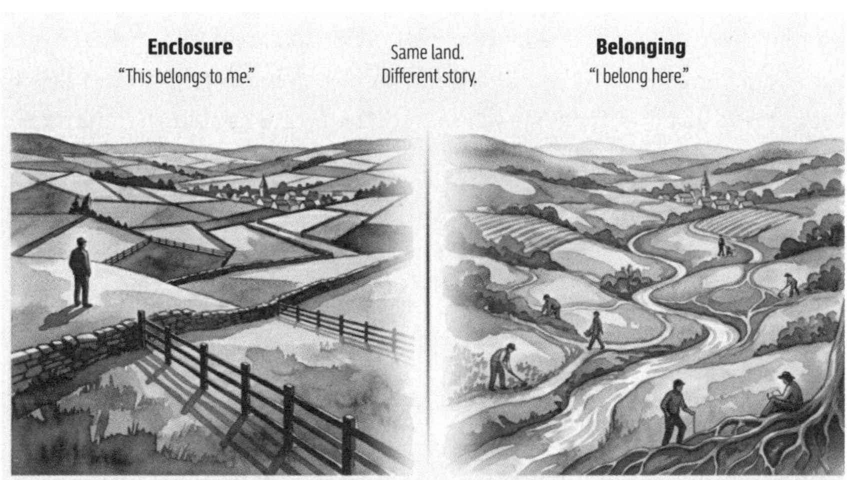

Figure 32. Enclosure Versus Belonging—Two Ways of Relating to Land

belong here, to this place, these people, this web of life. And they belong to me, not as possession but as kin." A child belongs to their family. A river belongs to its watershed. A story belongs to the people who carry it. You belong to the land that feeds you, even as you tend it. Belonging implies reciprocity. It's not about holding title; it's about being held.

For centuries, the prevailing economic story has told us that freedom comes from ownership—that only when we control land, capital, or intellectual property can we be secure. And yet, this pursuit of exclusive control has eroded the very ground on which belonging grows. We have fenced off land from the communities who depended on it, privatized water and seeds, patented genetic material, locked away knowledge, and stripped culture from its context to sell it back as commodity.

What was once commons—the shared foundations of life—has been enclosed.

But here's what the enclosers never understood: You cannot own your way to belonging. The more you enclose, the more isolated you become. The more you extract, the more the web frays. True security—the kind that lasts across generations, that survives crisis, that makes life worth living—comes not from what you can exclude others from, but from what you share, tend, and regenerate together.

The commons persist wherever relationship persists. Wherever a community maintains a resource through mutual care. Wherever people remember they're part of something larger. Wherever the land is still recognized as alive, the water as sacred, the future as shared inheritance rather than private property.

The work of reclaiming the commons is the work of remembering how to belong.

Designing for Belonging

In earlier chapters, we explored ownership as justice (Chapter 4) and capital as custodian (Chapter 5): structures and flows that resist extraction and embed stewardship. But belonging goes further.

Ownership can still carry the residue of dominance: *This is mine, and I will take care of it.* Belonging shifts the emphasis: *I am part of this, and it is part of me.* It dissolves the hard boundary between steward and stewarded.

For the impact entrepreneur, designing for belonging means asking: Does this enterprise strengthen the web of relationships around its resource? Do stakeholders feel this is theirs in a lived sense, not only on paper? Is the design resilient enough that when leadership changes, the relationships endure?

When belonging is designed into an enterprise, the commons is no longer a tragedy waiting to happen. It becomes an evolving field of care.

Who Guards the Commons: The Invisible Stewards

Before we can reclaim the commons, we must recognize who has been protecting it all along—often without recognition, resources, or political support. The commons does not persist by accident. It persists because people tend it.

Ecological stewards include Indigenous land managers applying traditional ecological knowledge refined over millennia, foresters managing watersheds that prevent floods and purify water, regenerative farmers building soil that sequesters carbon and buffers climate extremes, marine stewards protecting coastal ecosystems that absorb storm impacts and support fisheries, and park rangers and conservation workers maintaining biodiversity.

Community custodians include local organizers building networks of mutual aid and collective action, credit union managers providing fair financial services that prevent predatory debt cycles, cooperative developers creating shared ownership of productive assets, community land trust stewards ensuring housing remains permanently affordable, and library workers maintaining free access to information and gathering spaces.

Knowledge keepers include open-source developers maintaining digital commons, Indigenous elders passing down cosmologies of reciprocity, archivists and historians preserving collective memory, scientists publishing openly rather than behind paywalls, and teachers building critical thinking and civic literacy.

Cultural guardians include artists preserving and creating culture that gives communities identity, faith leaders building moral communities and providing pastoral care, practitioners of traditional crafts and foodways, language revitalization activists, and storytellers maintaining oral histories.

Readers will recognize these stewards from Chapter 8, where we identified them as the real security providers. Here we see them in a different light: not just preventing harm, but tending the shared resources that make collective life possible.

These are not peripheral actors. They are the immune system of the commons—the people whose daily work prevents enclosure, maintains access, and ensures regeneration. And yet, they are systematically undervalued: underpaid, politically marginalized, and culturally invisible. Making them visible is the first step toward reclaiming the commons. Resourcing them adequately is the second.

Why the Commons Matter More Than Ever

In an age of polycrisis, the commons are not luxuries—they are survival infrastructure.

Climate stability is a global commons—when nations treat the atmosphere as an individual resource to exploit, everyone suffers, but when it is governed as shared inheritance, solutions become possible. *Public health* depends on commons: clean water, breathable air, functioning ecosystems, shared knowledge about disease prevention and treatment. *Democracy* rests on commons: public space for assembly, free press, transparent governance, civic education, the trust that makes collective action possible. *Economic resilience* requires commons: seed varieties, traditional knowledge, open-source technology, public infrastructure, the social fabric that enables cooperation.

When the commons erode, everything else becomes more fragile. Markets cannot function without trust. Innovation stalls without shared knowledge. Communities fracture without public space. Security collapses without ecological stability. This is why reclaiming the commons is not nostalgia—it is strategic necessity.

Building Commons for the 21st Century

Understanding why the commons matter is essential. But the urgent question is how to protect and rebuild them. Around the world, practitioners are developing new architectures, governance principles, and legal structures that make shared stewardship viable in modern contexts.

Architectures of 21st-Century Commons

Reclaiming the commons requires innovation, not just preservation. New architectures are being developed that knit shared resources back into community life.

Community land trusts hold land in perpetuity for community benefit—housing, agriculture, cultural preservation—removing it from speculative markets while ensuring long-term affordability and local control.[1] The Dudley Street Neighborhood Initiative in Boston, discussed in Chapter 4, exemplifies this: a community-controlled land trust in a historically disinvested neighborhood where residents govern land use, maintain affordable housing, and build local wealth. The model has been replicated globally.

Data commons and digital sovereignty enable communities to govern how their information is collected, used, shared, and monetized, resisting corporate enclosure of the digital commons. Barcelona's Decidim Platform provides an open-source participatory democracy system where citizens cocreate policy, propose budgets, and organize collective action, with the code itself freely available for any city to adapt.[2]

Energy cooperatives allow residents to collectively own and manage renewable infrastructure, keeping wealth local and ensuring energy access is a right, not a commodity. Grameen Shakti, mentioned in Chapter 3, provides sustainable renewable energy solutions and income to rural populations in Bangladesh. Cooperative Energy Futures in Minnesota brings solar energy to low-income communities and communities of color, with shared ownership ensuring that benefits—economic and environmental—stay local.[3]

Seed commons and agricultural knowledge enable farmers to maintain seed varieties as commons, resisting patent enclosure and preserving genetic diversity essential for climate adaptation. The Open Source Seed Initiative brings together farmers, plant breeders, and seed companies committed to keeping seed genetics free and open, ensuring no one can patent or restrict access to varieties shared through the commons.[4]

Open-source design and fabrication provides open-source blueprints—from prosthetics to renewable energy systems to affordable housing designs—allowing communities worldwide to build solutions locally rather than depending on proprietary technologies. WikiHouse offers open-source building designs that can be digitally fabricated locally, drastically reducing housing costs while maintaining quality and adaptability.[5]

Knowledge commons in science and medicine support researchers who commit to publishing openly, sharing data, and ensuring discoveries benefit humanity rather than remaining locked behind paywalls or patents. The Structural Genomics Consortium brings together scientists from multiple countries to share drug discovery research openly, accelerating medical breakthroughs while resisting pharmaceutical enclosure of knowledge.[6]

Principles for Modern Commons Governance

Building on the work of Nobel laureate Elinor Ostrom—whose eight design principles for commons governance earned her the 2009 Nobel Prize—and adding a ninth principle drawn from regenerative economic practice, effective commons governance requires attention to *foundation, maintenance,* and *integration* (see figure 33).[7]

Foundation requires three elements. *Clear boundaries* define the resource and its limits, identify who has rights of access and use, and

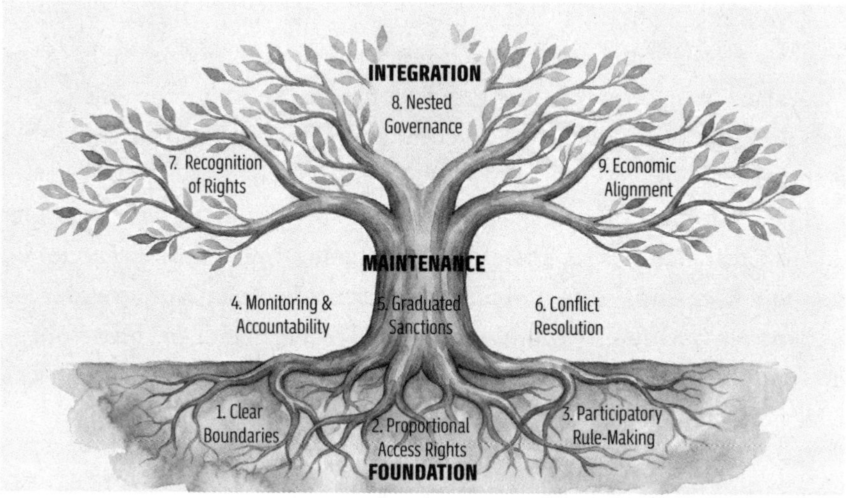

Figure 33. Commons Governance (Adapted from Elinor Ostrom's Research)

establish what responsibilities come with those rights. *Rules matched to local conditions* ensure governance fits the specific ecology, culture, and context, avoiding one-size-fits-all approaches and giving communities authority to adapt rules as conditions change. *Participatory decision making* ensures that those affected by rules help create them, that power is distributed rather than concentrated, and that diverse voices—including future generations and nonhuman stakeholders—are represented.

Maintenance requires three more elements. *Monitoring and accountability* track both the condition of the commons and patterns of use, making information transparent and accessible while ensuring monitors are accountable to the community rather than external interests. *Graduated sanctions* address violations proportionally, focusing on restoration and learning rather than just punishment and maintaining community cohesion while enforcing boundaries. *Conflict resolution mechanisms* provide accessible, fair processes for resolving disputes, keeping conflicts from undermining long-term cooperation and building capacity for dialogue and mediation.

Integration requires three final elements. *Recognition of rights* ensures that external authorities respect the community's right to organize, that legal frameworks protect commons from forced enclosure, and that property rights include commons rights, not just private ownership. *Nested governance* links local governance to regional, national, and global frameworks; makes decisions at the most local level possible; and coordinates across scales without centralized control. *Economic alignment* ensures that financial gain from the commons reinforces its renewal and that revenue models make the health of the resource inseparable from economic success, preventing extraction that depletes faster than regeneration.

Why Governance Principles Matter—and Why They're Not Enough

These governance principles—boundaries, participatory decision making, monitoring, graduated sanctions—sound technical. Managerial, even. They may seem to reduce belonging to bureaucracy, reciprocity to rules.

But watch what happens in commons that work. The principles become ceremony. Boundary setting becomes the ritual of acknowledging relationship. Participatory decision making becomes the practice of listening across difference and time—to elders, to children not yet born, to the river, to the forest, to the mycelia threading through soil. Monitoring becomes the discipline of attention, of noticing, of staying present to what's changing. Sanctions become the difficult conversations that keep community intact, that repair rather than exile, that hold people accountable to something larger than themselves.

We encountered the Haudenosaunee seven-generation principle earlier, as one example among many Indigenous governance traditions. Here we can see more fully what makes it work. The Confederacy has governed commons for more than a millennium, not because it has perfect rules but because governance itself is sacred practice. The clan mothers don't just manage resources—they carry responsibility to seven generations. Decisions aren't just efficient—they're prayers for the future.[8]

Robin Wall Kimmerer, botanist and member of the Citizen Potawatomi Nation, writes of the "Honorable Harvest"—the Indigenous practice of taking from the land only what you need, only what's given, and always with gratitude, always with reciprocity. "The Honorable Harvest," she explains, "asks us to give back, in reciprocity, for what we have been given. Reciprocity—returning the gift—is not just good manners; it's how the biophysical world works."[9]

This is commons governance as it was always meant to be: not rules imposed on nature, but participation in nature's own logic of reciprocity. Not management from above, but membership within. Not control, but kinship.

The technical principles matter because they encode wisdom. But the wisdom is this: We belong to each other. We belong to the land. We belong to the future. And that belonging isn't burden—it's the source of every real security, every lasting wealth, every life worth living.

Case Study: Indigenous Commons Governance

The most successful long-term commons governance systems are Indigenous—maintained for thousands of years through sophisticated cultural, spiritual, and practical frameworks.

The Haudenosaunee (Iroquois) Confederacy demonstrates that commons governance is sophisticated governance—not primitive or romanticized. The Great Law of Peace requires decisions be evaluated for their impact seven generations into the future. Clan mothers hold authority over land decisions, ensuring intergenerational continuity. Consensus-based governance distributes power and builds lasting agreements.

The Munduruku, Xipaya, Kayapó, and other Amazonian peoples have developed territorial mapping and monitoring initiatives using satellite imaging, drone surveillance, and GPS technology to document sacred sites, ecological corridors, and traditional territories. These tools are used to enforce land rights in court, negotiate benefit-sharing agreements, and plan regenerative economic activities.[10]

This demonstrates commons stewardship in the 21st century: rooted in ancient custodianship and seven-generation thinking, enabled by modern tools for legal and political weight, and generating livelihoods through preservation rather than sale. The lessons for the Impact Economy are clear: time horizons matter (short-term extraction versus long-term regeneration), cultural continuity and spiritual relationship strengthen material stewardship, women's leadership and intergenerational voice are essential, and legal recognition of Indigenous rights is not charity—it's climate strategy.

From Guardianship to Regenerative Reciprocity

Guardianship is essential—but it is not the endgame. The ultimate goal is *regenerative reciprocity*: a state in which the commons grows more resilient, more abundant, and more widely accessible over time.

For the impact entrepreneur, this means *seeing commons stewardship as competitive advantage*—enterprises rooted in commons protection build trust, resilience, and differentiation; long-term viability depends on maintaining the resources you depend on; and customers, employees, and investors increasingly value commons-positive business. It means *designing commons-based revenue models* that make the resource's health inseparable from financial success, where revenue flows fund regeneration rather than just extraction and distributed ownership ensures benefits stay with those who steward. It means *building cultural narratives that celebrate shared ownership*—challenging myths of individual success and private accumulation, telling stories of collective care and mutual prosperity, and making stewardship a marker of status and leadership.

When the commons is strong, everything else has a chance to flourish. When it is weak, every other system—from markets to governance to culture—is on borrowed time.

The Commons as Foundation for All Other Work

Everything explored in this book depends on the commons. Enterprises that heal (Chapter 3) cannot function without healthy ecosystems, functioning communities, and accessible knowledge. Ownership as justice (Chapter 4) recognizes that wealth concentration requires prior enclosure—and that reversing injustice means reclaiming commons. Capital as custodian (Chapter 5) can only serve regeneration if the resources being stewarded remain in commons, not privatized. Markets that reflect what matters (Chapter 6) depend on shared infrastructure, trust, and transparency—all commons functions. The Five Pillars of Real Security (Part III) protect the commons as core security infrastructure: watersheds, democratic institutions, knowledge systems, social cohesion. Culture, story, attention, and identity (Part IV) all depend on commons: shared narratives, public space, collective memory, the capacity to engage complexity.

The commons is not one domain among many. It is the substrate. It is what makes everything else possible.

Conclusion: Belonging as the North Star

Reclaiming the commons is not simply about resources. It is about reclaiming ourselves—our capacity to belong to something larger, to care for what we share, to pass on to future generations an inheritance richer than what we received. This requires moving from the myth of the separate self—the isolated owner accumulating private wealth—to the lived reality of the interdependent self, embedded in webs of reciprocity that make life possible.

I think of the old-growth forests—the ones that somehow escaped the saw, that still stand in scattered pockets, holding memory of what wholeness looked like. Walk into one and you can feel the difference. The air is cooler, damper. The silence has weight. The trees don't just grow—they commune, sending nutrients through fungal networks to young ones and failing neighbors, sharing what they have, receiving what they need. The whole forest is a conversation, an economy of gifts, a demonstration of belonging.

This is what we're building toward. Not the managed plantation—rows of same-age trees, extractable, expendable, efficient. The living commons—complex, resilient, generous, beautiful in ways that exceed any single purpose, alive in ways that make aliveness possible.

We are reclaiming this. Not returning to some imagined past, but recovering the principle: We belong to each other. We belong to the Earth. We belong to the generations coming after. That belonging is not a limit on our freedom—it's the only freedom worth having.

In the Impact Economy, the question is not "What can I own?" but "What am I part of?"

And the answer shapes everything that follows.

TOOL KIT: RECLAIMING THE COMMONS

Purpose: To embed commons stewardship into your enterprise, investment, or community so that use and renewal rise together.

1. Name the Commons You Depend On

   Identify the shared resources your work relies on across five domains: ecological (water, soil, air, biodiversity, climate stability), knowledge (open-source code, scientific research, traditional wisdom), cultural (language, stories, practices, public space), social (trust, civic infrastructure, networks of mutual aid), and digital (internet infrastructure, data commons, collaborative platforms).

2. Map Stakeholders—Including the Voiceless

   Who depends on these commons? Consider direct users (your organization, community members), indirect beneficiaries (downstream, adjacent, or future), nonhuman stakeholders

(CONTINUED)

(ecosystems, species, watersheds), and future generations. Ensure all are represented in governance, not just those with the loudest voices or most resources.

3. Assess Threats and Opportunities

   Examine enclosure pressures: Is the commons at risk of privatization, extraction, or degradation? Who benefits from enclosure, and what power do they hold? What legal, economic, or cultural forces threaten access?

   Then examine regeneration opportunities: Where could restoration strengthen the commons? What governance innovations could deepen stewardship? How could economic models reward rather than undermine commons health?

4. Choose Governance Structures

   Select models that protect shared resources from enclosure. For place-based commons: community land trusts, conservation easements with community governance, Indigenous land management agreements, cooperative ownership. For knowledge commons: open-source licensing (Creative Commons, GPL), patent pools, community protocols for traditional knowledge. For enterprise commons: multistakeholder cooperatives, public benefit corporations with mission locks, perpetual purpose trusts, steward ownership. For digital commons: data trusts with community governance, platform cooperatives, decentralized protocols.

5. Embed Commons Protection in Enterprise Design

   Align revenue models so they reinforce rather than deplete the commons through regenerative reinvestment (committing a percentage of profits to commons restoration), access covenants (legal agreements ensuring commons remain open and accessible), benefit sharing (distributing value to all who contribute to

(CONTINUED)

commons health), and anti-enclosure clauses (preventing future sale, privatization, or mission drift).

6. Build Monitoring and Accountability

   Track both commons condition and patterns of use. For ecological commons: biodiversity indices, water quality, soil health, carbon sequestration. For knowledge commons: openness metrics, citation patterns, contribution diversity. For social commons: trust levels, participation rates, conflict resolution effectiveness.

   Make data transparent through public dashboards, regular reports, community-accessible information, third-party verification, and participatory evaluation with those most affected.

7. Support the Guardians

   Resource those who protect the commons through fair compensation for stewardship labor, political recognition and protection from retaliation, capacity building (training, tools, networks), legal support when defending commons from enclosure, and cultural celebration (visibility, storytelling, awards).

Reflection Prompt

What is one commons you can help restore or protect in the next year—and how will you ensure its benefits remain shared across generations?

Connects To

This tool kit reveals the commons as the substrate for all other work—enterprises (Chapter 3), ownership (Chapter 4), capital (Chapter 5), and markets (Chapter 6) all depend on shared resources. Commons governance principles apply to attention (Chapter 13) and knowledge as much as to land and water. For integrating commons stewardship into your practice, see Chapter 16.

16
The Work of Reclamation

A Field Manual for Civilizational Renewal

We have traveled a long road together through these pages. We began with crisis—the fracturing of economic life under single-bottom-line thinking, the emergence of the Impact Economy as response and necessity. We explored possibility—enterprises that heal, ownership as justice, capital as custodian, markets

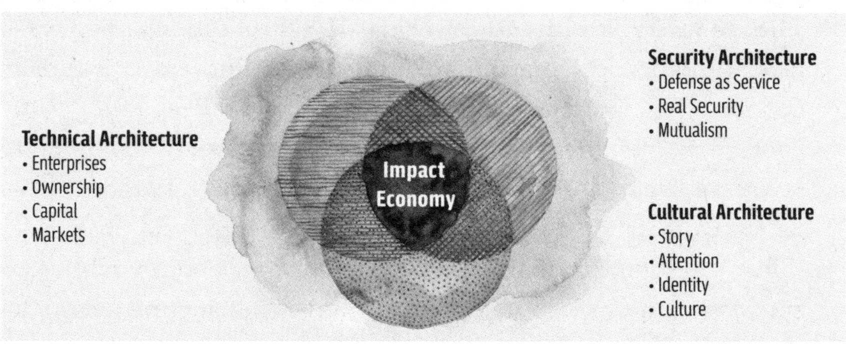

Figure 34. The Convergence

that reflect what matters. We reimagined protection—the Five Pillars of Real Security, mutualism over militarization, the recognition of who actually keeps us safe. We examined integration—the cultural infrastructure of story, attention, and identity without which no technical solution can endure. And we have just explored reclamation—the work of restoring the commons as foundation for all else.

Now we stand at a threshold. Behind us: diagnosis, design, demonstration. The architecture is clear. The blueprints exist. Working models prove the concepts viable. Ahead: the work itself. Not the work of imagination, but of implementation. Not the work of a few pioneers, but of a movement. Not the work of a decade, but of generations.

This is not the end of a book. It is an invitation to begin.

The Convergence: How It All Fits Together

The Impact Economy is not a collection of separate reforms. It is an integrated system—each element reinforcing the others, each necessary for the whole to function (see figure 34):

The technical architecture (Part II: Possibility) creates regenerative economic activity through enterprises that heal (Chapter 3); ensures power is distributed rather than concentrated through ownership as justice (Chapter 4); provides patient, aligned financing through capital as custodian (Chapter 5); and rewards regeneration over extraction through markets that reflect what matters (Chapter 6).

The security architecture (Part III: Protection) diagnoses how trillions spent on militarization fail to address real threats (Chapter 7); identifies *what* actually keeps us safe—public health, ecological stability, economic equity, democracy, community cohesion—and *who* keeps us safe—the invisible guardians, from health workers to ecosystem restorers to teachers and organizers (Chapter 8); makes the strategic case for cooperation over zero-sum competition (Chapter 9); and provides the operational model for embedding prevention and resilience through Defense as a Service (Chapter 10).

The cultural architecture (Part IV: Integration) creates the operating system for regenerative values through the culture we keep alive (Chapter 11), determines what becomes imaginable and legitimate through the stories that shape the possible (Chapter 12), protects the cognitive capacity to engage complexity through the attention commons (Chapter 13), and cultivates selves capable of interdependence through identities that remember the whole (Chapter 14).

The foundation for all (Part V: Reclamation) restores belonging rather than ownership as the basis for shared resources through reclaiming the commons (Chapter 15) and provides pathways for practitioners across all domains to participate in transformation through the work of reclamation (Chapter 16).

None of these works alone. Each depends on and strengthens the others. Structure requires culture. Culture requires security. Security requires prevention. Prevention requires healthy commons. Healthy commons require regenerative enterprises. Regenerative enterprises require stakeholder ownership. Stakeholder ownership requires patient capital. Patient capital requires markets that value what matters. And all of it requires practitioners who can see the whole and act from interdependence.

This is the architecture of transformation. This is the Impact Economy.

You cannot build healing enterprises without cultural support for valuing long-term regeneration over short-term extraction. You cannot protect attention commons without regulatory frameworks and alternative economic models. You cannot shift from militarization to mutualism without enterprises demonstrating that cooperation is strategic.

This is why the Impact Economy is civilizational work. It requires transformation at every level—technical, structural, cultural, psychological—simultaneously. The good news: You don't have to do it all yourself. You do your part, trust others to do theirs, and watch the system strengthen.

Pathways Forward: Where You Fit In

The Impact Economy needs many hands. Here are entry points for different actors:

FOR ENTREPRENEURS:

You are building the proof of concept—demonstrating that regenerative models work. Your work is to design enterprises with impact integrity from inception; lock mission into governance and ownership structures; build culture that values depth, relationships, and long-term stewardship; measure and share outcomes transparently; mentor others on the path; and resist pressure to compromise core values for growth.

Your leverage: When you succeed, you make alternatives imaginable. Every viable regenerative enterprise weakens the claim that extraction is inevitable.

FOR INVESTORS:

You control capital flows—the lifeblood of any economy. Your work is to deploy patient, catalytic capital aligned with regeneration, demand impact integrity rather than impact theater, support commons-based and distributed ownership models, fund cultural infrastructure (story, education, movement building) alongside enterprises, use governance rights to protect mission permanence, and measure success in systemic resilience rather than just financial returns.

Your leverage: Capital follows where you lead. When impact investing becomes mainstream, extractive models lose access to financing.

FOR POLICYMAKERS AND PUBLIC SECTOR LEADERS:

You shape the rules of the game—the legal, regulatory, and fiscal architecture. Your work is to redirect security spending toward prevention infrastructure; create enabling frameworks for cooperatives, benefit corporations, and commons trusts; regulate the attention economy and platform accountability; fund media literacy, civic education, and democratic infrastructure; implement carbon pricing and polluter-pays mechanisms; and support just transitions for workers in extractive industries.

Your leverage: Policy creates the conditions in which regenerative models can scale or remain marginal. You determine whether pioneers succeed or struggle against headwinds.

FOR CONSULTANTS AND COACHES:

You multiply impact by enabling others to build well—helping entrepreneurs, investors, and organizations translate values into operational reality. Your work is to guide clients toward systemic solutions rather than isolated interventions, help leadership teams develop structural integrity across all dimensions, facilitate stakeholder governance and accountability mechanisms, support measurement frameworks that capture genuine impact, craft narratives that make transformation legible and compelling, build organizational capacity for ongoing learning and adaptation, and connect clients to networks and resources for deeper implementation.

Your leverage: Each client you advise influences entire ecosystems—their supply chains, investors, communities, and employees. Quality consulting doesn't just improve individual organizations—it raises the bar for what good looks like across the field.

FOR EDUCATORS AND KNOWLEDGE WORKERS:

You shape consciousness—what people know, how they think, what they imagine possible. Your work is to integrate systems thinking, ecological literacy, and impact frameworks into curriculum; teach media literacy and attention protection as essential skills; share knowledge openly rather than behind paywalls; support narrative shifts toward interdependence and stewardship; mentor the next generation in regenerative practice; and build bridges across disciplines and sectors.

Your leverage: Education determines what becomes common sense in the next generation. You are planting seeds for cultural transformation.

FOR COMMUNITY LEADERS AND ORGANIZERS:

You build the relational infrastructure—trust, networks, collective power. Your work is to organize mutual aid and community resilience networks, reclaim and steward commons (land, knowledge, culture), build participatory governance structures, connect local efforts to regional and global movements, hold institutions accountable to community needs, and preserve and pass on cultural memory.

Your leverage: Movements don't start in boardrooms or legislatures—they start in communities. You create the social substrate for systemic change.

FOR ARTISTS, STORYTELLERS, AND CULTURAL WORKERS:

You shape imagination—what feels possible, beautiful, worth striving for. Your work is to create narratives that make regeneration compelling rather than just correct; make visible what extractive systems hide (true costs, better alternatives); celebrate pioneers and everyday stewards; use beauty, humor, and joy rather than just guilt and fear; build cultural movements that people want to join; and preserve and revitalize cultural traditions.

Your leverage: Culture is upstream from politics and economics. When regenerative culture becomes attractive, structural change follows.

FOR ALL OF US:

Regardless of your role, there is foundational work we all share. Inner work means cultivating whole identity (practicing interdependence, not just understanding it) and protecting attention (resisting algorithmic capture, creating space for depth). Relational work means telling better stories (sharing successes, naming challenges honestly) and building relationships across difference, across sectors, and across generations. Temporal work means practicing patience (this is long work, not a sprint) and holding hope and grief together (neither optimism nor despair, but determination).

The Movement Dimension: Building Power for Transformation

Individual action matters. Structural innovation matters. But without movement—organized collective power—the Impact Economy will remain a niche.

Movements create political will where it doesn't exist, shift culture at scale, build coalitions that transcend predictable divides, hold institutions accountable, protect pioneers from backlash, and celebrate wins while learning from losses.

The Impact Economy movement already exists in embryonic form: the B Corp community and certification infrastructure, cooperatives and solidarity economy networks, divestment campaigns targeting fossil fuels, land back and Indigenous sovereignty movements, climate justice organizing connecting equity and ecology, and democratic renewal efforts reclaiming governance. These are not separate movements—they are tributaries of the same river.

The work now is convergence: recognizing shared analysis, coordinating action, building institutions that can hold and scale collective power. This requires shared narrative (a story that names the system we're building, not just what we're against), infrastructure for coordination (platforms, convenings, shared resources), funding for organizing (movements need capital, not just enterprises), inclusive leadership (centering those most harmed by extraction), and strategic patience (playing the long game while celebrating near-term wins).

You don't have to build the whole movement. You have to show up for the part you can carry.

The Stakes and the Long View

Individual pathways and collective movements matter. But they gain meaning only in context—the context of what we stand to lose, what we might yet build, and the arc of time across which this work unfolds.

What's at Stake: Why This Matters Now

We are living through what historian Adam Tooze calls a "polycrisis"—multiple systemic breakdowns accelerating and compounding simultaneously.

Climate destabilization is breaching tipping points: melting ice sheets, collapsing ocean currents, intensifying storms, expanding droughts. The window for preventing catastrophic warming is closing. Ecological collapse is accelerating: biodiversity loss at rates unseen since mass extinctions, soil depletion undermining food security, ocean acidification destroying marine ecosystems. Social fragmentation is deepening: inequality at historic highs, trust in institutions at historic lows, polarization preventing collective action precisely when it's most needed. Democratic erosion is advancing: authoritarian movements gaining ground, disinformation overwhelming truth, concentrated wealth capturing governance.

These are not separate crises—they are manifestations of the same underlying system failure: an extractive economy optimized for short-term gain at the expense of long-term survival.

The Impact Economy is not a reform agenda. It is an emergency response. And the emergency is now.

Yet precisely because the crisis is so urgent, our response must be measured and sustained—we need both the fierce urgency of now and the patient determination of generations, both emergency action and civilizational strategy.

Here is what gives me hope: We have the knowledge—systems science, ecological economics, regenerative design, democratic innovation. The intellectual work is largely done. We have the technology—renewable energy, circular manufacturing, digital commons, distributed governance. The tools exist. We have the examples—thousands of enterprises, communities, and movements demonstrating that alternatives work.

What we need is not more proof of concept. What we need is the collective will to scale what works. And that will come from culture, from narrative, from identity, from movements—from the work explored in this book.

The Long View: Civilizational Time

This work will not be completed in our lifetimes. That is not pessimism. It is realism grounded in historical understanding.

Every major civilizational transformation—the Agricultural Revolution, the Renaissance, the Enlightenment, the Industrial Revolution—unfolded across generations. The people who planted seeds often did not see the harvest. The people who laid foundations often did not see the building completed.

We are planting seeds. We are laying foundations. And that is enough.

The question is not whether we will solve everything. The question is whether we will be good ancestors—whether we will pass on conditions slightly better than we inherited, knowledge hard-won and shared freely, institutions stronger and more just than those we received.

The seven-generation principle of the Haudenosaunee Confederacy offers guidance: Consider the impact of your decisions on the seventh generation yet to come. Will they inherit a living world or a depleted one? Democratic institutions or captured ones? Stories of courage or of cowardice? A commons expanded or enclosed?

This frame does not paralyze—it clarifies. It helps distinguish urgent from important, superficial from structural, extraction from regeneration. And it connects us across time: to those who came before us and built what we inherit, and to those who will come after and inherit what we build.

Reflection on Privilege and Responsibility

If you are reading this book, you likely have resources—education, time, capital, networks, safety—that billions do not. This is not guilt. It is fact. And it carries responsibility.

The Impact Economy cannot be built only by elites—it must be led by those most harmed by extraction and most invested in regeneration. But those with privilege have particular work to do: redistribute power and resources (use what you have to strengthen those with less), amplify marginalized voices (center those historically excluded from economic design), take risks that others cannot (use your safety net to experiment boldly), build bridges across difference (use your access to connect separated worlds), and hold institutions accountable (use your influence to demand change).

And crucially: Get out of the way when necessary. Not every space, not every decision, not every leadership role is yours to fill. Learn to recognize when your participation helps and when it hinders.

This work requires both humility and courage—humility to recognize what you don't know and cannot lead, courage to act boldly where you can.

The Invitation

This book has given you frameworks, examples, tool kits, and pathways. But frameworks don't transform systems—people do. So the question is not whether the Impact Economy is possible. The question is: *Will you help build it?* Not someday. Not when conditions are perfect. Not when you feel ready. Now. With whatever you have. In whatever role you occupy.

Because the truth is, we are out of time for preparation. This is the work.

Start where you are. If you lead an organization, begin the culture audit today. If you deploy capital, commit to one deeply aligned investment. If you teach, integrate one regenerative framework into your curriculum. If you organize, launch one mutual aid network or commons reclamation project. If you create culture, tell one story that makes regeneration beautiful. If you consume, shift one spending pattern toward regenerative enterprises.

Small actions compound. Individual choices aggregate. Pioneers become movements. The future is not written. It is *being* written—by millions of daily decisions, by choices to extract or regenerate, by courage to build alternatives or resignation to decline.

You are already writing it. The question is what you will write.

Conclusion: The Work of Reclamation

Reclamation is the work of making whole what has been fractured, of restoring what has been degraded, of reconnecting what has been severed.

We reclaim the commons from enclosure back to shared stewardship, ownership from extraction to justice, capital from speculation to custodianship, security from militarization to mutualism, culture from extraction to regeneration, story from inevitability to possibility, attention from capture to sovereignty, and identity from fracture to wholeness.

This is not nostalgia. We are not returning to some imagined past. We are building forward—integrating ancient wisdom with contemporary innovation, honoring what has endured while creating what must emerge.

The Impact Economy is not an alternative. It is the alternative—to collapse, to extinction, to civilizational failure. And it is being built now, by people just like you, in ten thousand places simultaneously.

This is not heroic. It is necessary.

This is not certain. It is possible.

This is not easy. It is worth doing.

Welcome to the work of reclamation.

Welcome, Impact Entrepreneur, to the breakthrough that defines us.

TOOL KIT: THE WORK OF RECLAMATION

Purpose: To translate everything in this book into immediate, concrete action in your life and work.

1. Assess Where You Are

   Personal inventory: What roles do you occupy (entrepreneur, investor, educator, organizer)? What resources do you control (capital, networks, knowledge, time, platform)? What power do you have (decision-making authority, influence, access)? What communities are you accountable to?

   Systems mapping: What systems are you embedded in? Where are the leverage points? Who are potential allies? What resistance will you face?

2. Choose Your Entry Point

   Based on your role and resources, select one to three high-impact actions from the pathways described in this chapter. Criteria for selection: aligns with your strengths and position, addresses genuine need or opportunity, builds power or capacity in the system, can be started within ninety days. Avoid taking on too much (leads to burnout), choosing what sounds impressive over what you can actually do, and working in isolation when collaboration would multiply impact.

3. Design for Integration

   How does your work connect to other dimensions of the Impact Economy? Technical plus cultural: If building enterprises, how are you cultivating regenerative culture? If deploying capital, how are you supporting narrative shift? Local plus systemic: If organizing locally, how are you connecting to regional/global movements? If working on policy, how are you grounding in community needs? Near-term plus long-term: What are you

(CONTINUED)

doing this quarter? What are you building across years? What are you protecting for generations?

4. Build Your Support Network

   This work is too hard to do alone. Participate in (create or join) peer learning communities, mentorship relationships (as mentor and mentee), movement organizations and coalitions, professional networks in your sector, and cross-sector collaborations. Commit to regular check-ins and accountability, honest feedback and learning from failure, mutual aid and resource sharing, and celebrating wins together.

5. Measure What Matters

   Track both process and outcomes. Process indicators: Are you maintaining alignment with values? Building relationships and trust? Learning and adapting? Sustaining your own well-being? Outcome indicators: What systems are stronger because of your work? Who has more power or capacity? What commons have been protected or reclaimed? What narratives have shifted?

6. Protect Your Sustainability

   This is lifelong work. Pace yourself. Practices for endurance: build rest and renewal into rhythm, celebrate progress rather than just completion, process grief and loss (they're inevitable), maintain sources of joy and meaning beyond the work, connect with nature and the nonhuman world, and hold hope and realism together.

7. Pass It Forward

   As you learn and grow: document what works (and what doesn't), share knowledge openly, mentor others earlier on the path, build institutions that outlast you, contribute to commons you benefit from, and be a good ancestor.

(CONTINUED)

8. Recommit Regularly

   Quarterly: review alignment with values and goals, assess what's working and what needs adjustment, connect with support networks, and recommit or pivot as needed. Annually: reflect on growth and impact, update strategy based on learning, deepen relationships and expand network, and celebrate the journey.

Reflection Prompt

When you imagine your descendants seven generations in the future looking back at your life's work, what do you most want them to inherit from you—and what is the first step you can take this week to begin building that inheritance?

Connects To

This final tool kit integrates everything we have discussed in these pages, translating the full architecture of the book into immediate action. Return to any earlier tool kit as needed: for enterprise design (Chapter 3), for ownership (Chapter 4), for capital (Chapter 5), for security (Chapter 10), for culture and identity (Chapters 11–14), for commons (Chapter 15). The work of reclamation is never finished; it spirals back through all these dimensions as you deepen your practice.

The work of reclamation spirals outward—from self to enterprise to movement to civilization. But it also spirals inward, to the question beneath all the frameworks: Why do we do this? What carries us through the difficulty? The answer, for me, involved a journey to a forest in Mexico—and the creatures who taught me what breakthrough actually looks like.

Breakthrough

In February 2000, I stood in the oyamel fir forests of Michoacán, Mexico, witnessing one of Earth's great mysteries (figure 35). We had come to honor Homero Aridjis—the extraordinary poet and tireless

Figure 35. Monarch Butterflies at Wintering Ground in Mexico

defender of these forests—with the John Hay Award.[1] We'd timed our visit to coincide with the monarch butterfly wintering, when millions of butterflies that had never been to Mexico before somehow found their way to these exact mountains, to these specific groves, following navigational instructions encoded in their bodies across thousands of generations.[2]

The drive up the mountain road gave us our first glimpse of what Homero was defending. Large trucks lumbered past us, beds stacked with mature oyamel firs, engines belching smoke. Illegal loggers, Homero told us quietly, his face tight with the exhaustion of endless battle. The sound of downshifting gears echoed through the forest as trucks hauled their loads toward distant mills—the grinding machinery of extraction, indifferent to the migration it threatened.

But then we continued upward, and the approach became magical—bright sun filtering through trees, hundreds of butterflies dancing around us in the warming air. Nothing prepared us for entering the grove itself.

Not hundreds. Not thousands. Not even millions. Tens of millions of monarch butterflies, so densely clustered on branches that the trees themselves seemed transformed—living, breathing, pulsing with orange and black wings. The weight was so concentrated that branches bowed nearly to breaking. Nearly. But they held.

We stood in silence, barely breathing, as butterflies landed on our shoulders, our hands, our hair. The air was filled with the sound of millions of wings—a rustling like leaves, like whispers, like prayers. So different from the mechanical grinding we'd heard below. This was the sound of life perpetuating itself, ancient and delicate and impossibly persistent.

Homero had dedicated much of his life to protecting these forests and the migration they enabled—fighting the illegal logging operations that even now were carving away at the edges of this sanctuary.[3] He understood something essential: that monarchs don't just visit Mexico—they depend on it. That the journey north to Canada and back again requires three to five generations of butterflies, each one born knowing how to continue a journey they've never made, guided by ancient coding and mysterious signals—shifts in light, changes in temperature, some inner compass pointing toward survival.

He understood that when you protect the wintering ground, you protect the entire migration. That everything depends on having a place to gather, to rest, to prepare for the journey ahead. And that every tree taken meant less shelter, less survival, less migration.

When we left the grove hours later, the trucks were still there on the road, still hauling, still extracting. The sound of downshifting gears followed us back down the mountain. The sound of pending extinction. The sound of silence being imposed on what should sing.

•

I've thought about those monarchs often over these twenty-five years.

About how something so delicate—wings you could tear with a breath—can break through seemingly impossible obstacles, travelling thousands of miles over mountains, through storms and drought.

About how tens of millions gathered together create enough collective weight to bend branches but not break them. About how each butterfly, following its own inner compass, participates in a breakthrough so much larger than itself.

About how they don't undertake this journey alone.

And about how beauty under siege is still beauty. How migration continues even as habitat shrinks. How ancient patterns persist even as extraction accelerates. How defenders like Homero keep fighting even as the trucks keep coming.

•

If you've read this far, you're preparing for your own migration. Not metaphorically—actually. You're leaving behind the extractive economy's logic, its promises, its certainties. You're heading toward something that doesn't fully exist yet, guided by an inner knowing that the current system is unsustainable and that alternatives must be built.

This is not an easy journey. The book you've just read is comprehensive, but comprehensiveness doesn't mean simplicity. Transforming economic systems requires technical innovation, cultural shift, security reimagining, identity transformation, and commons reclamation—simultaneously, across generations, in the face of resistance from those who benefit from extraction.

You will encounter skeptics who say it can't be done. Cynics who say it's already too late. Opponents who actively work to preserve the extractive status quo—like those trucks on the mountain road, grinding away at what sustains life because the immediate profit seems more real than the distant consequence. You will face setbacks. Some of your experiments will fail. Some of your allies will get tired and stop. Some days you'll question whether any of this matters.

But here's what I want you to know, standing here at the end of this book and the beginning of your work: *You're not alone.*

There are already tens of thousands of entrepreneurs in our network alone. Tens of thousands more who don't use that language but are doing this work—building regenerative enterprises, deploying patient capital, organizing cooperatives, protecting commons, shifting culture, teaching systems thinking, reimagining security. They're in over two hundred countries. They're in universities and boardrooms and community centers and Indigenous territories and accelerators and foundations and policy offices and farms and startups.

The wintering ground is real. The community exists. The pattern is forming.

The migration has already begun.

You're joining something in motion, something with momentum, something that's working. Not everywhere. Not completely. Not without difficulty. But working nonetheless. B Corps are scaling; ten thousand and growing by the month. Impact investing has reached $1.5 trillion. Benefit corporation legislation is spreading.[4] Cooperative models are proving viable. Communities are reclaiming land. Stories are shifting. Consciousness is changing.

And like monarchs, you're not just migrating—you're pollinating. Every conversation you have about stakeholder governance seeds possibility. Every regenerative model you build provides genetic material for others to adapt. Every connection you make between previously isolated innovators creates conditions for new solutions to emerge.

Monarchs don't just travel for their own survival; they enable the reproduction of entire ecosystems along their path. Their journey ensures that milkweed will bloom, that wildflowers will seed, that life will continue in their wake. This is what Impact Entrepreneurs do—not just building individual enterprises but pollinating an entire economy with regenerative possibilities.

The branches are bending under our collective weight. But they're holding.

And the journey, while arduous, follows ancient wisdom.

Monarchs don't migrate because someone taught them or convinced them or incentivized them. They migrate because it's coded into them—because their survival depends on it, because it's what their kind has always done, because something in them knows the way even when they've never traveled it before.

You picked up this book because something in you knows. Knows that extraction leads to collapse. Knows that alternatives are possible. Knows that transformation is both necessary and uncertain. Knows that the work is hard but worth doing.

That knowing—that inner compass—is enough to begin.

The mysterious signal has come.

The light is shifting. The temperature is changing. Something fundamental is moving in the world—climate breakdown accelerating, inequality deepening, democracy eroding, systems revealing their unsustainability. The old economic paradigm is entering its terminal crisis. The extractive economy is collapsing under its own weight.

Which means it's time to move.

Not because we're certain of success. Monarchs don't migrate with guarantees—they migrate because staying means death and moving means possibility. Not because the journey will be easy. It won't be. Not because we'll all make it. We won't—transformation always involves loss.

But because the alternative to migration is extinction. Because, gathered together, we're strong enough to make this journey. And because the Impact Economy—the world where enterprises heal and capital builds and markets reflect what matters and security comes from mutualism and culture sustains regeneration—is already being born in ten thousand places simultaneously.

You're not building from nothing. You're joining a migration already in motion.

And here's what the monarchs teach about where to begin: No single butterfly completes the full migration. The journey from Mexico to Canada and back takes generations—each one entering at a different point along the path, picking up where the previous generation left off, carrying it forward as far as they can (see figure 36). The butterfly that leaves the wintering ground is not the one that arrives. Yet each follows the same ancient pattern, each contributes to the same breakthrough, each is essential.

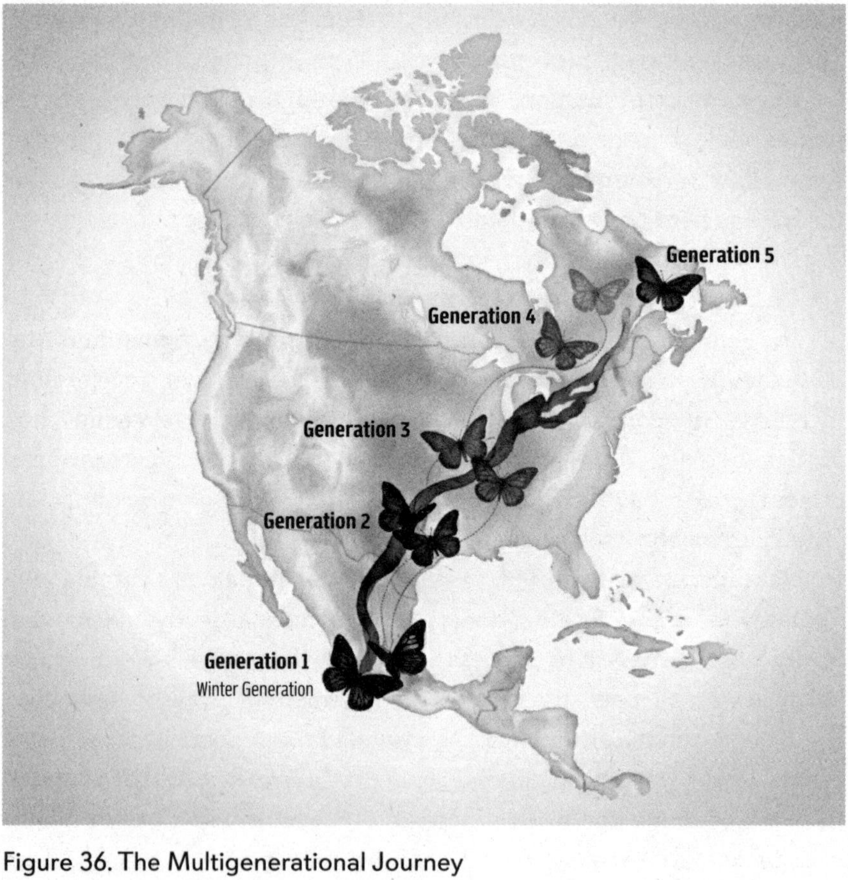

Figure 36. The Multigenerational Journey

You don't have to start at the beginning. There is no single beginning. You enter the stream where you are, with what you have, alongside whoever is already moving. The entrepreneur launching a regenerative business enters at a different point than the investor restructuring a portfolio, who enters at a different point than the teacher redesigning curriculum. Each is joining the same migration. The question isn't where you start—it's whether you start at all.

•

When I stood in that oyamel forest in Michoacán watching millions of monarchs prepare for their journey north, Homero said something I've never forgotten: *They return to a place they've never been. We must build a future we've never seen.*

That's the work of reclamation. Returning to patterns of reciprocity and regeneration that our ancestors knew but that we've forgotten. Building economic systems that have never existed at civilizational scale but that are already emerging in the spaces where extraction has failed. Following coding we inherit—from Indigenous wisdom, from ecological intelligence, from the deep knowledge that cooperation outperforms competition for genuine security.

We're not inventing the Impact Economy from scratch. We're remembering it. We're reclaiming it. We're letting it emerge through us.

And we're doing it together.

•

So here, at the end of this field manual and the beginning of your practice: Welcome to the gathering before the journey—our wintering ground. Draw strength here if you need to. Draw strength from knowing how many others are gathered with you. Study the frameworks. Master the tool kits. Build your network. Find your entry point.

And when that inner compass tells you it's time—when the light shifts and the temperature changes and you feel the pull toward transformation—trust it.

The trucks are still on the road. Extraction continues. The threats are real.

But so are we. So is this migration. So is the possibility of building what comes next.

Your wings are stronger than you know.
The journey is possible.
We're already on our way.
See you in the work.

—Laurie Lane-Zucker
Sheffield, Massachusetts

Acknowledgments

In 1993, I had the blessing of traveling to Port Royal, Kentucky, to spend several days celebrating the life's work of Wendell Berry, who was the first recipient (other than the award's namesake) of the John Hay Award. The Orion Society, which I was then leading, had established this award to recognize the highest contributions to environmental writing and to strengthening the relationship between people and nature. Our plan was to celebrate each year's recipient by going to either their home ground or one of their special places and convening a weekend gathering with thirty or forty other writers.

It was a wonderful way to confer an award, and it took us to some of the most memorable places and moments of my life: we visited Ann Zwinger in her beloved aspen grove in Colorado Springs, where she taught us to see the intricate choreography of high-altitude ecosystems; we sat zazen with Gary Snyder at his zendo in the Sierra Nevada foothills, learning that attention itself is ecological practice; we stood among tens of millions of monarch butterflies as they wintered in Michoacán with Homero Aridjis, witnessing one of Earth's great migrations; we walked through exotic palms with W.S. Merwin at his home in Maui, understanding that every garden is an act of hope; we heard Peter Matthiessen's stories of tracking snow leopards in the Himalayas while gathered in Bridgehampton, New York; we learned from Jane Goodall in Washington, DC, that kinship extends across species; we explored biodiversity's foundations with E.O. Wilson in Edgartown, Massachusetts; and we dreamed with Barry Lopez about wolves and the Arctic in Finn Rock, Oregon, where he showed us that bearing witness to the more-than-human world is a form of love. These journeys weren't tourism—they were pilgrimages to the edges where human consciousness meets the wild intelligence of the living world. They were my education in systems thinking, in the practice of attention, in what it means to see the whole. Everything in this book began there, at those thresholds.

At the award banquet in Port Royal, after our chairman, Marion Gilliam, and I had presented the award to Wendell, he was asked to share some thoughts with those gathered—many of whom he considered peers and wells of inspiration. His first words: "If I were to begin to subtract from myself the influence of each person in this room, I would very quickly disappear."

At the relatively tender age of twenty-eight, full of ambition and overweening self-confidence, I was astonished to hear one of the greatest contemporary American writers and poets demonstrate such profound humility. I wondered at the time whether he was being overly generous. Now, having reached the relatively ripe age of sixty this year, as I sit down to write these acknowledgments, I understand: If I were to begin to subtract the influence of everyone who has accompanied me on this journey, I would very quickly disappear.

So, at risk of disappearing before I finish these sentences, I will get to it—and will, for better or worse, leave out innumerable influences so that I may live to write another book and set of acknowledgments someday.

Family and Foundation

I wish to thank my father, Jack Zucker, and mother, Jane Lane-Zucker, who showed me that entrepreneurship, creativity, and healing were not separate callings. My brother Keith, family anchor, and sister Deirdre, Earth clinician. Christina Lane, the mother of my children and cofighter for justice. My children—Anna, Liam, and Silas—who teach me daily what it means to think in generations. Lori Haims, my dear friend and steady support through many years of building.

Early Influences

My oldest friend from nursery school, Rob Swan, who helped me understand the nature of a brand. My English teachers at Salisbury School, Bruce Blodgett and Ralph Menconi, who bludgeoned into me a love of language. My professors at Middlebury College and the Bread Loaf School of English, who used more subtle tactics to enliven that love even more—most significantly John Elder, who coined "place-based education" with me and remains a sage guide.

The Orion Years

Everyone associated with The Orion Society, especially Marion and Olivia Gilliam, Aina Barten, George Russell, Chip Blake, Jennifer Sahn, Peter Sauer, Emily Hiestand, Christopher Merrill, Karen Gagne, Jason Houston, Dale Abrams, Meagan Ledendecker, and the extraordinary writers who shaped my understanding of systems and story: Robert Michael Pyle, Scott Russell Sanders, Richard Nelson, Barry Lopez, Terry Tempest Williams, Wendell Berry, Pattiann Rogers, Kim Stafford, David James Duncan, Gary Paul Nabhan, David Abram, Bill McKibben, N. Scott Momaday, Ann Zwinger, Ofelia Zepeda, Simon Ortiz, Bill Kittredge, Annick Smith, Rick Bass, Robert Hass, Edward O. Wilson, Peter Matthiessen, Alison Deming, and so many others who showed me that transformation requires changing not just structures but consciousness itself.

The Wisdom Path

My former colleagues at the Seven Pillars House of Wisdom, especially Pir Zia Inayat-Khan and Corin Girard, and all the Sufi, Christian, Jewish, Muslim, Buddhist, Hindu, Indigenous, and other wisdom scholars who contributed to our work.

The Entrepreneurial Journey

Crucial supporters during my entrepreneurial years and the founding of the Triad Institute, Hotfrog, and Impact Entrepreneur: Marion Rockefeller Weber, whose visionary "flow funding" models and patient capital helped me get Hotfrog off the ground; Susan Engelhard O'Connor, Ken Wilson, Gleb Raygorodetsky, Jon and Mike Doolittle, Margot Brandenberg, Heather Grady, Phillip Fisher, and Doug Miller, who believed in what we were building when few others could see it.

The Impact Entrepreneur Community

To the tens of thousands of members of the Impact Entrepreneur network across over two hundred countries: you claimed the identity, you built the movement, you proved that "impact entrepreneur" is not just what we do but who we are.

My colleagues, past and present, at Impact Entrepreneur—Oscar Pozuelos, Mandy Gardner, Andrea McGrath, Carol Caruso, Sara Minard, Michelle Pomerantz, and all our amazing interns, Molly, Adam, Ellie, Dzidedi, Harrison, and Mady—who turned vision into operational reality and built the cultural infrastructure that makes transformation possible.

Fellow Travelers in the Impact Economy

To the luminous practitioners, investors, scholars, and field builders whose passion and commitment have driven the impact economy forward—you have been collaborators, coconspirators, and sources of inspiration throughout this journey: Jackie Abramian, Rosemary Addis, Philo Alto, Adwoa Asare, Melanie Audette, Gigi Aulesbrook, Clarisse Awamengwi, Ross Baird, David Bank, Zuleyma Bebell, Justin Bellame, Saoussen Ben Cheikh, Genevieve Bennett, Janine Benyus, Amit Bouri, Antony Bugg-Levine, Deborah Burand, Bill Burkhart, Allie Burns, Laura Callanan, Susan Chaffin, Tom Chappell, Mark Chasan, Ben Cohen, Stephanie Cohn Rupp, Calandra Cruickshank, Agnes Dasewicz, Elizabeth Boggs Davidsen,

Edward Dugger, Lubna Maria Elia, John Elkington, Ebuka Emebinah, Jed Emerson, Richard Feiner, Anne Field, Ian Fisk, Willy Foote, Rodney Foxworth, Cecilia Foxworthy, Deborah Frieze, John Fullerton, Steven Godeke, Catherine Griffin, Stephanie Gripne, Jordana Grunfeld, Richard Hartung, Brigit Helms, Jeffrey Hollender, Juli Iacuaniello, Dmitriy Ioselevich, Jason Jay, Gayle Jennings O'Byrne, Kevin Jones, Lisa Jones, Elizabeth Kaetzel, Rob Kaplan, Erika Karp, Megan Kashner, Iva Kaufman, Sarah Kearney, Christian Kingombe, Charly Kleissner, Regina Kline, Andy Kuper, Allison Lee, Christina Leijonhufvud, Luni Libes, Rachel Lim, Ana Rita Magalhães, Gillian Marcelle, Patience Marime-Ball, Ashish Mehta, Clara Miller, Nathalie Molina Niño, Sara Murdock, Deb Nelson, Jacqueline Novogratz, Sara Olsen, Matt Onek, Chintan Panchal, Aunnie Patton Power, Judithe Registre, Jane Reisman, Anne Richie, Jonathan Rose, Gideon Rosenblatt, Ainurul Rosli, Robert Rubinstein, Stuart Rudick, Fran Seegull, Rohini Seshasayee, Durreen Shahnaz, Jenny Snape, Joel Solomon, David Stead, Mitchell Strauss, Isabelle Swiderski, Nicole Systrom, Devin Thorpe, Brian Trelstad, Mitch Tyson, Selen Ucak, Evan Vahouny, Stuart Valentine, Kim Venkataraman, Steve Waddell, Isabella Wang, Michael Whelchel, Bentley Wilson, Susan Witt, Ming Wong, Jane Woodward, Eva Yazhari, Matt Yuttaworakool, Julianne Zimmerman, and Richard Zimmerman. Your work makes the impact economy real.

To the impact investing pioneers, B Corp founders, cooperative organizers, community land trust innovators, and all the practitioners profiled in these pages, thank you for building the alternatives we desperately need.

This Book

Before Impact Entrepreneur had a website, it had a domain name: impactalchemist.com. I chose it because alchemy felt like the right metaphor for what Impact Entrepreneurs and investors do—blending values to create something greater than the sum of its parts, a higher gestalt. I eventually secured impactentrepreneur.com and let the alchemist go. But the alchemy stayed.

It returned, unexpectedly, in the form of a publisher.

Steve Piersanti of Berrett-Koehler saw what this book could become before I did. When I brought him the manuscript—passionate, sprawling, a manifesto for civilizational transformation—he read it with the kind of attention that changes what it touches. "It's great," he said, "but people don't buy manifestos, generally." Over the months that followed, Steve guided the work through a series of transmutations that would have made any alchemist proud. First, he urged me to build out the field manual dimension—the tool kits, frameworks, and practical pathways that give readers something to do with the ideas beyond just thinking about them. Then, crucially, he pushed me to weave in my own stories: the Forgotten Language Tour, the monarch butterflies in Michoacán, the painting in Tajikistan, the collapse of Hotfrog, the afternoon at Point Reyes the day after Lehman Brothers fell. He understood that a book arguing for the integration of structure and culture had to demonstrate that integration—that the personal narratives weren't decoration but load-bearing architecture. This book would quite simply not be this book without Steve. I am forever grateful for his vision, his patience, and the potent alchemy he brought to every conversation.

Mark Annett, Zach Gajewski, and Kathy Sheiern read the manuscript with care and generosity, providing comprehensive feedback that strengthened the book at a critical stage.

Rachel Wheeler provided copyediting of extraordinary precision and intelligence. Her work went far beyond grammar and consistency—she caught factual errors, questioned claims that needed better sourcing, identified structural redundancies I had missed, and improved the manuscript on virtually every page while preserving the voice throughout. Working with her was a genuine collaboration, and the book is measurably better for her care.

At Berrett-Koehler, Jeevan Sivasubramaniam and Katelyn Keating shepherded the production process with patience and responsiveness, embracing the book's unconventional watercolor illustrations—not the usual business book graphics, to put it mildly—with openness and good humor. Ashley Ingram brought receptiveness and skill to the cover design and layout, translating the book's earth-tone aesthetic into a physical object worthy of its contents. Kristen Frantz, Christy Kirk, Sarah Nelson, and Elsa Frantz have brought energy and creativity to the marketing effort, and Catherine Lengronne has championed the book's international potential through subsidiary rights.

The Long View

Finally, to those I haven't named but whose influence runs through every page: the Indigenous knowledge holders whose seven-generation thinking preceded and grounds this work; the ancestors who fought for justice and passed down tools we still use; the children and future generations for whom we're building these alternatives; and the more-than-human world—the watersheds and forests and mycelia and migrations—that models regeneration for those willing to pay attention.

This book emerged from a web of relationship. If it has value, the value belongs to everyone named here and the thousands I couldn't name. If it disappears me a little by showing how much I owe to others, that seems exactly right. Transformation is always collective work. The "I" who started this acknowledgment is really a "we" that has been becoming for thirty-five years.

To all of you: Thank you for building these wings with me.

Glossary

Key Concepts and Terminology

This glossary contains key terms used throughout the book, presented in alphabetical order.

attention commons The shared cognitive infrastructure that enables deep thinking, sustained focus, and collective sensemaking. As discussed in Chapter 13, the attention commons—under siege from algorithmic capture and designed distraction—requires active protection as essential security infrastructure. Reclaiming attention is not individual discipline but collective resistance to systems designed to fragment consciousness.

B Corporation (B Corp) A certification (not legal structure) administered by B Lab for companies meeting rigorous standards of social and environmental performance, accountability, and transparency. Distinct from benefit corporation legal status. As of early 2026, over ten thousand Certified B Corps globally demonstrate that stakeholder value can be operationalized at scale.

benefit corporation A legal corporate structure (available in more than forty US states and several countries) requiring companies to consider stakeholder impact alongside shareholder returns, protecting mission through governance documents. Unlike B Corp certification, this is a permanent legal status that survives leadership changes and sale. Impact Entrepreneur, PBC, is a public benefit corporation.

blended finance Capital structures combining public, philanthropic, and private funds, each absorbing different risk/return profiles to make regenerative investments viable. A climate resilience project might combine philanthropic grants for planning, concessional public loans for construction, and market-rate bonds for operations. Blended finance recognizes that the most effective infrastructure often requires cooperation across sectors, with each capital type playing to its comparative advantages. Central to redirecting capital flows from reaction to prevention.

capital as custodian Capital deployed with patient time horizons, mission alignment, structural protections against extraction, and accountability to stakeholders beyond shareholders. Contrasts with speculative capital seeking maximum short-term returns. As discussed in Chapter 5, custodial capital acts as steward rather than owner, building rather than extracting.

catalytic capital Investment structured to absorb early risks that conventional capital won't take—first-loss positions, below-market rates, longer time horizons, flexible terms. Functions as the "icebreaker" that makes subsequent investment possible in marginalized communities, unproven models, or infrastructure with diffuse returns. Often philanthropic or public in origin, catalytic capital de-risks opportunities so that patient private capital can follow. Essential for financing enterprises that heal before they achieve conventional viability metrics.

commons Shared resources—land, water, knowledge, culture, democratic institutions, attention, the atmosphere—governed collectively rather than owned privately. The central argument of Chapter 15 is that these resources must be reclaimed: moving from ownership logic (exclusive control) to belonging practice (reciprocal relationship), making shared resources more abundant and resilient over time through regenerative governance.

community land trust (CLT) A legal structure holding land in perpetuity for community benefit, removing it from speculative markets while ensuring long-term affordability and local control. Residents may own buildings but not land, preventing displacement while building community wealth.

cultural infrastructure The stories, identities, symbols, and shared frameworks that make new economic structures legible, desirable, and sustainable. Includes narrative, identity formation, community, and the attention capacity to engage complexity. Just as load bearing as financial infrastructure; determines whether technical innovations remain marginal or become movement.

Defense as a Service (DaaS) An operational framework for genuine security through prevention infrastructure (public health, ecosystem restoration, economic equity, democratic resilience, community cohesion) rather than militarized reaction. Treats security as distributed capacity requiring ongoing investment in root causes, not fortress logic defending symptoms. Applicable at municipal, enterprise, portfolio, and national scales. DaaS is explored in depth in Chapter 10.

ecotone An ecological term for boundary zones where two ecosystems (such as forest and meadow) meet. Used metaphorically in this book to describe threshold moments where old systems dissolve and new forms can emerge—neither system's rules fully apply; maximum creativity and vulnerability coexist.

enterprises that heal Business models where regeneration is core to operations—not an add-on or offset but embedded in how the enterprise creates value. Healing enterprises cannot succeed without simultaneously improving ecosystem health, community well-being, and worker dignity. Contrasts with "less bad" approaches (reducing harm while maintaining an extractive core) and with philanthropy (giving away wealth generated through extraction). Explored in Chapter 3 as the foundational building block of the Impact Economy.

ESG (environmental, social, governance) A framework adding environmental, social, and governance metrics to investment analysis.

Progress over single-bottom-line thinking, but insufficient for transformation. Critiques include that it is often backward-looking (reporting past performance, not preventing future harm), siloed (treating E, S, and G concerns as separate rather than interdependent), compliance-oriented (checking boxes rather than transforming structures), and gameable (optimizing for scores while maintaining an extractive core). A company can score high on ESG while extracting unsustainably and lobbying against climate policy. Systemic intelligence goes deeper.

externalities Costs (or benefits) imposed on parties not involved in a transaction—pollution affecting downwind communities, climate damage from carbon emissions, health costs from processed food. The extractive economy systematically externalizes costs: What cannot be monetized does not count on the balance sheet. Markets designed for regeneration must internalize externalities through carbon pricing, true-cost accounting, extended producer responsibility, and polluter-pays policies—making visible what extraction renders invisible.

extractive economy/extractive capitalism An economic system optimized for maximum short-term extraction of value from ecosystems, communities, and future generations, externalizing costs and concentrating benefits. Treats nature, labor, and commons as inputs to be depleted. Contrasts with regenerative approaches that create conditions for ongoing flourishing.

Five Pillars of Real Security The framework identifying genuine security infrastructure. The Five Pillars are: ecological stability (healthy ecosystems that buffer against disasters and regulate climate), public health capacity (systems preventing illness and enabling rapid response), economic equity (distributed prosperity preventing desperation), democratic infrastructure (transparent governance maintaining trust), and community cohesion (social bonds enabling mutual aid). Weakness in any one destabilizes the whole. These pillars organize Part III and inform the Defense as a Service approach.

greenwashing/impact-washing Marketing practices claiming social or environmental benefit without substantive operational change. Performative impact lacking structural integrity—allows companies to give the appearance of supporting regeneration while maintaining extractive practices. Addressed through authentic measurement, third-party verification, and stakeholder accountability.

Impact Economy A comprehensive economic system where enterprises heal, ownership distributes power, capital acts as custodian, markets reflect true value, security comes from mutualism, and culture sustains regenerative practices. Not a sector but a civilizational alternative to extraction—operational and scaling, not aspirational.

impact entrepreneur Someone committed to transforming systems through innovation—an identity, not just a job title. A systems-minded changemaker who sees the whole, acts from interdependence, and builds enterprises/initiatives that address root causes rather than symptoms. Coined by the author in 2011, now claimed by tens of thousands globally.

impact integrity Alignment between stated values and operational reality—what you claim and what you do, your story and your structure. Requires authentic measurement, transparent accountability, stakeholder governance, and structural protections that outlast individual commitment. The difference between genuine transformation and performative change.

impact investing Capital deployment seeking measurable social and environmental benefit alongside financial return. Ranges from market-rate-seeking with impact as constraint to concessionary capital prioritizing impact. At $1.5+ trillion globally as of 2025, demonstrates that finance can serve regeneration, though the field still struggles with impact-washing and measurement rigor.

interdependent identity A sense of self rooted in ecological, social, and temporal connection—recognizing that you exist within living systems rather than separate from them. Contrasts with the extractive economy's "fractured self": compartmentalized, competitive, self-maximizing, suffering from ecological amnesia, social atomization, and temporal compression. Interdependent identity enables sustained commitment to regeneration because caring for systems becomes caring for self. Cultivated through practices that expand time horizons, deepen relational awareness, and restore belonging. Central to Chapter 14.

leverage points Places in complex systems where small interventions can create large change. Donella Meadows identified a hierarchy: the weakest leverage comes from adjusting parameters (taxes, subsidies); stronger leverage from changing feedback loops, information flows, and system rules; and the strongest leverage from shifting the mindset or paradigm from which the system arises. Narrative is how paradigms travel, making stories the deepest leverage point. Impact entrepreneurs cultivate systemic intelligence partly to identify leverage points where their efforts can cascade into broader transformation.

mission lock/mission permanence Legal and governance mechanisms protecting enterprise mission from future compromise, ensuring values survive leadership changes, investor pressure, and acquisition attempts. Achieved through benefit corporation status (requiring stakeholder consideration), steward ownership (separating economic rights from control), covenant agreements (mission requirements tied to capital terms), stakeholder governance (distributed decision-making power), and anti-dilution provisions. Without mission lock, even enterprises founded with regenerative intent can drift toward extraction under market pressure.

mutualism A security strategy based on cooperation and mutual benefit rather than zero-sum competition and militarization. As discussed in Chapter 9, mutualism recognizes that genuine safety comes from addressing root causes collectively, that distributed resilience outperforms concentrated defense, and that the defended fortress is ultimately more vulnerable than the mutually secured community.

narrative infrastructure The myths, metaphors, and mental models that make new possibilities believable and desirable. Just as physical infrastructure (roads, utilities) enables economic activity, narrative infrastructure enables cultural transformation. Stories legitimize structures of power, define the horizon of change, and embed incentives in culture. The Impact Economy requires renovating narrative infrastructure—cultivating stories that normalize reciprocity, stewardship, and interdependence rather than extraction and dominance. Chapter 12 explores this as the deepest leverage point for systemic change.

patient capital Investment with time horizons measured in decades rather than quarters, prioritizing long-term value creation over short-term extraction. Willing to accept lower returns or delayed returns in exchange for mission alignment, stakeholder benefit, and regenerative outcomes. Essential for enterprises that heal, which build value slowly but sustainably.

place-based education Pedagogy rooting learning in local community, culture, and ecology. Coined by the author Dr. John Elder in 1995, it has evolved from a marginal concept to a mainstream framework. By 2015, the term had migrated to finance as "place-based investing," demonstrating how cultural infrastructure spreads across domains.

platform cooperative A digital platform owned and governed by its users—workers, customers, or both—rather than extractive investors. Demonstrates that alternatives to surveillance capitalism exist and function (see examples in Chapter 6). Platform cooperatives apply traditional cooperative principles to the digital economy, proving that democratic ownership scales in networked contexts.

polycrisis Multiple systemic breakdowns (climate, democracy, pandemic, inequality, information) accelerating and compounding simultaneously—not separate challenges but interconnected manifestations of extractive system failure. Demands integrated response across economic, cultural, and security dimensions.

Prevention Dividend The measurable return on investment generated by addressing root causes rather than reacting to crises. Research consistently demonstrates strong returns: disaster preparedness yields $4–$7 saved per dollar invested; ecosystem restoration generates $7–$30 in economic returns; pandemic preparedness produces $1,102 in economic gain per dollar spent. The framework makes prevention as visible, measurable, and politically compelling as reaction—central to the Defense as a Service operating model. See also Prevention Ratio, the diagnostic complement that measures current reactive-to-preventive spending allocation.

Prevention Ratio The proportion of an organization's, community's, or government's security-related spending directed toward addressing root causes (prevention) versus reacting to crises and symptoms (reaction). Most institutions discover their Prevention Ratio is heavily skewed toward reaction—often 80–90 percent. Making the ratio visible and tracking it over time converts abstract commitments to prevention into concrete budgetary accountability. The Prevention Ratio is a diagnostic complement to the Prevention Dividend: the Ratio measures current allocation; the Dividend quantifies the returns available from improving it. Central to the Defense as a Service operating model.

regenerative (versus sustainable) Sustainability asks, "How do we maintain?" Regeneration asks, "How do we restore, enhance, make more alive?" Sustainability accepts current degradation as a baseline and minimizes further harm. Regeneration refuses that baseline and insists on active healing—participating in life's pattern of creating more life, more complexity, more resilience over time.

Notes

Why Impact Entrepreneurs?

1 On climate tipping points and their increasing proximity, see Intergovernmental Panel on Climate Change (IPCC), *Climate Change 2023: Synthesis Report. Contribution of Working Groups I, II and III to the Sixth Assessment Report of the Intergovernmental Panel on Climate Change* (IPCC, 2023). For the most comprehensive current assessment of tipping point risks, see Timothy M. Lenton et al., *Global Tipping Points Report 2023* (University of Exeter, 2023), which identifies five major tipping systems already at risk at current warming levels.

2 On ecosystem risk and extinction rates, see Intergovernmental Science-Policy Platform on Biodiversity and Ecosystem Services (IPBES), *Global Assessment Report on Biodiversity and Ecosystem Services* (IPBES Secretariat, 2019). The report found that approximately one million animal and plant species are threatened with extinction, and that nature is declining at rates unprecedented in human history. The current rate of species extinction is tens to hundreds of times higher than the average over the past ten million years.

3 On wealth inequality, see Oxfam International, *Inequality Inc.: How Corporate Power Divides Our World and the Need for a New Era of Public Action* (Oxfam, 2024). The report documents that the world's five richest men have more than doubled their fortunes since 2020, while nearly five billion people have become poorer during the same period. See also World Inequality Lab, *World Inequality Report 2022* (World Inequality Lab, 2021).

4 On the corrosion of civic trust, see Edelman, *2023 Edelman Trust Barometer* (Edelman, 2023). The twenty-third annual survey, conducted across twenty-eight countries, found that lack of faith in societal institutions—triggered by economic anxiety, disinformation, and failure of leadership—has contributed to deep polarization. The *2024 Edelman Trust Barometer* (Edelman, 2024) found that innovation has become a new wedge issue, further exacerbating trust issues and instability. Trust in government has particularly declined among

election skeptics, falling to 19 percent, compared to 63 percent among those who believe elections are legitimate.

5 For accounts of these pioneering enterprises, see Tom Chappell, *The Soul of a Business: Managing for Profit and the Common Good* (Bantam, 1993); Anita Roddick, *Business as Unusual: The Journey of Anita Roddick and The Body Shop* (Thorsons, 2000); Ben Cohen and Jerry Greenfield, *Ben & Jerry's Double-Dip: Lead with Your Values and Make Money, Too* (Simon & Schuster, 1997); and Jeffrey Hollender, *Built for a Better World* (Fast Company Press, 2026).

6 On the Unilever acquisition of Ben & Jerry's, see Ben & Jerry's Homemade, Inc., *Proxy Statement*, July 5, 2000, filed with the US Securities and Exchange Commission (SEC). Ben Cohen's reflections on the personal toll of the sale—including his comment that "one could say that losing Ben & Jerry's literally broke my heart"—are drawn from the author's conversation with Cohen during an Impact Entrepreneur webinar. Cohen underwent emergency bypass surgery in early 2001, shortly after the sale closed; contemporaneous reports noted speculation about stress from the acquisition as a contributing factor. Legal scholars Antony Page and Robert A. Katz have argued that the company's defensive mechanisms, including a poison pill and staggered board, could technically have blocked the acquisition (see Antony Page and Robert A. Katz, "The Truth About Ben and Jerry's," *Stanford Social Innovation Review*, Fall 2012). However, the distinction between having legal tools and being able to deploy them without devastating practical consequences is precisely the gap that benefit corporation legislation and other structural innovations aim to close.

7 The Body Shop was acquired by L'Oréal in March 2006 for £652.3 million. Anita Roddick's "Trojan horse" characterization appeared in an interview with *The Guardian* following the sale announcement (Claudia Cahalane, "'I Believe They Are Honourable and the Work They Do Is Honourable,'" *The Guardian*, November 3, 2006): As reported, "she sees herself as a kind of 'Trojan horse' who by selling her business to a huge firm will be able to influence the decisions it makes." See also "L'Oréal Buys Body Shop for £652m," *The Guardian*, March 17, 2006.

Part I

1 Terry Tempest Williams, *Refuge: An Unnatural History of Family and Place* (Pantheon Books, 1991), 149. The full passage reads: "I pray to the birds because I believe they will carry the messages of my heart upward. I pray to them because I believe in their existence, the way their songs begin and end each day—the invocations and benedictions of Earth. I pray to the birds because they remind me of what I love rather than what I fear. And at the end of my prayers, they teach me how to listen."

2 David Abram, "The Ecology of Magic," *Orion*, Summer 1991. This essay was later included in Theodore Roszak, Mary E. Gomes, and Allen D. Kanner, eds., *Ecopsychology: Restoring the Earth, Healing the Mind* (Sierra Club Books, 1995), and subsequently expanded as the foundation for Abram's book *The Spell of the Sensuous: Perception and Language in a More-Than-Human World* (Pantheon Books, 1996).

3 Barry Lopez, *Of Wolves and Men* (Scribner, 1978). Lopez writes: "The wolf exerts a powerful influence on the human imagination. It takes your stare and turns it back on you." Throughout his book, Lopez explores how wolves "have a high degree of social organization" and "have evolved a system of communication and communal interaction which stabilizes these social relationships," with "packs develop[ing] distinct personalities."

4 Aldo Leopold, *A Sand County Almanac: And Sketches Here and There* (Oxford University Press, 1949), 224–225. This passage articulates what Leopold called "the land ethic," the culminating essay of the collection.

5 The First National People of Color Environmental Leadership Summit was held October 24–27, 1991, in Washington, DC. The summit produced the "Principles of Environmental Justice," a foundational document that articulated the framework connecting environmental degradation with racial and economic injustice. For the full text, see EJnet.org, "Principles of Environmental Justice," ejnet.org/ej/principles.html.

6 Donella H. Meadows, *Thinking in Systems: A Primer*, ed. Diana Wright (Chelsea Green Publishing, 2008). Though published posthumously (Meadows died in 2001), this work distills her decades of systems thinking research, including her influential essay "Leverage Points: Places to Intervene in a System" (1999).

7 This quotation is widely attributed to Albert Einstein but cannot be verified in his published works. The earliest documented version appears in *Ram Dass Newsletter*, Spring 1970. See Alice Calaprice, ed., *The Ultimate Quotable Einstein* (Princeton University Press, 2011), 474, where it is listed among "Probably Not by Einstein." The sentiment, regardless of origin, captures a principle central to systems thinking.

Chapter 1

1 Muhammad Yunus and Grameen Bank were jointly awarded the Nobel Peace Prize in 2006 "for their efforts to create economic and social development from below." See Nobel Prize, "Nobel Peace Prize 2006," nobelprize.org/prizes/peace/2006/summary/. For Yunus's own account of the structural innovations underlying Grameen Bank, see Muhammad Yunus with Alan Jolis, *Banker to the Poor: Micro-Lending and the Battle Against World Poverty* (PublicAffairs, 1999).

Chapter 2

1 For documented accounts of the persistence of child labor in global supply chains despite corporate compliance programs, see Richard M. Locke, *The Promise and Limits of Private Power: Promoting Labor Standards in a Global Economy* (Cambridge University Press, 2013). The systemic nature of the problem—rooted in poverty, education access, and governance capacity—is analyzed in the International Labour Organization's *World Report on Child Labour 2015* (ILO, 2015).

2 Ray Anderson founded Interface, Inc., in 1973 and launched Mission Zero in 1994 after reading Paul Hawken's *The Ecology of Commerce* (HarperBusiness, 1993). Anderson's account of Interface's transformation is documented in Ray Anderson with Robin White, *Confessions of a Radical Industrialist: Profits, People, Purpose—Doing Business by Respecting the Earth* (St. Martin's Press, 2009). Anderson died in 2011. Interface achieved its Mission Zero goal in 2019 and has since announced a "Climate Take Back" initiative, aiming to become carbon negative. See Interface, "Our Climate Commitment," interface.com/US/en-US/sustainability/sustainability-overview.html.

3 See The Natural Step, "Interface: The Journey of a Lifetime" (2013), and Interface, "Interface Announces Mission Zero Success," *PR Newswire*, November 4, 2019.

Part II

1 The Mahican (also spelled Mohican) are an Eastern Algonquian people whose name derives from *Muh-he-con-neok*, meaning "people of the waters that are never still," referring to the tidal flows of the Hudson River. For the etymology of regional place names, see Lion G. Miles, "The Red Man Dispossessed: The Williams Family and the Alienation of Indian Land in Stockbridge, Massachusetts, 1736–1818," *New England Quarterly* 67, no. 1 (March 1994): 46–76.

2 William Edward Burghardt Du Bois (1868–1963) was born in Great Barrington, Massachusetts, on February 23, 1868. His connection to the Berkshire landscape is explored in David Levering Lewis, *W. E. B. Du Bois: Biography of a Race, 1868–1919* (Henry Holt, 1993), particularly chapters 1–3. Du Bois's own reflections on the landscape that shaped him appear in *Dusk of Dawn: An Essay Toward an Autobiography of a Race Concept* (Harcourt, Brace, 1940). The W. E. B. Du Bois Center in Great Barrington preserves his boyhood homesite.

3 The Schumacher Center for a New Economics, founded in 1980 and based in Great Barrington, Massachusetts, continues the legacy of E. F. Schumacher, author of *Small Is Beautiful: Economics as if People Mattered* (Harper & Row, 1973). Susan Witt has served as executive director since 1980. See centerforneweconomics.org.

4 BerkShares, Inc., launched in September 2006 as a local currency for the southern Berkshire region of Massachusetts. Over $11 million in BerkShares have circulated through the local economy. See Jared Spears, "BerkShares: A Local Currency for the Berkshire Region," Schumacher Center for a New Economics, centerforneweconomics.org/apply/local-currencies-program/berkshares/.

5 John Fullerton is founder and president of Capital Institute (capitalinstitute.org) and author of *Regenerative Economics: Revolutionary Thinking for a World in Crisis* (New Society Publishers, 2025). His framework of regenerative design principles informed the Race Brook Lodge gathering.

Chapter 3

1 The Haudenosaunee (Iroquois) Confederacy's Great Law of Peace (*Gayanashagowa*) includes the principle of considering the impact of decisions on descendants seven generations into the future. See Oren Lyons, "An Iroquois Perspective," in Christopher Vecsey and Robert W. Venables, eds., *American Indian Environments: Ecological Issues in Native American History* (Syracuse University Press, 1980), 171–174.

2 *Rāhui* is a Māori practice of temporary resource restriction to allow ecosystem regeneration. For contemporary applications in New Zealand resource management, see Mere Roberts et al., "Kaitiakitanga: Māori Perspectives on Conservation," *Pacific Conservation Biology* 2, no. 1 (1995): 7–20.

3 *Ubuntu*, often translated as "I am because we are," represents an African philosophy of humaneness and interconnection. See Desmond Tutu, *No Future Without Forgiveness* (Doubleday, 1999), where Tutu writes: "A person with *ubuntu* is open and available to others, affirming of others, does not feel threatened that others are able and good."

4 *Wu wei* (無為), often translated as "nonaction" or "effortless action," is a central concept in Taoist philosophy, particularly in the *Tao Te Ching*, attributed to Laozi. See Edward Slingerland, *Effortless Action: Wu-wei as Conceptual Metaphor and Spiritual Ideal in Early China* (Oxford University Press, 2003).

5 Ray Anderson's transformation of Interface, Inc., discussed in Chapter 2, is documented in Ray Anderson with Robin White, *Confessions of a Radical Industrialist: Profits, People, Purpose—Doing Business by Respecting the Earth* (St. Martin's Press, 2009). Interface's service-based carpet tile leasing model ("Evergreen Services Agreement") began in 1995.

6 MUD Jeans, founded by Bert van Son in the Netherlands in 2012, operates a "Lease A Jeans" circular model where customers can lease jeans and return them for recycling. See mudjeans.eu and Ellen MacArthur Foundation, *A New Textiles Economy: Redesigning Fashion's Future* (EMF, 2017).

7 Patagonia, Inc., was founded by Yvon Chouinard in 1973. In September 2022, Chouinard transferred ownership to the Patagonia Purpose Trust and the

Holdfast Collective, a nonprofit organization. See Yvon Chouinard, *Let My People Go Surfing: The Education of a Reluctant Businessman*, 2nd ed. (Penguin, 2016), and Yvon Chouinard, "Earth Is Now Our Only Shareholder," September 14, 2022, patagonia.com/ownership/.

8 Fairphone achieved B Corp certification in 2015. For more on the company's philosophy and goals, see Fairphone, "Our Impact," fairphone.com/en/impact/.

9 See Lauren Kaori Gurley, "Everlane Lays Off Employees Who Tried to Unionize," *Vice*, March 27, 2020, and Chavie Lieber, "Everlane's Radical Transparency Claim Fell Apart," *Business of Fashion*, July 15, 2020.

10 Tanka Bar, founded in 2006 by Karlene Hunter of the Oglala Lakota Nation and Mark Tilsen, produces meat bars using buffalo from Native-managed herds. The enterprise supports prairie ecosystem restoration and economic development on the Pine Ridge Indian Reservation. See tankabar.com.

11 Riversimple Movement Ltd., founded by Hugo Spowers in the UK in 2001, develops hydrogen fuel cell vehicles under a "sale of service" model. The company's governance structure includes six custodians representing different stakeholder groups. See riversimple.com.

12 Grameen Shakti ("Rural Energy") was founded in 1996 as a not-for-profit company under Grameen Bank. See gshakti.org; Right Livelihood Foundation, "Grameen Shakti," rightlivelihood.org/the-change-makers/find-a-laureate/grameen-shakti/; and Ashden, "Grameen Shakti," ashden.org/awards/winners/grameen-shakti/.

Chapter 4

1 Mondragon Corporation was founded in 1956 in the Basque region of Spain; for more information, see the case study later in this chapter. Cooperative Home Care Associates (chcany.org) was founded in the South Bronx in 1985. Both are discussed in Hilary Abell, *Worker Cooperatives: Pathways to Scale* (Democracy Collaborative, 2014). See also Peter Walsh, Michael Peck, and Ibon Zugasti, "Why the U.S. Needs More Worker-Owned Companies," *Harvard Business Review*, August 8, 2018.

2 REI (Recreational Equipment, Inc.), founded in 1938 as a consumer cooperative, has over 23 million members and operates more than 180 retail locations. Members receive annual dividends ("Co-op Member Rewards") based on purchases. See REI, "About REI," rei.com/about-rei.

3 The Dudley Street Neighborhood Initiative (DSNI), founded in 1984, became the first community organization in the United States to gain eminent domain authority in 1988. The Dudley Neighbors Inc. community land trust has developed over 225 units of affordable housing. See Peter Medoff and Holly Sklar, *Streets of Hope: The Fall and Rise of an Urban Neighborhood* (South End Press, 1994).

4 The Champlain Housing Trust, formed in 2006 through the merger of Burlington Community Land Trust (founded 1984) and Lake Champlain Housing Development Corporation, is one of the largest community land trusts in the United States, with over 2,800 affordable homes in its portfolio. See Champlain Housing Trust, "About," getahome.org/about/.

5 Ecosia, a search engine founded in Berlin in 2009, operates under steward ownership through the Purpose Foundation. The company donates 100 percent of profits to tree planting and has funded the planting of over 200 million trees. See ecosia.org and Purpose, "Steward-Ownership," purpose-economy.org/en/whats-steward-ownership/.

6 The Robert Bosch Stiftung (Foundation) GmbH holds 94 percent of Robert Bosch GmbH, one of the world's largest suppliers of automotive components. The Carl Zeiss Foundation, established in 1889, owns both Carl Zeiss AG and SCHOTT AG. The Novo Nordisk Foundation, established in 1989, controls Novo Nordisk A/S, a global healthcare company. These purpose trusts demonstrate multigenerational mission protection at industrial scale. See Jens Lowitzsch, ed., *The PEPPER IV Report: Benchmarking of Employee Participation in Profits and Enterprise Results in the Member and Candidate Countries of the European Union* (Free University of Berlin, 2009).

7 Bears Ears National Monument, established by President Obama in December 2016 and reduced by President Trump in 2017, was restored by President Biden in October 2021. The Bears Ears Commission, comprising representatives from five tribal nations (Hopi, Navajo, Ute Mountain Ute, Ute Indian Tribe, and Zuni), advises on comanagement. See US Department of the Interior, Bureau of Land Management, "Bears Ears National Monument," blm.gov/visit/bears-ears-national-monument.

8 In 2019, the City of Eureka, California, transferred 202 acres of Tuluwat Island (formerly "Indian Island") to the Wiyot Tribe, marking the first voluntary return of land to a tribe by a local government without compensation. The site was the location of the 1860 massacre of Wiyot people. See *Indian Country Today*, "City of Eureka Agrees to Return Sacred Land to Wiyot Tribe," October 21, 2019.

9 RUNWAY Roots (formerly The Runway Project), founded by Jessica Norwood in 2016, provides pre-seed "Believe in You Money"—low-interest loans and mentorship—to Black entrepreneurs, addressing the "friends and family" funding gap created by racial wealth inequalities. Shared Capital Cooperative (formerly Northcountry Cooperative Development Fund), founded in 1978, provides loans exclusively to cooperatives throughout the United States. Borrower cooperatives participate in governance by electing board members. The Northeast Farmers of Color Land Trust (NEFOC), founded in 2018, works to return land to Black, Indigenous, and people of color (BIPOC) farmers in the

northeastern United States through a community land trust model. See runway .family, sharedcapital.coop, and nefoclandtrust.org.

10 A full history is provided at Mondragon, "All Our History," mondragon -corporation.com/en/history/.

Chapter 5

1 RSF Social Finance, founded in 1984 (originally Rudolf Steiner Foundation), provides loans, grants, and investments to enterprises working toward social and ecological health. RSF pioneered transparent pricing, bringing borrowers and lenders together quarterly to set interest rates collaboratively. See rsfsocialfinance.org.

2 Zebras Unite, founded in 2017 by Jennifer Brandel, Mara Zepeda, Astrid Scholz, and Aniyia Williams, advocates for an alternative to "unicorn" venture capital culture. The movement supports "zebra" companies that are profitable and improve society. See Zebras Unite, "Zebras Fix What Unicorns Break," *Medium*, March 8, 2017, and zebrasunite.coop.

3 Beneficial State Bank, founded in 2007 in Oakland, California, is a CDFI and B Corp owned by nonprofit foundations. The bank's products and services are intentionally designed to optimize positive social and environmental outcomes; extractive lending investments are excluded. See Beneficial State Bank, "About Us," beneficialstatebank.com/about-us.

4 Self-Help Credit Union, founded in Durham, North Carolina, in 1980, is one of the nation's largest community development lenders, having provided over $9 billion in financing to underserved borrowers. See self-help.org.

5 Triodos Bank, founded in the Netherlands in 1980, finances only enterprises that create social, environmental, or cultural value. The bank publishes details of every loan and investment on its website. See Triodos, "Know Where Your Money Goes," triodos.com/en/know-where-your-money-goes.

6 Toniic (toniic.com) is a global network of impact investors. ANDE (Aspen Network of Development Entrepreneurs, andeglobal.org) connects small and growing businesses with capital and support. Investors Circle (investorscircle .org) has facilitated over $275 million in investments to impact enterprises since 1992. SWAN Impact Network (swanimpact.org) is a national angel group investing in early-stage, purpose-driven startups.

Chapter 6

1 Margaret Thatcher's statement "there is no such thing as society" appeared in an interview with *Woman's Own* magazine titled "Aids, education and the year 2000!" published on October 31, 1987. The full quotation is: "There is no such thing [as society]. There are individual men and women and there are families."

2 Adam Smith, *The Theory of Moral Sentiments* (1759; repr., Cambridge University Press, 2002), opening lines. Smith's earlier work on moral philosophy is essential context for *An Inquiry into the Nature and Causes of the Wealth of Nations* (1776). The "invisible hand" appears in both works but serves different argumentative purposes. See Dennis C. Rasmussen, *The Problems and Promise of Commercial Society: Adam Smith's Response to Rousseau* (Penn State University Press, 2008).

3 The EU Emissions Trading System (EU ETS), launched in 2005, is the world's largest carbon market. Verified emissions in covered sectors fell approximately 47 percent between 2005 and 2023. See European Environment Agency, "EU Emissions Trading System (ETS) Data Viewer," eea.europa.eu /en/analysis /maps-and-charts/emissions-trading-viewer-1-dashboards.

4 Fashion Revolution, founded in 2013 following the Rana Plaza factory collapse in Bangladesh that killed 1,134 garment workers, organizes the annual "Who Made My Clothes?" campaign. See fashionrevolution.org and the Fashion Transparency Index, published annually since 2016.

5 For more information, see Center for Good Food Purchasing, "Oakland Unified School District Adopts the Good Food Purchasing Program," goodfoodpurchasing .org, and Oakland Unified School District, "Our Food," ousd.org/nutrition-services /our-food.

6 The Brixton Pound, launched in 2009 in Brixton, South London, was a local complementary currency designed to support independent local businesses. The physical currency was retired in 2020, though the digital version continued. See brixtonpound.org.

7 The Long-Term Stock Exchange (LTSE), founded by Eric Ries and approved by the SEC in 2019, requires listed companies to adopt policies promoting long-term thinking, specifically mandating commitments to five core principles including stakeholder consideration and long-term strategy. See ltse.com.

8 B Lab, the nonprofit behind B Corp certification, was founded in 2006. As of early 2026, over ten thousand companies in more than a hundred countries are Certified B Corps. See bcorporation.net.

9 The GDPR took effect May 25, 2018. Germany's Renewable Energy Act (*Erneuerbare-Energien-Gesetz*, EEG) was enacted in 2000, establishing feed-in tariffs that drove global solar cost reductions. The Montreal Protocol on Substances that Deplete the Ozone Layer, part of the Vienna Convention for the Protection of the Ozone Layer, was agreed in 1987; in 2009, these became the first and only global environmental treaties to achieve ratification by all UN member parties. The Danish deposit return scheme, established in 2002, is widely recognized as one of the best in the world.

10 Kudumbashree ("Prosperity of the Family"), launched by the Government of Kerala in 1998, organizes women through a three-tier community network. The

program helped Kerala become the first Indian state to declare elimination of extreme poverty, achieved in November 2025. See kudumbashree.org and Kerala State Planning Board reports.

11 Platform cooperativism was conceptualized by Trebor Scholz. See Trebor Scholz, *Platform Cooperativism: Challenging the Corporate Sharing Economy* (Rosa Luxemburg Stiftung, 2016). For additional information on the examples cited here, see stocksy.com, upandgo.coop, fairbnb.coop, and drivers.coop.

Part III

1 W. S. Merwin, "Witness," in *The Rain in the Trees* (Alfred A. Knopf, 1988). Merwin (1927–2019) served as US Poet Laureate from 2010 to 2011 and received the Pulitzer Prize for Poetry in 1971 and 2009.

2 *Orion* magazine was founded in 1982 as a standalone journal. In 1992, the author was asked by Board Chairman Marion Gilliam to help him establish The Orion Society, a new 501(c)(3) organization into which the magazine folded. As the founding director (1992–2004), the author led the Society in publishing *Orion* magazine and *Orion Afield* magazine; pioneering place-based education; launching the Orion Grassroots Network (which at its zenith included over one thousand member organizations); creating the Forgotten Language Tour (1992–2003), which brought environmental writers and poets to communities across North America, and the John Hay Award; and organizing numerous leadership summits and conferences, including the 1996 "Watershed: Writers, Nature, and Community" conference at the US Library of Congress and the 1999 millennium conference "Fire & Grit: Working for Nature and Community" at the National Conservation Training Center. See *Orion* magazine archives, orionmagazine.org.

3 McKibben's *The End of Nature* (Random House, 1989) was the first book for a general audience on climate change. McKibben later founded 350.org (2008) and Third Act (2021).

4 The organized campaign to manufacture doubt about climate science is documented in Naomi Oreskes and Erik M. Conway, *Merchants of Doubt: How a Handful of Scientists Obscured the Truth on Issues from Tobacco Smoke to Global Warming* (Bloomsbury Press, 2010). See also Union of Concerned Scientists, *The Climate Deception Dossiers* (UCS, 2015).

5 Stockholm International Peace Research Institute (SIPRI), "Trends in World Military Expenditure, 2024," SIPRI Fact Sheet/release, April 2025, reporting global military expenditure of approximately $2.718 trillion in 2024 (current US dollars).

Chapter 7

1 The calculation that redirecting approximately 10 percent of global military spending could make decisive progress toward eliminating extreme poverty

draws on United Nations, *Financing for Sustainable Development Report 2023* (UN/DESA, 2023), and SIPRI analyses of military versus development spending. The SDG financing gap is estimated at $4.2 trillion annually; $270 billion represents roughly 6 percent of this gap but could catalyze additional investment.

2 The International Monetary Fund (IMF) estimated global GDP losses from COVID-19 at approximately $12.5 trillion through 2024, with the World Bank estimating total economic impact exceeding $20 trillion when including long-term effects. See IMF, *World Economic Outlook*, various editions 2020–2024. The Johns Hopkins Coronavirus Resource Center documented over seven million confirmed deaths globally.

3 The $7–$30 return on investment for ecosystem restoration is documented in United Nations Environment Programme, *Becoming #GenerationRestoration: Ecosystem Restoration for People, Nature and Climate* (UNEP, 2021). See also Rudolph S. De Groot et al., "Benefits of Investing in Ecosystem Restoration," *Conservation Biology* 27, no. 6 (2013): 1286–1293.

4 Siddharth Narayan et al., "The Value of Coastal Wetlands for Flood Damage Reduction in the Northeastern USA," *Scientific Reports* 7 (2017): 9463. The study found that coastal wetlands prevented over $625 million in direct property damages during Hurricane Sandy. New Jersey alone avoided an estimated $425 million in damages due to wetland presence.

5 The program was initiated in 1997. See National Research Council, *Watershed Management for Potable Water Supply: Assessing the New York City Strategy* (National Academies Press, 2000).

6 See Global Preparedness Monitoring Board, *A World in Disorder: Global Preparedness Monitoring Board Annual Report 2020* (World Health Organization, 2020), and World Bank and World Health Organization, *Analysis of Pandemic Preparedness and Response (PPR) Architecture, Financing Needs, Gaps and Mechanisms*, prepared for the G20 Joint Finance and Health Task Force (World Bank, 2022).

7 Viroj Tangcharoensathien et al., *Universal Coverage Scheme in Thailand: Equity Outcomes and Future Agendas to Meet Challenges*, World Health Report (2010) Background Paper No. 43 (World Health Organization, 2010). See also Supon Limwattananon, Viroj Tangcharoensathien, and Phusit Prakongsai, "Catastrophic and Poverty Impacts of Health Payments: Results from National Household Surveys in Thailand," *Bulletin of the World Health Organization* 85, no. 8 (2007): 600–606.

8 W. E. B. Du Bois, *Black Reconstruction in America, 1860–1880* (Harcourt, Brace and Company, 1935; repr., Free Press, 1998), 602.

9 For a description of the long-term effects of the Perry Preschool Project, see James J. Heckman, "Skill Formation and the Economics of Investing in

Disadvantaged Children," *Science* 312, no. 5782 (2006): 1900–1902. Research by Heckman and colleagues has identified returns of between 7 and 13 percent for this and similar programs; see James J. Heckman et al., "The Rate of Return to the High/Scope Perry Preschool Program," *Journal of Public Economics* 94, nos. 1–2 (2010), 114–128, and Jorge Luis García et al., "Quantifying the Life-Cycle Benefits of an Influential Early Childhood Program," *Journal of Political Economy* 128, no. 7 (2020): 2502–2541.

10 Sónia Gonçalves, "The Effects of Participatory Budgeting on Municipal Expenditures and Infant Mortality in Brazil," *World Development* 53 (2014): 94–110. Gonçalves found that Brazilian municipalities using participatory budgeting between 1990 and 2004 channeled significantly larger budget shares to sanitation and health services, accompanied by measurable reductions in infant mortality. See also Ioanni Delsantea and Luciana Inês Gomes Miron, "Urban Growth, Regeneration and Social Inclusion in Porto Alegre: The City Entrance Integrated Programme Case Study," *UPLanD: Journal of Urban Planning, Landscape & Environmental Design* 2, no. 2 (2017), 239–254.

11 The Vietnamese-American community of Village de l'Est in New Orleans East rebuilt remarkably quickly after Hurricane Katrina struck in 2005. Researchers attribute this to dense social networks, strong community institutions (particularly the Mary Queen of Vietnam Church), and established mutual aid practices. See Eric Tang, "A Gulf Unites Us: The Vietnamese Americans of Black New Orleans East," *American Quarterly* 63, no. 1 (2011): 117–149, and Karen J. Leong et al., "Resilient History and the Rebuilding of a Community," *Journal of American History* 94, no. 3 (2007): 770–778.

12 Approximately 50 percent of shallow-water corals died during the mass bleaching events in the Great Barrier Reef in 2016 and 2017. See Terry P. Hughes et al., "Global Warming Transforms Coral Reef Assemblages," *Nature* 556 (2018): 492–496.

13 Uluru (formerly Ayers Rock) is a sacred site of the Anangu people in Australia's Northern Territory. *Tjukurpa* (Dreamtime) refers to the Anangu creation period and continuing spiritual law. Climbing Uluru was permanently closed to visitors on October 26, 2019, at the request of traditional owners. See Parks Australia, "Uluru-Kata Tjuta National Park," uluru.gov.au.

14 The Kangaroo Island bushfires (December 2019–February 2020) burned approximately 211,000 hectares (48 percent of the island's land area). See South Australia Country Fire Service reports and conservation assessments, 2020.

15 Researchers from the University of Sydney initially estimated that nearly one billion animals died in the 2019–2020 "Black Summer" bushfire season; a subsequent analysis by the World Wildlife Fund (WWF) estimated that approximately three billion animals were killed or displaced. See Lily M. van Eeden et al., *Impacts of the Unprecedented 2019–2020 Bushfires on Australian Animals* (WWF-Australia, 2020).

16 See Australian Government, Department of Defence, *2020 Defence Strategic Update* (Commonwealth of Australia, 2020).

17 National Institute of Building Sciences, *Natural Hazard Mitigation Saves: 2019 Report* (NIBS, 2019). The study analyzed twenty-three years of federal mitigation grant funding and found savings of $6 for every $1 invested in FEMA mitigation grants, with riverine flood mitigation returning $7 per $1 and building code improvements returning $4 per $1.

18 Helen Ding et al., *The Roots of Prosperity: The Economics and Finance of Restoring Land* (World Resources Institute, 2018). This finding is corroborated by Organisation for Economic Co-operation and Development, *Biodiversity: Finance and the Economic and Business Case for Action* (OECD, 2019), and the UN Decade on Ecosystem Restoration Finance Task Force.

19 Jameel Institute, Imperial College London, epidemiological-economic modeling research presented at Center for Global Development, October 2023. The study projected outcomes for COVID-like pandemic scenarios and found expected economic gains in averted GDP loss of $1,102 per dollar spent on preparedness (United States estimate).

20 Longitudinal studies have shown that high-quality early childhood programs can yield returns of between 7 and 13 percent. See James J. Heckman et al., "The Rate of Return to the High/Scope Perry Preschool Program," *Journal of Public Economics* 94, nos. 1–2 (2010), 114–128, and Jorge Luis García et al., "Quantifying the Life-Cycle Benefits of an Influential Early Childhood Program," *Journal of Political Economy* 128, no. 7 (2020): 2502–2541. Returns accrue through reduced special education costs, lower crime rates, improved health outcomes, higher earnings, and increased tax revenue.

21 Commission on a Global Health Risk Framework for the Future, *The Neglected Dimension of Global Security: A Framework to Counter Infectious Disease Crises* (National Academies Press, 2016). See also Institute for Economics and Peace, *Global Peace Index* annual reports on conflict prevention cost-effectiveness.

22 Costa Rica abolished its military on December 1, 1948, following a brief civil war, under President José Figueres Ferrer. The decision was enshrined in Article 12 of the 1949 Constitution. See Martha Honey, *Hostile Acts: U.S. Policy in Costa Rica in the 1980s* (University Press of Florida, 1994).

23 Per the United Nations Development Programme, life expectancy at birth in Costa Rica is 80.8 years, compared with 79.3 years in the United States. The country has a literacy rate of 98 percent, and a quarter of the national territory is preserved by the National System of Conservation Areas. Costa Rica is sixth in the global happiness rankings, according to the 2025 World Happiness Report. See United Nations Development Programme, *Human Development Report 2025* (UNDP, 2025), Statistical Annex, Table 1; UNESCO Institute for

Statistics, "Adult Literacy Rate, Population 15+ Years, Both Sexes—Costa Rica," *UIS Data Browser*, databrowser.uis.unesco.org; World Bank Group, "How Costa Rica Is Investing in a Landscape Approach to Build a Sustainable Future," March 21, 2022; and John F. Helliwell et al., eds., *World Happiness Report 2025* (Oxford University Centre for Wellbeing Research, 2025).

Chapter 8

1 Community health workers (CHWs) are lay health workers who provide health education, outreach, and basic services within their communities. The WHO estimates over five million CHWs operate globally. See World Health Organization, *WHO Guideline on Health Policy and System Support to Optimize Community Health Worker Programmes* (WHO, 2018).

2 The CCC, established by President Franklin D. Roosevelt in 1933, employed approximately three million young men during its nine-year existence. CCC workers planted over three billion trees, constructed trails and fire lookouts, and built much of the infrastructure still used in American public lands. See Neil M. Maher, *Nature's New Deal: The Civilian Conservation Corps and the Roots of the American Environmental Movement* (Oxford University Press, 2008).

3 Farmer-to-farmer (*campesino a campesino*) agroecology networks originated in Central America in the 1970s and have spread throughout Latin America. See Eric Holt-Giménez, *Campesino a Campesino: Voices from Latin America's Farmer to Farmer Movement for Sustainable Agriculture* (Food First Books, 2006), and La Vía Campesina, "Agroecology," viacampesina.org.

4 Restorative justice practices originated in Indigenous traditions and were formalized in New Zealand's juvenile justice system in 1989. Studies consistently show reduced recidivism compared to conventional incarceration. See Lawrence W. Sherman and Heather Strang, *Restorative Justice: The Evidence* (Smith Institute, 2007), and Danielle Sered, *Until We Reckon: Violence, Mass Incarceration, and a Road to Repair* (The New Press, 2019).

Chapter 9

1 The New Patriotism series included Wendell Berry's *In the Presence of Fear: Three Essays for a Changed World* (Orion Society, 2001); Wendell Berry and David James Duncan's *Citizens Dissent: Security, Morality, and Leadership in an Age of Terror* (Orion Society, 2003); Barry Lopez, Richard Nelson, and Terry Tempest Williams's *Patriotism and the American Land* (Orion Society, 2002); and Terry Tempest Williams's *The Open Space of Democracy* (Orion Society, 2004). Berry's central argument—that a society dependent on centralized systems and fossil energy is structurally fragile regardless of military expenditure—anticipated the "fortress thinking" framework developed in this chapter. Through the Triad Institute, I subsequently published David James Duncan's

God Laughs & Plays: Churchless Sermons in Response to the Preachments of the Fundamentalist Right (Triad Books, 2006), a National Bestseller and Push-cart Prize winner that extended The New Patriotism series's challenge to the militarized security paradigm.

2 The Global Scenario Group, convened by the Stockholm Environment Institute, developed scenarios including "Fortress World" and "Great Transition" in the 1990s and 2000s. See Paul Raskin et al., *Great Transition: The Promise and Lure of the Times Ahead* (Stockholm Environment Institute, 2002). Paul Raskin is founding director of the Tellus Institute.

3 See Institute for Economics and Peace (IEP), *Global Peace Index 2024* (IEP, 2024). See also IEP, *The Economic Value of Peace* (2024).

4 Nordic countries integrate civil preparedness into national security strategy through organizations like Sweden's Civil Contingencies Agency (MSB), Finland's National Emergency Supply Agency, and Norway's Directorate for Civil Protection. These systems emphasize volunteer networks, food security planning, and community resilience. See Bengt Sundelius and Jesper Grönvall, "Strategic Dilemmas of Biosecurity in the European Union," *Biosecurity and Bioterrorism* 2, no. 1 (2004): 17–23.

5 Community-owned renewable energy cooperatives proliferated across Germany following the 2000 Renewable Energy Sources Act (EEG). By 2020, approximately 40 percent of Germany's renewable energy capacity was citizen-owned. See Craig Morris and Arne Jungjohann, *Energy Democracy: Germany's Energiewende to Renewables* (Palgrave Macmillan, 2016).

6 The Meru Herbs cooperative, founded in the 1990s, has grown to include over four hundred member households. See meruherbs.com and Nicola Taylor, "True Impact Starts Here—the Story of Meru Herbs," November 5, 2025, trueorigin.org.uk/true-impact-starts-here.

7 African Risk Capacity (ARC), established by the African Union in 2012, is a sovereign disaster risk insurance pool. Member states pay premiums and receive rapid payouts following verified climate disasters, enabling faster response than traditional humanitarian appeals. See arcafrica.org.

Chapter 10

1 Menominee Tribal Enterprises (MTE) has practiced sustained-yield forestry in Wisconsin since 1854, harvesting over 2 billion board feet of timber while actually increasing standing timber volume from approximately 1.2 billion board feet in 1854 to over 1.9 billion board feet 160 years later. The Menominee forest maintains greater biodiversity than surrounding managed lands. See Menominee Tribal Enterprises, "The Forest Keepers," mtewood.com, and Dave Logan Mausel, T. Waupochick and Marshall Pecore, "Menominee Forestry: Past, Present, Future," *Journal of Forestry* 115, no. 5 (2017): 366–369.

2 The United Nations Monetary and Financial Conference, commonly known as the Bretton Woods Conference, was held July 1–22, 1944, at the Mount Washington Hotel in Bretton Woods, New Hampshire. It established the International Monetary Fund and the International Bank for Reconstruction and Development (World Bank). See Benn Steil, *The Battle of Bretton Woods: John Maynard Keynes, Harry Dexter White, and the Making of a New World Order* (Princeton University Press, 2013).

3 Defense as a Service, Prevention Dividend, and Prevention Ratio are trademarks of Laurie Lane-Zucker. The frameworks are released for public use under the principle that paradigm shifts require many builders; the trademarks protect quality and coherence as the approaches scale.

Part IV

1 The term "impact entrepreneur" was coined by the author in 2011 when founding his company, Impact Entrepreneur. The term has since been adopted across the field, appearing in university programs, foundation strategies, and professional identities globally.

2 Kevin Kelly, *What Technology Wants* (Viking, 2010). Kelly defines the "technium" as "the greater, global, massively interconnected system of technology vibrating around us," which has its own wants, tendencies, and urges.

3 Robin Wall Kimmerer, *Braiding Sweetgrass: Indigenous Wisdom, Scientific Knowledge, and the Teachings of Plants* (Milkweed Editions, 2013). Kimmerer, a member of the Citizen Potawatomi Nation and Professor of Environmental and Forest Biology at SUNY College of Environmental Science and Forestry, explores how Indigenous languages encode different relationships with the natural world.

4 Writers who participated in the Forgotten Language Tour (1992–2003) included Bill McKibben, Terry Tempest Williams, Gary Snyder, Wendell Berry, Barry Lopez, David James Duncan, Pattiann Rogers, Robert Michael Pyle, Scott Russell Sanders, Richard Nelson, Ann Zwinger, and dozens of others. The tour brought environmental writers and poets to communities across North America through The Orion Society.

5 The term "place-based education" was coined by Laurie Lane-Zucker and John Elder at Middlebury College in the mid-1990s. See David Sobel, *Place-Based Education: Connecting Classrooms and Communities* (Orion Society, 2004), and Gregory A. Smith, "Place-Based Education: Learning to Be Where We Are," *Phi Delta Kappan* 83, no. 8 (2002): 584–594.

6 Place-based investing emerged in the 2010s as the financial application of place-based education concepts. The Federal Reserve Bank of San Francisco has published extensively on place-based investment strategies.

7 In ecological succession, pioneer species are the first organisms to colonize an area after a disturbance (fire, flood, volcanic activity). They modify the environment, creating conditions for other species to establish. See Eugene P. Odum and Gary W. Barrett, *Fundamentals of Ecology*, 5th ed. (Cengage Learning, 2005).

Chapter 11

1 The concept of organizational culture as "the pattern of assumptions, values, and behaviors" draws on Edgar H. Schein, *Organizational Culture and Leadership*, 5th ed. (Wiley, 2017). Schein identifies three levels of culture: artifacts (visible), espoused values (stated), and underlying assumptions (unconscious).

2 Patagonia's cultural practices are documented in Yvon Chouinard, *Let My People Go Surfing: The Education of a Reluctant Businessman*, 2nd ed. (Penguin, 2016), and Vincent Stanley and Yvon Chouinard, *The Responsible Company: What We've Learned from Patagonia's First 40 Years* (Patagonia Books, 2012). The "Let My People Go Surfing" flex-time policy and environmental internship programs are described in company materials; see patagonia.com.

3 1% for the Planet was founded by Yvon Chouinard and Craig Mathews in 2002, though Patagonia had been donating 1 percent of sales since 1985. As of early 2026, over 11,600 businesses and environmental organizations participate globally. See onepercentfortheplanet.org.

4 In September 2022, Yvon Chouinard transferred ownership of Patagonia (valued at approximately $3 billion) to the Patagonia Purpose Trust and Holdfast Collective, a 501(c)(4) nonprofit dedicated to fighting the environmental crisis. See Yvon Chouinard, "Earth Is Now Our Only Shareholder," September 14, 2022, patagonia.com/ownership/.

5 Mondragon's cultural and educational infrastructure, including Mondragon University (founded 1997), is documented in Keith Bradley and Stephen Hill, "The Mondragon System: Cooperation at Work," *ILR Review* 45, no. 4 (1992): 692–702, and in Mondragon Corporation's annual reports. The solidarity fund for struggling cooperatives (*Fondo Central de Intercooperación*) is a distinctive feature of the system.

Chapter 12

1 See Donella Meadows, "Leverage Points: Places to Intervene in a System," donellameadows.org/archives/leverage-points-places-to-intervene-in-a-system/. Meadows identifies twelve leverage points in increasing order of effectiveness, with changing the paradigm or mindset from which the system arises as the second most powerful (after transcending paradigms entirely). The essay, originally published in 1999, was later included in *Thinking in Systems: A Primer* (Chelsea Green, 2008).

2 According to Gallup polling, support for same-sex marriage in the United States increased from 27 percent in 1996 to 60 percent in 2015, as the Supreme Court prepared to rule on its legality. See Justin McCarthy, "Record-High 60% of Americans Support Same-Sex Marriage," Gallup.com, May 19, 2015. See also Marc Solomon, *Winning Marriage: The Inside Story of How Same-Sex Couples Took on the Politicians and Pundits—and Won* (ForeEdge, 2014).

3 The narrative shift around tobacco is documented in Allan M. Brandt, *The Cigarette Century: The Rise, Fall, and Deadly Persistence of the Product That Defined America* (Basic Books, 2007). The 1964 report of the Surgeon General's Advisory Committee on Smoking and Health marked a turning point, but significant regulatory change took decades more.

4 The Land Back movement encompasses diverse efforts to return land to Indigenous stewardship. See David Treuer, "Return the National Parks to the Tribes," *The Atlantic*, April 12, 2021, and the NDN Collective's LANDBACK campaign (ndncollective.org/landback/). Standing Rock (2016–2017) galvanized international attention to Indigenous sovereignty and environmental protection.

5 The term "greenwashing" was coined by environmentalist Jay Westerveld in 1986. "Impact-washing" emerged more recently to describe similar practices in impact investing. See Tariq Fancy, "The Secret Diary of a 'Sustainable Investor'," *Medium*, August 2021, for a critique by a former BlackRock sustainable investing executive.

Chapter 13

1 The concept of the "attention economy" was developed by Herbert A. Simon and elaborated by Michael H. Goldhaber. For surveillance capitalism specifically, see Shoshana Zuboff, *The Age of Surveillance Capitalism: The Fight for a Human Future at the New Frontier of Power* (PublicAffairs, 2019).

2 Variable ratio reinforcement schedules, first described by B. F. Skinner, are widely used in social media design. See Natasha Dow Schüll, *Addiction by Design: Machine Gambling in Las Vegas* (Princeton University Press, 2012), and Adam Alter, *Irresistible: The Rise of Addictive Technology and the Business of Keeping Us Hooked* (Penguin Press, 2017).

3 Initial reporting based on a whistleblower's account suggested Cambridge Analytica had harvested data from approximately fifty million Facebook users for political targeting. Facebook later disclosed that it believed the breach had affected up to eighty-seven million users. See Carole Cadwalladr and Emma Graham-Harrison, "Revealed: 50 Million Facebook Profiles Harvested for Cambridge Analytica in Major Data Breach," *The Guardian*, March 17, 2018, and BBC, "Facebook Scandal 'Hit 87 Million Users'," April 5, 2018.

4 Research by time tracking software provider RescueTime shows the average knowledge worker checks in on email or IM every six minutes, and 40 percent

never get more than thirty minutes of uninterrupted worktime in a day. See Jory MacKay, "Communication Overload: Our Research Shows Most Workers Can't Go 6 Minutes Without Checking Email or IM," *RescueTime Blog*, July 12, 2018.

5 Finland's media literacy curriculum, integrated from primary school through university, is described in Eliza Mackintosh, "Finland Is Winning the War on Fake News. What It's Learned May Be Crucial to Western Democracy," *CNN*, May 22, 2019. Finland consistently ranks highest in the Media Literacy Index produced by the Open Society Institute—Sofia.

6 Basecamp's attention-protective practices are described in Jason Fried and David Heinemeier Hansson, *It Doesn't Have to Be Crazy at Work* (HarperBusiness, 2018). The company has implemented "Library Rules" hours, forty-hour work weeks, and asynchronous-first communication. For case studies of Patagonia's and Mondragon's organizational cultures, see Chapter 11.

7 The GDPR took effect May 25, 2018. The Digital Services Act (DSA) was adopted in 2022, requiring algorithmic transparency from large platforms. France's "right to disconnect" law (El Khomri law) was enacted in 2016.

Chapter 14

1 The concept of the "market self" draws on Charles Taylor, *Sources of the Self: The Making of the Modern Identity* (Harvard University Press, 1989), and Zygmunt Bauman, *Consuming Life* (Polity, 2007). See also Alain de Botton, *Status Anxiety* (Vintage, 2005).

2 The Tajikistan Civil War (1992–1997) resulted from the collapse of the Soviet Union and competing regional, political, and ideological factions. Robert Middleton and Huw Thomas's *Tajikistan and the High Pamirs* (Odyssey Books, 2008) provides historical context.

3 The Transition Towns movement was founded by Rob Hopkins in Totnes, England, in 2006. See Rob Hopkins, *The Transition Handbook: From Oil Dependency to Local Resilience* (Green Books, 2008), and *The Transition Companion: Making Your Community More Resilient in Uncertain Times* (Chelsea Green, 2011). As of early 2026, the movement has spread to sixty-seven countries with thousands of local initiatives; see transitionnetwork.org.

Part V

1 B Lab was founded in 2006 by Jay Coen Gilbert, Bart Houlahan, and Andrew Kassoy. The first B Corporations were certified in 2007, with approximately twenty-five "founding B Corps" including Hotfrog. As of early 2026, over ten thousand companies in more than a hundred countries have been certified. See bcorporation.net.

2 The term "impact investing" was coined at a 2007 Rockefeller Foundation conference. As of 2025, the GIIN estimated the impact investing market at over

$1.5 trillion (see GIIN Impact Investor Survey reports, 2024 and 2025). Investors Circle (investors-circle.org), founded in 1992, is one of the oldest impact investor networks in the United States. It has facilitated over $275 million in investments to more than 350 hundred enterprises. The Social Venture Network (svn.org, now part of Social Venture Circle) was founded in 1987.

3 Lehman Brothers filed for bankruptcy on September 15, 2008. It was the largest bankruptcy in US history ($639 billion in assets). Bear Stearns was acquired by JPMorgan Chase in March 2008. Merrill Lynch was sold to Bank of America on September 14, 2008. AIG received an $85 billion federal bailout on September 16, 2008. See Andrew Ross Sorkin, *Too Big to Fail: The Inside Story of How Wall Street and Washington Fought to Save the Financial System—and Themselves* (Viking, 2009).

4 Abram is an ecologist, philosopher, and sleight-of-hand magician whose work explores the relationship between perception, language, and ecological consciousness. See David Abram, *The Spell of the Sensuous: Perception and Language in a More-Than-Human World* (Vintage, 1996), and *Becoming Animal: An Earthly Cosmology* (Vintage, 2010).

5 The Global Impact Investing Network (GIIN) was founded in 2009. See thegiin.org.

6 The United Nations Sustainable Development Goals (SDGs) were adopted in September 2015 as part of the 2030 Agenda for Sustainable Development. The 17 goals and 169 targets provide a shared framework for global development priorities. See sdgs.un.org/goals.

Chapter 15

1 Community land trusts originated in the US civil rights movement, with New Communities Inc. (Georgia, 1969) as an early model. The Burlington Community Land Trust (1984, now Champlain Housing Trust) pioneered the urban CLT model. See John Emmeus Davis, ed., *The Community Land Trust Reader* (Lincoln Institute of Land Policy, 2010).

2 Decidim (decidim.org) is a free, open-source participatory democracy platform developed by the Barcelona City Council beginning in 2016. The name means "let's decide" in Catalan. As of 2026, it has been adopted by over four hundred institutions in more than thirty countries.

3 Cooperative Energy Futures (cooperativeenergyfutures.com) is a community-owned clean energy cooperative founded in 2009 in Minneapolis, Minnesota, originating from pilot programs at Macalester College. For discussion of Grameen Shakti's model of community-based solar energy, see Chapter 3.

4 The Open Source Seed Initiative (OSSI), founded in 2012, uses an "open source pledge" to ensure seed varieties remain freely available and cannot be patented. See osseeds.org and Jack Kloppenburg, "Re-Purposing the Master's

Tools: The Open Source Seed Initiative and the Struggle for Seed Sovereignty," *Journal of Peasant Studies* 41, no. 6 (2014): 1225–1246.

5 WikiHouse, founded by Alastair Parvin in 2011, is an open-source construction system allowing homes to be digitally fabricated locally. See wikihouse.cc and Alastair Parvin, "Architecture for the People by the People," TED Talk, 2013.

6 The Structural Genomics Consortium (SGC), founded in 2004, is a public-private partnership committed to open-access drug discovery research. All data and materials are released without restriction. See thesgc.org.

7 Elinor Ostrom, *Governing the Commons: The Evolution of Institutions for Collective Action* (Cambridge University Press, 1990). Ostrom received the Nobel Prize in Economic Sciences in 2009 for her analysis of economic governance, especially the commons. Her eight design principles for commons governance have been widely applied and extended. The ninth principle presented here—economic alignment—draws on regenerative economic practice to address how financial incentives can reinforce rather than undermine commons health.

8 The Haudenosaunee Confederacy has governed through the Great Law of Peace (*Gayanashagowa*) for over a thousand years. The seven-generation principle requires considering the impact of decisions on seven generations into the future. See Oren Lyons, "An Iroquois Perspective," in Christopher Vecsey and Robert W. Venables, eds., *American Indian Environments: Ecological Issues in Native American History* (Syracuse University Press, 1980), 171–174.

9 The "Honorable Harvest" is described in Robin Wall Kimmerer, *Braiding Sweetgrass: Indigenous Wisdom, Scientific Knowledge, and the Teachings of Plants* (Milkweed Editions, 2013). The practice includes taking only what is needed, using everything taken, giving back, and expressing gratitude.

10 The Monitoring of the Andean Amazon Project (MAAP), launched in 2015 by Amazon Conservation, uses satellite imagery and remote sensing to provide real-time deforestation alerts to Indigenous communities including the Kayapó, Munduruku, and others. See maapprogram.org. For a broader analysis of Indigenous adoption of earth-observation technologies for territorial defense, see also Nidia Catherine González and Markus Kröger, "The Adoption of Earth-Observation Technologies for Deforestation Monitoring by Indigenous People: Evidence from the Amazon," *Globalizations* 20, no. 3 (2023): 415–431.

Breakthrough

1 Homero Aridjis (born 1940) is a Mexican poet, novelist, environmental activist, and former ambassador. He cofounded Grupo de los Cien (Group of 100), an organization of artists and intellectuals defending the monarch butterfly and its habitat. He received the John Hay Award from The Orion Society in 2000.

2 The eastern North American monarch butterfly (*Danaus plexippus*) migration spans approximately three thousand miles, from Canada to central Mexico. The migration requires three to five generations, with no individual completing the full round trip. Monarchs winter in oyamel fir (*Abies religiosa*) forests in the mountains of Michoacán and the State of Mexico. See Lincoln P. Brower et al., "Decline of Monarch Butterflies Overwintering in Mexico," *Biological Conservation* 166 (2012): 297–302.

3 The Monarch Butterfly Biosphere Reserve, established in 1986 and expanded in 2000, was designated a UNESCO World Heritage Site in 2008. Illegal logging remains a significant threat despite legal protections. The reserve encompasses approximately 56,259 hectares in the states of Michoacán and Mexico.

4 Impact investing has grown from approximately $50 billion in 2010 to over $1.5 trillion in 2025, according to GIIN estimates. As of early 2026, there are over 10,500 Certified B Corps, spanning over 100 countries and more than 160 industries. Benefit corporation legislation has been adopted in more than forty US states and internationally.

Index

A

Abram, David, 2, 3, 57, 218, 250
abundance mindset, 195
accountability/transparency
 algorithmic, 104, 105, 224
 in the commons, 267, 274
 in core architecture, 54–55
 demanding market, 105, 107
 for flow of capital, 87, 90
 in impact economy, 12
 in impact measurements, 82
 mandating, 103
 and ownership, 68
 in regenerative businesses, 49
 to stakeholders, 82
 in supply chains, 100
adaptability/flexibility, 52
addictiveness, online platform, 220
advertisers, targeting by, 219, 220
affordable housing, 69–70
African Risk Capacity, 158
Aga Khan Trust for Culture, 229
agricultural commons, 266
agroecology networks, 144
aid, mutual, 117, 128–129, 157, 159
algorithmic amplification, 220
aliveness, security via, 131–132, 159
Amazon Web Services, 166
analysis paralysis, 28
Anderson, Ray, 25–26
Are.na, 224
Aridjis, Homero, 289–291, 295
Arizmendiarrieta, José María, 68
arms races, 155
asymmetric power, 81
attention commons
 algorithmic regulation in, 224–225
 capture/fragmentation of, 217
 defined, 305
 as narrative infrastructure, 189, 217–218
 reclaiming the, 218, 221–224
 security and capture of, 221
Australia, 129–131
authoritarianism, x, 129

B

Basecamp, 223
B Corps, xiv, 13, 50, 51, 93, 102, 107, 108, 183, 189, 245, 247, 249, 255, 281, 292, 305
Bear Stearns, 248
behavior, identity and, 227
belonging
 architecture of, 64
 as foundational, 271–272
 and kinship, 73
 from ownership to, 74, 261–263
Ben & Jerry's, xiii
Beneficial State Bank, 82
benefit corporations, xiv, 18, 50, 102, 292, 305
BerkShares, 37, 39, 101, 126
Berry, Wendell, 2, 3, 150, 350
binaries, false, 212
biodiversity, 125, 129
biodiversity loss, 4, 130, 133
B Lab, 245, 255, 258, 305
Black/Brown communities
 in care work, 140
 economic equity for, 126
 enterprises owned by, 67, 68
 historical amnesia about, 228

blended finance, 84, 306
The Body Shop, xiii–xiv
breakthrough, regenerative
  economy based on, xi
  inevitability of, xv
  as reclamation, 258, 259
  recognition and, 38
  slow magic of, 181
Bretton Woods, 173, 174
budgeting, participatory, 128
burnout culture, 48, 194
business models
  adaptable/flexible, 52
  assessing your, 60
  in custodial economies, 82
  for impact economy, 12–13, 37
  of integrity, 49–53
  mission encoded into, xiii–xiv, 13, 15, 247
  ownership options in, 65, 72
  peace as, 161
  regenerative, xii, 10, 46–48, 196
  systemic-intelligence-informed, 28–29
  See also enterprise building

C

Cambridge Analytica, 220
capital
  capital innovation, xii, 38
  custodial. *see* custodial capital
  designing equitable flows of, 83–84
  as moral actor, 85–86
  patient, 24, 28, 41, 49, 72, 194, 277, 292
  perpetual purpose capital, 83
  power and flow of, 6, 79–80, 81, 87
  private capital realignment, 134
  redirecting flow of, 40, 133–134
  self-assessments on, 88–91
capitalism, 10–11, 104, 308
care work, 140, 143, 144–145, 148, 160
catalytic capital, 83, 134
change
  B Corps and scaling, 102
  as communal journey, 291–295
  of consciousness, 3–4
  of culture, 189
  disruption required for, 173–174
  economic transformation, x, 252–258
  via embedded values, xv
  in the face of polycrisis, 161
  frogs as symbolizing, 252–255
  grassroots cultural changes, 201–203
  of identity, 186–187, 188
  integrated thinking for, 185–187
  language for framing, 202
  as leverage point, 207–208
  liminal spaces required for, 2–3
  via naming something, 180
  via narrative, 207, 208–210
  perceptual shifts for, 3
  personal contribution to, 16
  piecemeal vs. systemic, 22–23, 41
  from profit-driven to systemic thinking, 30
  radical/wholesale, 252–255
  resistance to, 114, 211–213, 292
  structural, 9–10
  time required for, 283
Chappell, Tom, xiii, 300
Chappell, Kate, xiii
child labor, 21–22
Chouinard, Yvon, 50
Christensen Fund, 229, 247
circular business models, 47
Civilian Conservation Corps (CCC), 144
Civil War, 127
climate change, 129, 209–210
coaches/consultants, xviii, 279
Cognitive Defense, 222–223
cognitive security, 221, 222–223
Cohen, Ben, xiii–xiv, 300
collective action, 105, 238
collective unconscious, 255
commodification, 80–81, 100
commons, the
  belonging to, 261–263, 271–272
  collective action in, 105
  culture as, 15, 203
  defined, 306
  digital commons, 65
  extractive depletion of, 11
  as foundational, 271
  genuine security for, 124
  governance of, 77, 266–270, 273, 274
  importance of, 264–265
  markets and, 104–106
  narrative commons, 210–211
  and ownership justice, 63
  protection of, 15
  reclamation of, 261–274
  stewarding the, 29
  of the 21st century, 265–266
community/cooperation
  civic connectors, 140, 141

in the commons, 105–106
community investment, 84–85
cultural transformation in, 291–295
for defense, 166
for digital platforms, 105
dynamic stability via, 4, 157
in energy use, 265
identity work in, 242–243
infrastructure of, 157
and land ownership, 73
multisector investment entities, 134
and ownership justice, 65, 68–69
in power distribution, xii, xv
in regenerative markets, 101, 109
security via, 117, 124, 128–129, 132, 156–160, 233
shared risk/return, 82
social rewards for, 160–161
strength of, 160
and systems thinking, 17
community custodians, xx, 263, 280
community development financial institutions (CDFIs), 86
community health workers, 143
community investment, 84–85
community land trusts (CLTs), 66, 69–70, 73, 265, 306
compartmentalized thinking, 184–185
competition
collaboration and, 105–106
in extractive cultures, 228
patience and, 84
via regenerative practices, 103
complexity manufacturing, 212
complex systems, 22, 28
compliance-oriented initiatives, 23
compromise, safeguards against, 76
conflict prevention, 157
conflict resolution, 267
conscious capitalists, 11
consciousness, 35–37, 254
consumer cooperatives, 66
contemplative practices, 239
Cooperative Energy Futures, 266
Costa Rica, 134–135
costs
exposing true, 213
externalized, 22, 99, 308
of fractured identities, 229
internalized, 100, 107
of militarization, 154–155, 158
of prevention vs. reaction, 133, 135–136
redirecting flow of capital, 133–134
of security spending, 145
of threat/response mismatches, 121–123, 130–131
of violence vs. peace, 155–156
courage
humility and, 284
to redesign systems, 10
COVID-19, 122, 143
creativity, 224
culture
architecture for, 199
attention commons in, 221, 223
boundaries for, 200
as the commons, 203
core practices of regenerative, 280
cost of extractive systems to, 232
cross-cultural engagement, 238
cultural coherence, 15
custodians of, xix, 140, 142, 264
degradation of, 197–199
extractive pattern of, 193–194, 256–257
feedback loops in, 200
flexible workplace, 223
as foundational, 189, 191
grassroots changes to, 201–203
of impact economy, 15, 249–251, 256–257, 292
infrastructure of, 180–181, 184, 192, 199, 205, 307
of integrity, 52
intentional design of, 199–201
norms in, 192
as pioneer work, 187
political suppression of, 231
reclamation of, 259
regenerative pattern of, 13, 47–48, 195–197
self-assessments on, 204–206
spiritual wisdom in, 183
to support security providers, 145
transforming institutional, 239
transmission methods for, 192, 200
See also society
currencies, alternative, 37–38, 101
custodial capital
architecture of, 81–83
capital as moral actor, 85–86
defined, 306
extractive pattern vs., 41, 80–81
functions of, 82–83

custodial capital (*continued*)
in impact economy, 15
power and flow of capital, 79–80, 87
scaling, 84–85
self-assessments on, 88–91

D

dangers, and threat/response mismatches, 119–124
data commons, 265
data privacy, 103, 105, 224
Decidim Platform, 265
decision-making
collective, 238
by consensus, 198
distributed, 76
in extractive cultures, 193
markets as evidence of, 98–99
morality of, 52–53, 80, 85–86
deep work, 220
defense
cognitive, 222–223
cooperation for, 166
fortress-style, 152, 153
misallocated response to threats, 119–124, 130–131, 135–137, 146, 155
via mutualism, 15, 153, 156–160, 162–163, 166–167, 310
See also security
Defense as a Service (DaaS)
advantages of, 166–167
defined, 307
foundation of, 167–172
service economy logic in, 166
system architecture of, 172–173
toolkit for building, 175–177
defensiveness, fear and, 113, 114
delay, defense as, 122, 136
democracy
attention capture vs., 221
basis for true racial, 126
and the commons, 264
democratic infrastructure, 116, 124, 127–128, 132, 136, 233
erosion of, x, 120
range of action in, 182
security via, 153
digital commons, 265
digital markets, 104–105, 107
Digital Services Act, 224
disinformation, 222–223
dissonance, 236
displacement, 231–232
distraction, online, 219–220
distributed authority, 195
distributed capacity, 167–168
distributed ownership, 71–72, 76, 126, 270
diversity, 31
Drivers Cooperative, 105
Du Bois, W.E.B., 35–37, 126, 127
Dudley Street Neighborhood Initiative, 66, 69, 265

E

ecological practices, 238
ecological stability, 116, 124, 125, 136, 140, 233, 264
ecological stewards, 2, 140, 263
economic diasporas, 231
economic systems
architecture of, 15
attention economy, 219–220, 223
equity and resilience of, 126–127
extractive. *see* extractive economies
identity as shaped in, 227, 228
integrity rewarded in, xiii
interdependent, 157
invisible labor in, 144–145
market architecture in, 106
of peace, 155–156
reclamation of, 257
as reflective of mindset, 227
regenerative. *see* regenerative economy
shift to new, 248–249
stewards of healthy, 140
transformation of, x, xii, xv, 250, 291–295
wealth concentration in, x, 11, 64, 87, 99, 123, 126
ecosystems
businesses in, 54
cost of a lost, 232
ecology of safety for, 140–142
failure to protect, 129–131
of identity, 234–235, 238, 242
interdependent outcomes in, 10, 116
as living infrastructure, 131–132
positioning enterprises in, 17
relational awareness of, 36–37
security via healthy, 124, 125
tipping points in, ix–x

ecotones, 115, 248, 307
education
and attention cultivation, 222
core practices of regenerative, 279
by failures, 250
for impact economy, xix
as invisible labor, 144–145
by the past, 238
place-based education, xiv, 181, 229, 246, 311
ROI for investment in, 127
and the service economy, 148, 160
Elder, Dr. John, 181
energy cooperatives, 265
enterprise building
commons protected in, 273
for conflict prevention, 157
cultural infrastructure for, 184
and growth pressure, 197
for impact economy, 17, 276–277
outcomes shaped by, 10
for radical transformation, 252–255
resources for, xvii
structural innovation, 12
values-based, xiii–xiv
environmental collapse
bearing witness to, 4
climate crisis narratives, 209–210
human denial of, 114, 118
lack of timely response to, 254, 255
and ownership injustice, 64
polycrisis, ix–x, 13, 145, 161, 233, 258, 264, 282, 311
and preventative resilience, 169–170
from profit-driven economies, 22
response to, 258, 293
ROI of preventing, 132–133
and threat/response mismatches, 119–124
urgency of, 282–283
environmental issues
desecration of place, 3
ecological commons, 104
ecosystem health, 125
environmental justice, 5
information asymmetry on, 99
nature/human interconnection, 114, 115
undervalued/invisible laborers for, 144–145
equity, economic, 116, 124, 126, 136, 233
ESG (environmental, social, governance) practitioners, x, 12, 23, 82, 101, 211, 307–308
EU Emissions Trading System, 100
Everlane, 54–55
exit imperatives, 81, 83
extractive economies
alternatives to, xi, xv, 10, 13, 38, 57, 258
attention as used in, 218, 219
backlash from, xiv, 211–212, 292
business-as-machine in, 54
collapse of, 38
compartmentalized thinking in, 15–16, 184–185
defensive protection of, 114–115
defined, 10–11, 308
in digital markets, 104–105
ESG/impact measures in, 23
externalized costs of, 22, 99
extractive cultural pattern, 193–194
extractive/impact economy ecotone, 115
flow of capital in, 80–81, 86
fractured identity of, 228–229, 234
fragility of, 248
harm done by, x, 13, 290, 293, 295
in housing market, 70
inequity in, 126–127
leaving behind, 291
markets in, 58, 93, 99–100
mindset of, 22–23, 246
narratives of, 208
ownership in, 72–73
power in, 65
as profit driven, 22, 44
reckoning with history of, 67–68
stewardship vs., 75
success metrics in, 44
treating symptoms of, 5–6, 11–12, 22
undervalued/invisible laborers in, 144–145

F

Facebook, 220
failures, 70, 250
Fairbnb, 105
Fairphone, 51–52, 57, 102–103
Fairtrade, 108
Fashion Revolution, 100
fear, 113, 114, 160–161, 197
feedback literacy, 21, 24, 25–26, 30, 31, 200
Finland, 222
Flinders Chase National Park, 129–131

focus, 218–219, 221
food security, 125, 144
Forgotten Language Tour, 112, 113, 181, 246
fortress-style security, 152, 153
fossil fuel dependency, 150
fractured identity, 228–229, 235
frog totem, 252–255
Fullerton, John, 38, 40

G

gaps, closing, 59, 60–62
gender factors, 140
General Data Protection Regulation (GDPR), 103
generosity, 159
GIIN, 255
Global Scenario Group, 151
governance
- of the commons, 104, 266–270, 273
- cooperative, 65–67
- of digital platforms, 105
- in distributed ownership, 76
- ESG, x, 12, 23, 82, 101, 211, 307–308
- of flow of capital, 87
- local, 129
- loss of trust in political, 122
- in regenerative businesses, 49
- security and, 135
- by stakeholders, 74
- values protected by, 51
- *See also* Indigenous governance/stewardship

Grady, Heather, 38
Grameen Shakti, 56, 57, 143, 265
Great Barrier Reef, 129
Greenfield, Jerry, xiii–xiv
greenwashing, 211, 309
ground of consciousness, 35–37
growth pressure, 197
guardianship vs. reciprocity, 270

H

happiness index, 134, 159
Haudenosaunee Confederacy, 45, 268, 283
healing
- via changing perception, 250
- in core architecture, 55–56
- vs. doing less harm, 6, 11, 22, 38, 44–46
- enterprises that heal, 43–61, 307
- and reckoning with history, 67–68
- in regenerative businesses, 46–48
- via spiritual/cultural wisdom, 183
- as strategy, 57–58
- via systems thinking, 6–7

healthcare access, 126
health guardians, 140, 141, 143
hierarchy as control, 193
Hissar Historical and Cultural Reserve, 231
historical amnesia, 228
historic injustice, 67–68
homecoming, 240–241
Hotfrog, 245, 246, 247, 252, 256–257
Hollender, Jeffrey, xiii, 301
housing initiatives, 69–70
humility, 284
Hurricane Katrina, 114, 129, 324
Hurricane Sandy, 125
hyperindividualism, 193, 228

I

identity
- behavior as determined by, 227
- at community scale, 239–240
- cultivating whole identity, 238–239
- economy as reflecting, 227
- of extractive systems, 228–229
- of the impact economy, 239–240
- as impact entrepreneur, 179–180, 184–187, 251–252, 256
- interdependent, 234–235, 309–310
- journey from fractured to whole, 235–237
- narrative and, 190
- self-assessments, 241–243
- system transformation via, 188

immediacy trap, 142
impact economy
- basis of, xiii, 6, 252, 255, 276–277
- capital as moral actor in, 85–86
- civic redesign via, 7
- cognitive security in, 221
- communal journey into, 291–295
- cultural support for, 249–250
- currency for, 37–38
- defined, 309
- eight layers of, 14–15
- evolution of, 255
- extractive/impact economy ecotone, 115
- financial success in, 46, 57–58, 102
- five pillars of, 233–234
- impact integrity in, 44, 48–52
- inner transition to, 239–240
- mapping the, 37–40

markets in, 94, 100–101
metrics for, 87
mission in structure of, 13, 15
narrative battle tactics for, 213
patience in, 84, 134
practices to sustain, 258
radical transformation into, 252–255, 258
as regenerative, xi
and re-rooting into place, 233
service to builders of, xii–xiii
transition to identity of, 239–240

Impact Entrepreneur, PBC, ix

Impact Entrepreneur Magazine, xv

impact entrepreneurs
breakthrough of, ix, xi
core practices of, 12–13, 278
cultural infrastructure for, 184, 187
DaaS as built by, 174
defined, 11, 309
evolutionary journey of, 13, 49, 291–295
examples of, xiii, 37, 49–52
identity as, 179–180, 251–252, 256
narrative crafting by, 213, 214–216
need for, 13–14
scaling impact by, 106
self-assessment for, 17–19
system architecture by, xii, 7, 9
systems intelligence of, 6, 16, 29

impact investing, 6, 86, 89, 245, 249, 278, 309

impact measurement, 23

impact-washing, 211, 309

inclusivity, 76

Indigenous governance/stewardship, 67, 68, 73, 77, 171, 209, 263, 269–270

Indigenous history, 228

inequality, 126, 136, 228

injustice
and ownership, 64, 126
racial, 126
reckoning with historic, 67–68
self-assessments, 136
systemic, 127

insect apocalypse, 4

Institute for Economics and Peace, 155–156

integrity
audits, 59
of capital flows, 88
closing gaps in, 61
crises in, 62
impact integrity, 44, 48–52, 309
integrity triage, 62
and morality of decisions, 52–53
ongoing alignment to, 52
and resilience, 53

intelligence
ancient regenerative wisdom, 45
of elders, 34
of mutualism, 156
required for change, 8
without power, 28
See also systemic intelligence

interdependence
celebrating, 163
economy as reflecting mindset of, 227
vs. extractive mindset, 229, 256
human/nature, 114, 115
in impact economy, 10, 256
Indigenous wisdom on, 45
in regenerative culture, 15, 48, 194–195
security via, 116, 124, 140, 152, 156, 160, 174
stabilization via economic, 157
and stewardship mindset, 65
See also relationships/relational awareness

Interface Carpets, 100

intergenerational connection, 129, 238

investors/investment
in community, 84
core practices of, 278
in cultural reclamation, 259
ESG analysis for, 12
impact investing, 6, 86, 89, 245, 249, 278, 309
in peace, 156
place-based, 182
public investment reallocation, 133
in regenerative businesses, xvii, 245
ROI of DaaS, 167
in secure systems, 117, 148
threat/response mismatches, 119–124, 130, 146, 147
See also ROI (return on investment)

J

Journey Toward Wisdom, 183

justice
economic equity and resilience, 126–127
environmental, 5
as interconnected, 36–37
narratives in fight for, 208
ownership justice, xii, 73, 75–77
restorative justice facilitators, 144
self-assessments, 136

K

Kangaroo Island, 129–131
Kelly, Kevin, 180
Kimmerer, Robin Wall, 180, 268
kinship, 72–73, 75
knowledge commons
  governance of, 266, 273
  investment in building, 90
  keepers of, 140, 141, 263
  lack of protection of, 119
  markets and, 104
  monitoring/accountability in, 274
  reclamation of, 221, 224, 265
  regenerative security via, 146
  resources via, 283
  in science/medicine, 266
knowledge transfer, 129
knowledge workers, 220, 279
Kudumbashree Program, 104

L

labor
  in digital markets, 105
  information asymmetry on, 99
  invisible, 144–145
  in regenerative security field, 144–148
land, cooperative ownership of. *See* community land trusts (CLTs)
land-back movements, 68, 77, 171, 209
Lane-Zucker, Laurie, xvi, 296
Latin America, 144
leadership
  core practices of regenerative, 278–279
  redesigning systems of, 9
  resources for regenerative, xvii–xx
  shared, 284
Lehman Brothers, 248
leverage points, 5, 16, 27, 28, 29, 30, 202, 207, 248, 278, 286, 310
liminal spaces, 2
linear thinking, 15
Long-Term Stock Exchange, 101
Lopez, Barry, 4, 150
Lyons, Oren, 151, 152, 154

M

MacArthur Foundation, 182
Māori wisdom, 45
markets
  architecture of, 106, 109
  and the commons, 104–106
  digital, 104–105
  extractive, 22, 25, 39, 58, 93
  hidden aspects of, 99–100
  identity in extractive, 228–229
  integrity-rewarding, xiii
  moral grounds for, 94–98
  myth of laissez-faire, 94–99
  profit in regenerative, 28
  as reflecting what matters, xv, 6, 41, 93, 98–99, 107
  regenerative, 100–101, 102–103
  regulation of, 103–104
  self-assessment on integrity in, 107–109
  to serve the collective, 7
  as set of choices, 93, 98, 104, 106
  solving social problems via, 10, 11
  systemic intelligence in, 29
  transformation of, xii, 15, 40, 102, 108
Mastodon/Fediverse, 224
materials, regenerative, 47
McKibben, Bill, 112
Meadows, Donella, 207–208
meaning, 142, 203, 224, 229, 232, 233, 234, 236, 240, 251, 259, 287
mechanistic thinking, 193–194
media literacy, 222–223, 224, 225
Merrill Lynch, 248
Meru Herbs, 157
Merwin, W.S., 111, 113
messenger assassination, 212
microfinance, 9
migration, 289–295
militarized mindset
  alternatives to, 134–135, 156–160
  and fortress-style security, 150–153
  gravitational pull of, 154
  in the knowledge commons, 146
  limits/costs of, 154–155
  as misallocated response to threat, 121, 130
  moving out of, 162–163
  myth of military security, 122–123
  reactive vs. preventative, 133
misallocated response to threats, 119–124, 130–131, 135–137, 146, 147
mission
  in culture, 52
  in custodial economies, 82
  drift, 90
  embedded, xiii–xiv, 13, 15, 75

embedding permanence of, 18, 50, 51, 72, 75, 82, 197, 278, 310
evolution of, 13
in extractive enterprises, 81
investments aligned to, 86, 87
mission-driven business, 247
protection of, 18, 76, 89, 90
monarch butterflies, 245, 289–295
Mondragon, 68, 201, 223
monopolies, 99, 104
Montreal Protocol, 103
morality
as basis for markets, 94–98
capital as moral actor, 85–86
of decision-making, 52–53
of ownership, 74
Mount Everett, 34
movement building, xi, xii, 10, 278, 281
movement consciousness, 12, 17
MUD Jeans, 46
multistakeholder cooperatives, 66, 134
mutual aid, 117, 128–129, 157, 159
mutual benefit protocols, 169
mutualistic security, 15, 153, 156–160, 162–163, 166–167, 310

N

narrative(s)
attention as infrastructure of, 189, 217–218, 222
changed perspectives via, 183
co-opting the, 211
cultural transmission via, 189, 192, 280
identity formation via, 185–187, 188
and imagination, 214
narrative battles, 210–213
narrative infrastructure, 207, 215, 311
nature/human interconnection, 114, 115
Nelson, Richard, 150
New Orleans East, 130
New Patriotism, The, 150–151
New York City, 125
Nordic Civil Preparedness Networks, 157
norms, cultural, 192, 214
Nova Vida, 70–71

O

open-source development, 106, 265, 266
opportunity mapping, 158
Orion magazine, 2, 4, 5
The Orion Society, 5, 112, 149, 150, 181, 299
Ostrom, Elinor, 266, 267
overwhelm, 237–238
ownership
and belonging, 64, 74, 261–263
and cooperative power, xii, 65–67
and cultural infrastructure, 199
distributed ownership, 71–72, 76, 126, 270
and economic equity, 126
and enterprise models, 72
in impact economy, 15, 38
justice, xii, 73, 75–77
as kinship, 72–73
of land, 73
power and ownership, 71–72
in regenerative businesses, 49
and systems thinking, 41
as traditional defense mindset, 166

P

pandemic response, 123, 132
paradigm shifts, 6, 41, 114, 173, 207–208
parasocial relationships, 220
participatory budgeting, 128
Patagonia, 13, 49–51, 57, 106, 196–197, 223, 258
patience, 81–82, 84–85
patient capital, 24, 28, 41, 49, 72, 194, 277, 292, 311
pattern recognition, 21, 25–26, 38, 40
peace, 155–156, 160, 161
performance culture, 194
Perry Preschool Project, 127
perspectives
diverse perspectives, 31
on flow of capital, 88, 134
healing via changed, 250
of long-term place/time, 34–35, 134, 194
paradigm shifts via changed, 3, 207–208
of short-term gains, 81
wisdom via diverse, 183
philanthropy
in business models, 196–197
corporate charity, 44
by impact entrepreneurs, 38
for mission-driven business, 248–249
resources, xvii
place
disconnection from, 231–233
as ground of consciousness, 34–37
and identity of wholeness, 230
impact of ancestral, 94–95
investing based on, 182

place (*continued*)
ownership of vs. belonging to, 261–263
place-based commitments, 82
place-based education, xiv, 181–182, 229, 246, 311
place-based writing, 229
systems based on, 234
transformation via, 182–183
platform cooperatives, 105, 107, 108, 221, 311
platforms, online, 217, 218–219, 220
politics
of attention capture, 220, 221
core practices of regenerative, 278
of military spending, 123
reaction vs. prevention in, 133
resisting authoritarian, 129
Soviet, 231
pollinator crisis, 4
polycrisis, x, 145, 161, 233, 258, 264, 282, 311
poverty, 231
power
of attention capture, 219–220
building collective, xii, 238
concentrating, 71–72
and flow of capital, 79–80, 81, 87
ground-up systems of, xi
and historic harm, 228, 235
intelligence without, 28
isolated, 160
and morality of decisions, 52–53
naming structures of, 75
narratives to legitimize, 208
and ownership, 64–65, 71–72
of procurement, 108
and reaction vs. prevention, 133
in regenerative businesses, 49
trust and cooperative, 70
premortems, 31
prestige hierarchy, 143
Prevention Ratio, 168, 312
prevention vs. reaction, 132–133, 135–137, 140, 142, 167, 312
private sector, 133, 246
privilege, responsibility and, 284
procurement, regenerative, 101, 108
product design, 47, 60
profit
business driven by, 22, 44, 80
commons-based, 270
for cooperation, 160–161
from human attention, 217–218
in impact economy, 46, 57, 71
patience with, 81–82, 84–85
via peace, 157–158
redefining returns, 88
shared risk/return, 82
short-term gains, 81, 99–100
public benefit corporations (PBC), 134
public health capacity, 116, 124, 125–126, 132, 233
purpose trusts, xiv, 13, 50, 62, 67, 72, 73, 75, 89, 197, 205, 273
Pyle, Robert Michael, 2, 4, 230

R

Raskin, Paul, 151, 152
Raygorodetsky, Gleb, 247
reclamation
call to, 284–285
of civilization, 259
of the commons, 261–274
cultural, 257
how to participate in, 275–288
self-assessment on, 286–288
Reconstruction, 126
regenerative agriculture, 125, 139, 144
regenerative economy
ancient roots of, 45
architecture of, 188–189
basis of, 10, 252–255
capital as moral actor in, 85–86
certification systems for, 100–101, 108
closing gaps for, 59, 60–62
culture in, 13, 47–48, 195–197, 201–203
in digital markets, 105
ecosystems of, 54
entrepreneurs to build, xii, 10
vs. extractive economies, xi
financial success in, 13, 46, 57, 102
how to scale, 35, 41
in impact economy, 15
integrity in, 44, 48–52
mapping systems for, 37–40
markets in, 58, 94, 100–101
narratives of, 208
reciprocity in, 270
redirecting capital to, 134
structural redesign for, xi
from sustainability to, 45–46, 312
systemic-intelligence-informed, 28–29
transition to identity of, 239–240
See also breakthrough, regenerative

Regenerative Organic, 100, 108
relationships/relational awareness
  about ownership, 74
  in capital flows, 84, 90
  in the commons, 262
  and community cohesion, 129
  in community investment, 84–85
  friends vs. online "friends", 220
  identity based in, 236
  of interpenetration, 34–36, 41
  and morality of decisions, 52–53
  mutualism and, 156, 159
  in regenerative businesses, 49
  self-assessment on, 136
  and shared stewardship, 65–67
  in systemic intelligence, 21, 23–24, 25–26
  transactional relations, 228
religious suppression, 231
renewable energy, 103
Renewable Energy Act, 103
resilience
  and the commons, 264
  to disinformation, 222–223
  via distributed capacity, 166
  guardians of, 135, 139–144
  in impact economy, 84, 172
  integrity and, 53
  of mutualism, 156
  preventative climate, 169–170
  security and, 116, 119, 123, 124, 126, 137, 160
  social assessments for, 161
resource competition, 228
resource misallocation, 119–124
responsibility, 235, 237, 284
restorative finance, 68
restorative justice facilitators, 144
revenue-based financing, 83
rights, 268
risk
  extraction and externalized, 99
  mutualism to face, 158
  risk-absorbing architecture, 83
  risk intolerance, 81
  risk/return sharing, 82, 89
Riversimple, 56
Rockefeller Brothers Fund, 149
Rockefeller family, 247
Rockefeller Foundation, 182
Rockefeller Philanthropy Advisors, 38
Roddick, Anita, xiii–xiv, 314
ROI (return on investment)
  of community cohesion, 129–130
  for DaaS, 166–167, 170–172
  of democratic infrastructure, 128
  of ecosystem health, 125
  of mutualism, 159–160
  myopic focus on, 246
  of prevention vs. reaction, 132–133, 312
  of public health security, 126
  of social equity, 127
root causes, addressing, 36–37
rootedness, 231–233
RSF Social Finance, 84, 258

S

safety
  ecology of, 140–142
  fortress-style security, 152, 153–154
  and happiness, 159
  See also security
same-sex marriage, 208
scarcity mindset, 159, 175–177, 193
Schumacher Center for a New Economics, 37
scroll, infinite online, 220
security
  and aliveness, 131–132, 159
  alternatives to military, 134
  via ancient wisdom, 174
  cognitive, 221, 222–223
  for the commons, 263–264
  via DaaS, 165–177
  via democracy, 153
  five pillars of real, 111, 116–117, 124–129, 136, 147–148, 153, 233, 308
  guardians of, 135, 139–144
  limits/costs of military, 154–155
  military mindset on, 122–123, 150–154
  via mutualism, 156–160
  need for new models of, 113–115, 117–118
  prevention vs. reaction, 142, 167–172
  protection delivery mechanisms, 167–172
  public health, 125–126
  via redirecting flow of capital, 133–134
  and resource misallocation, 119–124
  threat/response mismatches, 119–124, 130, 135–137
  value shift for real, 152, 153
  visibility for providers of, 145
  as a web, not fortress, 124
  workforce for regenerative, 144–148
  See also defense

seed commons, 266
self-assessments
 on the commons, 272–273
 on culture, 204–206
 for DaaS building, 175–177
 of flow of capital, 88–91
 for healing/regenerative businesses, 60–62
 of identity, 241–243
 for impact entrepreneurs, 17–19
 integrity audits, 59
 on markets, 107–109
 of misallocated defense, 135–137
 on reclamation of civilization, 286–288
 on regenerative culture, 204–206
self-interest, 94–98
service economy, 160
Seven Pillars House of Wisdom, 183, 246, 299
Seventh Generation, 258
Shared Capital Cooperative, 82
shared stewardship, 65–67
short-term gains, 81, 99–100, 134, 193
siloed initiatives, 23
single-bottom-line-thinking, 22–23, 30, 44
slow media, 221
Smart Growth America, 182
smartphone supply chains, 51
Smith, Adam, 94–98
social entrepreneurs, 11
social media, 219–220, 224
social myopia, 228
Social Venture Network (SVN), 245, 247
society
 cognitive security in, 223
 converging breakdowns in, ix–x
 genuine security for, 116, 125–126
 happiness index in, 134
 humans as social beings, 235
 invisible resilience guardians in, 142–143
 narratives as blueprints for, 208
 new security model for, 116–118
 online, 219–220
 protection of/by, 119
 public health capacity of, 125–126
 redesign of, 7
 social commons, 104
 threat/response mismatches for, 120
 See also culture
Soviet Union, 231
stakeholders
 in B Corps, 245
 of the commons, 272
 decision-making by, 52
 expanding stakeholder voice, 61
 governance by, 74
 narrow focus on, 81
 for regenerative business, 47
 and shared stewardship, 65–67
 stakeholder integration, 12
 in systems thinking, 30
standards, baseline, 103
Standing Rock, 209
status quo, 192, 214
stewardship
 of attention, 221–222
 and belonging, 261–263
 in business models, 196
 of capital, 80, 83
 for the commons, 263–264
 vs. extraction, 75
 guardians of security, 135, 139–144
 identity based in, 237
 vs. ownership, 73, 74
 shared, 63, 65–67
 as true wealth, 88
stock markets, 101
Stocksy United, 105
storytelling, 52
structural causality, 21, 25–26
Structural Genomics Consortium, 266
structural innovation
 for accountability, 68
 for belonging, 262–263
 and cultural change, 248–251, 257
 cultural infrastructure plus, 184, 187
 for flexibility, 52
 for impact economy, 276–277
 by impact entrepreneurs, 12, 17, 18
 for integrity, 50–51, 52
 layers of, 10
 for ownership justice, 75–77
 to protect the commons, 273
 for regeneration, 46–48
 systemic-intelligence-informed, 28–29
subconsciousness, 254
Substack, 223
success
 of B Corps, 102
 celebrating regenerative, 203
 in changing the narrative, 208–210
 via culture, 191–192
 of distributed ownership, 71
 extractive metrics for, 44

via integrity in design, 53
via regenerative business, 46, 57
supply chains
DaaS to transform, 170
information asymmetry on, 99
integrity embedded into, 51–52
mutualism in, 157
in regenerative business, 47
transforming your, 60
transparent, 49, 100
surveillance capitalism, 104
sustainability
in cultural rhythms, 196
greenwashing via, 199
via healing systems, 57
limited thinking of, 38
regeneration vs., 45–46, 312
sustainable business leaders, 11
SWAN Impact, 86
system architecture
of belonging, 64
for cooperation/mutualism, 157
for culture, 199
for custodial capital, 83–84
of Defense as a Service, 172–173
extractive vs. custodial, 81–83
in impact economy, 15, 256–257
by impact entrepreneurs, xii, 7
injustice in, 127
integrity in, 44, 48–52
investment in truly secure, 117
of markets, 98–99, 103–104, 106
mission in structure of, 13, 15
for prevention, 133
for real security, 145
redesign of, 9
to reflect what matters, 93–94, 145
for regeneration, 46–48
regulation in, 103–104
security infrastructure, 133–134
threat/response mismatches in, 120–121, 130–131
transparency in, 54–55
systemic intelligence
business models based on, 37, 41
case studies, 25–26
on climate change, 115
for complex systems, 22
conceptual tools for, 27
defined, 23–25
economic transformation via, 4–7
embodied practices for, 27
evolution of, 4–7
how to cultivate, 26–27, 30–32
identifying failures in, 32
of impact entrepreneurs, 12, 16, 185
and leverage points, 207–208
limitations of, 28–29
organizational practices for, 27
problem-solving via, 29–30
reading signals for, 31
in regenerative culture, 195
vs. single-bottom-line-thinking, 21–22
transformation via, 182–183

T

Tajikistan, 229, 230–231
Tanka Bar, 56
Taoist wisdom, 45
Theory of Moral Sentiments, The (Smith), 96, 97
threat assessment, 158, 273
time horizon expansion
attention capture vs., 221
in custodial economies, 81–82, 88
Long-Term Stock Exchange, 101
security via, 221
self-assessment on, 31
in systemic intelligence, 21, 24
tipping points, environmental, ix–x, 123, 146, 152, 282, 313
tobacco regulation, 208
Tom's of Maine, xiii
Tooze, Adam, 282
Transition Towns movement, 239–240
transparency/accountability, 12, 49, 51, 54–55
Triad Institute, 245, 246, 300
trust
and long-term partnerships, 54
loss of social, 122, 123
and resilience, 53
safety and social, 159
trust capital, 53

U

Ubuntu, 45
Uluru, 129
unconscious, collective, 255
unemployment, 231
unions, 54–55, 198
Universal Coverage Scheme, 126
UN Sustainable Development Goals, 255
Up & Go, 105

V

values
- in attention commons, 224
- behavior as determined by, 227
- businesses founded on moral, xiii-xiv, 50
- vs. capturing of attention, 219
- culture aligned to, 196–197
- embedded into structure, 50–51
- and flow of capital, 80, 81
- future as requiring shift in, 152
- markets as evidence of, 98–99
- of the uncommodifiable, 100
- undervalued/invisible laborers, 144–145
- values-aligned banks, 86

visibility bias, 142

W

watershed management, 125
wealth
- building community, 69–70
- concentration of, x, 11, 64, 87, 99, 123
- harm done by concentrated, 126
- hoarding of, 80
- racial inequities in, 127
- stewardship as true, 88
- as "worth", 228

W.E.B. Du Bois Center, 35–36
Weinstein, Randy, 34, 35, 37, 126
wholeness
- with boundaries, 237–238
- cultivating whole identity, 238–239
- vs. extractive mindset, 228
- homecoming to, 240–241
- of interdependent identity, 234–235
- via rootedness in place, 230, 233–234
- transition to identity of, 239–240

wildfire, 129–131
Williams, Terry Tempest, 2, 3, 150, 182
Wilson, Ken, 247
wisdom
- ancient, 45
- cultivation of, 183, 236
- stewardship via, 263

witness, bearing, 2–4
Witt, Susan, 37, 40
worker cooperatives, 66
World Health Organization (WHO), 126
Worn Wear program, 13, 50, 196
writing as witness, 2–4, 229

Y

Yunus, Muhammad, 9

About the Author

Laurie Lane-Zucker is the founder and President of Impact Entrepreneur, PBC, and the person who, in 2011, gave a name to the movement this book describes. He recognized that a new kind of entrepreneur was emerging—not adding social good to business, but building enterprises where financial return and systemic regeneration are inseparable. He called them "impact entrepreneurs," and with that naming, helped crystallize a movement now spanning over two hundred countries.

It wasn't the first time he'd named something into existence. In the mid-1990s, he and a colleague coined "place-based education," language that transformed how educators understood the relationship between learning and location. He understood early what this book argues throughout: Transformation begins when you can name what's emerging.

Through Impact Entrepreneur, Lane-Zucker has built a platform serving tens of thousands of systems-minded changemakers worldwide. *Impact Entrepreneur Magazine*, educational programming, and partnerships with notable innovators have documented and amplified the voices transforming our economy from single-bottom-line extraction to triple-bottom-line regeneration.

As a multiple award-winning publisher, editor, and writer, Lane-Zucker has had the privilege of collaborating with acclaimed authors, editing and contributing forewords to their bestselling works. His New Patriotism book series, conceived in the aftermath of September 11 to challenge the militarized security paradigm through the work of America's finest writers, included Wendell Berry's *In the Presence of Fear*, Barry Lopez's and Richard Nelson's *Patriotism and the American Land*, and Terry Tempest Williams's *The Open Space of Democracy*. Through the Triad Institute, he published David James Duncan's *God Laughs & Plays*, a National Bestseller, among other works.

Between these chapters, Lane-Zucker founded the Triad Institute, a global think tank advancing "triadic thinking"—the capacity to hold simultaneous rootedness in place alongside sophisticated understanding of national and global systems. He later served as executive director of Seven Pillars House of Wisdom, working with scholars and wisdom keepers from diverse spiritual traditions to explore how contemplative practice and ecological healing are inseparable. These experiences reinforced his belief that structural transformation requires cultural and spiritual foundations—a conviction that shapes every chapter of this book.

Recognizing that real change requires new language for old problems, his latest innovations—Defense as a Service, Prevention Dividend, and Prevention Ratio, described for the first time in this book—reframe security itself, from militarized protection to regenerative prevention.

Lane-Zucker has organized over a hundred conferences and summits—from the landmark 1996 Watershed Conference at the Library of Congress and 1999 Millennium Conference at the National Conservation Training Center, to programs with the Rockefeller Brothers Fund, Rockefeller Philanthropy Advisors, Mission Investors Exchange, and Aga Khan Trust for Culture—each one revealing patterns in how systems change happens. Through founding Hotfrog, a founding B Corporation that completed the first equity transaction on an impact investment exchange, he learned that building new economic infrastructure requires both visionary thinking and practical tools.

This field manual emerges from decades of naming, framing, and building movements. It's for those ready to move beyond critique to construction, beyond impact-washing to genuine transformation. The Impact Economy doesn't need more theory—it needs practical tools wielded by people who understand that changing the world begins with changing the words we use to describe what's possible.

This book distills not just Lane-Zucker's journey but the collective wisdom of thousands of practitioners he has interviewed, edited, advised, and learned from across six continents—from Istanbul to Sydney, from Silicon Valley to social enterprises in rural villages.

Laurie Lane-Zucker lives in Sheffield, Massachusetts, where he continues to name—and build—the future.

About Impact Entrepreneur

Impact Entrepreneur is a global network of systems-minded changemakers—entrepreneurs, investors, scholars, and practitioners—building, financing, teaching about, and otherwise using entrepreneurship and finance to transform the economy from extraction to regeneration.

Since 2011, we have grown to serve over seventy thousand members across more than two hundred countries through a multifaceted platform that includes *Impact Entrepreneur Magazine*, live webinars with impact luminaries, field-building summits, and LinkedIn's largest community dedicated to impact entrepreneurship.

Continue Your Journey

This book is a beginning, not an end.

Visit impactentrepreneur.com/breakthrough to access:

FREE RESOURCES:

- *The Reader's Companion:* Navigation guides, framework summaries, and reading group questions
- *The Implementation Roadmap:* Self-assessment, ninety-day sprints, and practical pathways for applying the book's frameworks

- *The Instructor's Supplement:* Syllabi, discussion questions, and assignments for educators
- *Book Graphics:* High-resolution figures and diagrams for presentations and teaching

IMPLEMENTATION SUPPORT:

For practitioners and organizations ready to go deeper, Impact Entrepreneur offers facilitated Implementation Cohorts and customized workshops. Defense as a Service consulting—helping cities, corporations, foundations, and communities redirect resources from reactive defense to regenerative security—is also available.

Join the Movement

Subscribe to our magazine. Join our LinkedIn community. Attend our webinars. Connect with practitioners worldwide who are proving, every day, that the Impact Economy is not just possible—it's already being built.

The frog is jumping. Will you?

About the Art

My mother, Jane Lane-Pryor, was an accomplished watercolorist who exhibited nationally, including twice in the American Watercolor Society's prestigious traveling exhibition, and won awards from institutions such as the National Audubon Society. I grew up surrounded by her work: bold abstractions alive with color and geometric energy, atmospheric woodland scenes where greens bled and merged with the quiet authority of wet-on-wet technique, and stark, brooding landscapes where she gave most of the canvas to darkness and let the earth emerge below like a whisper. Her range was extraordinary. She could fill a miniature with the chromatic intensity of stained glass or surrender a full sheet to shadow and negative space with equal confidence. Watching her, I absorbed something about that medium that I would only appreciate decades later: watercolor demands partnership with the material. You cannot dominate it the way you can oil or acrylic. You lay down color and then negotiate with water, with gravity, with time. The paint has its own intelligence.

I inherited many things from my mother—her love of the natural world, her conviction that beauty is not decoration but a form of truth-telling, her belief that creativity and healing are not separate callings. But I did not inherit her hand. It would be generous to compare my own facility with a brush to a three-year-old's finger painting. For most of my adult life, I assumed that the visual arts were something I could appreciate and champion but never practice.

Then, as I was writing this book, something unexpected happened.

I had been searching for a visual language that could carry the book's ideas without reducing them to corporate graphics or stock photography. I wanted something that felt handmade, organic, imperfect in the way living systems are imperfect. Something that evoked the natural world this book is ultimately about protecting. And something that signaled to readers, from the first page, that this is not a conventional business book offering mechanistic solutions.

Watercolor was the obvious aesthetic. But I could not paint.

What I could do was see. Thirty-five years of working with artists, writers, and visual thinkers had taught me to envision what I wanted. I knew what these images needed to *feel* like. I knew the emotional register, the palette, the compositional logic. I carried the creative intention clearly, even if I lacked the manual technique to execute it.

AI-assisted image generation gave me a way to bridge that gap. Using Nano Banana AI as the primary generation tool, I developed a process of extensive iteration—crafting detailed prompts, evaluating dozens of variations for each concept, selecting and refining until an image captured the specific emotional and intellectual resonance I was after. This was not a matter of typing a sentence and accepting what appeared. Each of the dozens of illustrations in this book required scores of iterations, as I refined prompts, adjusted compositions, and searched for the moment when a generated image crossed the threshold from technically adequate to genuinely expressive.

But generation was only the beginning. Every image then moved into a second stage of substantial manual work in Pixelmator Pro, Adobe Illustrator, and Canva, where I added hand-applied typography designed for visual consistency across the entire book, made composition adjustments, corrected elements that the AI had rendered imprecisely, and optimized each illustration for black-and-white and grayscale printing—a demanding translation that required reimagining each piece for a medium where luminance and contrast must do the work that color performs.

There is a resonance between this creative process and the book's central argument that I did not plan but have come to appreciate. The book argues that the most powerful transformations happen when human intention partners with systemic intelligence, when we learn to guide complex systems rather than dominate them. The illustrations emerged through exactly that kind of partnership: human creative vision directing a computational process, then human craft refining the results. Neither the AI nor I could have produced these images alone. The collaboration yielded something that belongs to both and to neither.

I think my mother would have understood. She knew that watercolor's beauty comes precisely from the negotiation between the painter's intent and the medium's own behavior, the way pigment blooms unpredictably when it meets wet paper, the way darkness pools and gathers its own weight, the way a wash of green can suggest an entire forest if you trust the water to do its work. Her paintings taught me that the most powerful creative acts are collaborations with the material, not conquests of it. That is what these illustrations are as well.

The watercolor aesthetic was chosen for reasons that go beyond personal history. The soft edges and organic washes mirror the book's argument: that the rigid boundaries between economy and ecology, between profit and purpose, between self-interest and collective well-being are constructs we can dissolve. Watercolor, unlike the clean vectors and hard edges of conventional business graphics, suggests permeability. It evokes the natural world, where boundaries are gradients rather than walls, where systems interpenetrate rather than stand apart. It says: *This is different. Pay attention differently.*

The grayscale rendering in the printed book adds a further dimension. Stripped of color, the illustrations take on a timelessness—evoking the nature writing and field guides that inspired this work, the ink drawings in Aldo Leopold's *A Sand County Almanac*, the hand-drawn maps in Barry Lopez's *Arctic Dreams*. Black and white is the medium of the essentials, what remains when ornamentation falls away.

One image in the book requires special mention. Figure 28, *The Displaced*, is a watercolor rendering based on an original painting I acquired at the Hissar Historical and Cultural Reserve in Tajikistan in 2005, while developing place-based education programs in Central

Asia. As described in Chapter 14, that painting has hung in my office for twenty years, visible over my shoulder in every webinar I've hosted, silently testifying to the human cost of displacement and the dignity that persists within it. Reproducing it in the book's watercolor style was a deliberate choice to weave the personal and the political, to honor the unnamed artist who painted it, and to remind readers that the people affected by extractive systems are not abstractions.

I want to say something about what this creative process made possible, because it connects to the book's deepest commitments. For most of publishing history, a book of this scope with thirty-six original illustrations would have required either an institutional budget or inherited wealth. The alternative, commissioning that many custom pieces from a professional artist, was simply not feasible given our timeline and resources. AI-assisted tools democratized that capacity, allowing an author with clear creative vision but limited manual skill to produce a book with a level of visual richness that would otherwise have been impossible.

That democratization of creative capacity is itself a small example of the broader theme this book explores: that tools, when designed and used with intention, can distribute power and possibility more widely. The question is never whether to use powerful tools. It is whether we use them in service of extraction or regeneration, of concentration or distribution, of domination or partnership.

These illustrations were made in partnership. I offer them in that spirit.

•

Technical Note: All thirty-six illustrations were created by the author through a hybrid process. Base images were generated using Nano Banana AI, with prompts crafted to achieve specific compositional, emotional, and conceptual goals for each figure. Generated images were then substantially refined in Pixelmator Pro for composition, correction, and grayscale optimization, and further developed in Adobe Illustrator and Canva for typography, graphic refinement, and final design.

Multiple prompts were used for each illustration, ranging from initial concept exploration to targeted refinements of composition, lighting, perspective, and stylistic consistency. No illustration was used as generated; all underwent significant post-production work to achieve the visual coherence and intentionality the book requires.

Berrett-Koehler
PUBLISHERS

Dear Reader,

Welcome to the Berrett-Koehler Community—a global network of changemakers creating positive impact in their lives, organizations, and communities.

Our Mission: Connecting People and Ideas to Create a World That Works for All

We believe transformation is possible. While outdated paradigms of self-interest, exclusion, and hierarchy continue to hold back our communities and organizations, we know that change can happen. That's why we connect people with actionable ideas from leading experts who are already creating the solutions we need.

The BK Way

We're an independent publisher that practices what we publish. Our books, digital resources, and community offerings provide practical pathways for building more just, equitable, and sustainable organizations and lives. Whether you're transforming your workplace, community, or personal practices, our publications meet you where you are with tools that work.

But we don't just talk about positive change—we live it. Through "The BK Way," we put stewardship and purpose before profit. As a benefit corporation, we're legally committed to benefiting all our stakeholders: authors, readers, employees, communities, and the environment.

As our gift to you, claim your free bestselling ebook at bkconnection.com/welcome. You'll also receive fresh leadership insights delivered to your inbox from bkconnection.com/blogs/the-bk-exchange.

You Make the Difference

We're grateful to our readers, authors, and community members, who bring our mission to life every day. Your stories of transformation inspire us and show others what's possible.

Share how BK publications are making a difference in your world at bkconnection.com/impact.

Your friends at Berrett-Koehler

Join the Berrett-Koehler Community

Are you passionate about supporting independent publishing and reading diverse voices and perspectives? Join the BK Community Membership Program and become a part of a vibrant literary community. To support mission-based publishing while saving up to 30 percent on all books and attending exclusive events, visit ideas.bkconnection.com/bkcommunity-join to learn more and become a member.

MIX
Paper | Supporting responsible forestry
FSC® C005010
FSC www.fsc.org